The Editors

CAROLE GERSON was born in Montreal in 1948. She took her B.A. (1970) from Simon Fraser University, M.A. (1972) from Dalhousie University, and Ph.D. (1977) from the University of British Columbia. Her many publications include *Three Writers of Victorian Canada* (1983) and *A Purer Taste: The Writing and Reading of Fiction in English in Nineteenth-Century Canada* (1989). She is a member of the Department of English, Simon Fraser University, Burnaby, British Columbia.

GWENDOLYN DAVIES was born in Halifax in 1942. She took her B.A. (1963) from Dalhousie University [King's], M.A. (1969) from the University of Toronto, and Ph.D. (1980) from York University. Her many publications include *Studies in Maritime Literary History, 1760-1930* (1991) and *Myth and Milieu: Atlantic Literature and Culture: 1918-1939* (1993). She is a member of the Department of English, Acadia University, Wolfville, Nova Scotia.

THE NEW CANADIAN LIBRARY

General Editor: David Staines

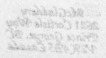

CANADIAN POETRY

From the Beginnings
Through the First World War

Selected and with an Afterword by
Carole Gerson and Gwendolyn Davies

M&S

Copyright © 1994 by McClelland & Stewart Inc.

Afterword copyright © 1994 by Carole Gerson
and Gwendolyn Davies

Canadian Cataloguing in Publication Data

Main entry under title:

Canadian poetry from the beginnings through the First World War

(New Canadian library)
Includes bibliographical references and index.
ISBN 0-7710-3450-4

1. Canadian poetry (English).* I. Gerson, Carole. II. Davies,
Gwendolyn. III. Series.

PS8289.C35 1994   C811'.008   C93-095458-0
PR9195.23.C35 1994

Cover design by Andrew Skuja
Typesetting by M&S, Toronto
The support of the Government of Ontario through the
Ministry of Culture, Tourism and Recreation is acknowledged.
The publishers acknowledge the support of the Canada Council and
the Ontario Arts Council for their publishing program.

Every effort has been made to contact the copyright holders of
material in this book. Any oversights, upon notification, will be
corrected in subsequent editions.

Printed and bound in Canada by Webcom Limited

McClelland & Stewart Inc.
The Canadian Publishers
481 University Avenue
Toronto, Ontario
M5G 2E9

1 2 3 4 5   98 97 96 95 94

Editorial Preface

In this anthology of English-language Canadian poetry from the early years through the First World War, we attempt to reproduce the most authoritative texts available. Drawing upon the scholarly principles embodied in D.M.R. Bentley's edition of Isabella Valancy Crawford's "Malcolm's Katie: A Love Story," Gerald Lynch's edition of Oliver Goldsmith's "The Rising Village," Desmond Pacey and Graham Adams's edition of Charles G.D. Roberts's poetry, and Laurel Boone's edition of selected works by William Wilfred Campbell, we follow the standard principle that the last publication of a poem during an author's lifetime represents his or her final intention. If the author's final intended version exists only in manuscript, this text is reproduced.

After the early deaths of Crawford and Archibald Lampman, their poems were frequently altered by well-meaning editors. It is therefore difficult to ascertain their final intentions. With many poems by these two writers we return to the versions that appeared in periodicals or survive in manuscript, occasionally retaining a few later changes in punctuation that render the poem more coherent. With several poems by Duncan Campbell Scott, we restore explanatory notes that situate the poems within their original contexts.

The two parts of this anthology are arranged chronologically, with authors introduced by the date of publication of the first poem included. A date in round brackets denotes the year of a poem's first known publication, and a date in square brackets denotes its known or estimated date of composition. A question mark after a date indicates a probable decade, e.g., (186?); a dash after a date indicates a certain decade, e.g. (186–).

*   *   *

The editors would like to thank the following for their consultation and assistance during the compilation of this anthology: Joyce Banks, National Library of Canada; Archives staff, New Brunswick Museum; D.M.R. Bentley, University of Western Ontario; Deborah Blacklock, Sandra Djwa, Kathy Mezei, Letia Richardson, and Charles Watts, Simon Fraser University; Laurel Boone, Fredericton, New Brunswick; Peter Buck, McClelland & Stewart; Cyril Byrne, Padraig O Siadhail, and Terry Whalen, Saint Mary's University; the staff of the Public Archives of Nova Scotia; John Charles, Kristjana Gunnars, and Bruce Peel, University of Alberta; Judy Dietz and Diane O'Neill, Art Gallery of Nova Scotia; Carolyn Donnelly, Ottawa, Ontario; Klay Dyer, Gerald Lynch, and David Staines, University of Ottawa; Len Early, York University; Mary Flagg, University of New Brunswick; Tom Gerry, Laurentian University; Edith Haliburton, Sue Rauth, Alexis Yanaky, and Helena Malton, Acadia University; Mary Lu MacDonald, Halifax, Nova Scotia; Theresa McIntosh, National Archives of Canada; Bruce Meyer, University of Toronto; Carman Miller, McGill University; W.H. New and Laurie Ricou, University of British Columbia; Michael Peterman, Trent University; Cheryl Siegel, Vancouver Art Gallery; Ann de G. Tighe, Art Gallery of Greater Victoria; and Thomas Vincent, Royal Military College, Kingston.

Contents

PART TWO: CONTINUATIONS

Part One

Foundations

ROBERT HAYMAN

1575–1629

Born in Devonshire, England, and educated at Oxford University, Robert Hayman associated with literary circles in London before he was appointed governor of the colony at Harbour Grace, Newfoundland. From 1618 to 1628 he spent ten successive summers and one fifteen-month stretch in Newfoundland, where he composed the first English poetry written in what would become Canada. His book of verses and epigrams, *Quodlibets Lately Come Over From New Britaniola, Old Newfound-Land. Epigrams, and Other Small Parcels, Both Morall and Divine*, was published in London in 1628.

From Quodlibets
Book 1, no. 117

A Skeltonicall continued ryme, in praise of
my New-found-Land

Although in cloaths, company, buildings faire,
With *England*, *New-found-land* cannot compare:
Did some know what contentment I found there,
Alwayes enough, most times somewhat to spare,
With little paines, lesse toyle, and lesser care,
Exempt from taxings, ill newes, Lawing, feare,
If cleane, and warme, no matter what you weare,
Healthy, and wealthy, if men carefull are,
With much much more, then I will now declare,
10 (I say) if some wise men knew what this were,
(I doe beleeve) they'd live no other where.

(1628)

Book 2, no. 79

The foure Elements in Newfound-Land.
To the Worshipfull Captaine *John Mason*,
who did wisely and worthily governe there divers yeeres

The Aire, in *Newfound-Land* is wholesome, good;
The Fire, as sweet as any made of wood;
The Waters, very rich, both salt and fresh;
The Earth more rich, you know it is no lesse.
Where all are good, *Fire, Water, Earth, and Aire*,
What man made of these foure would not live there?

(1628)

Book 2, no. 101

To the first Planters of *Newfound-land*

What ayme you at in your *Plantation*?
Sought you the *Honour* of our *Nation*?
Or did you hope to raise your owne *renowne*?
Or else to adde a Kingdome to a *Crowne*?
Or *Christs* true *Doctrine* for to propagate?
Or drawe Salvages to a blessed state?
Or our o're peopled *Kingdome* to relieve?
Or shew *poore men where* they may *richly live*?
Or poore mens children godly to maintaine?
10 Or aym'd *you at your owne sweete private gaine*?
All these you had *atchiv'd* before this day,
And all these you have balk't by your delay.

(1628)

Book 2, no. 103

To my very loving and discreet Friend,
Master *Peter Miller* of Bristoll

You askt me once, What here was our chiefe dish?
In Winter, Fowle, in Summer choyce of Fish.
But wee should need good Stomackes, you may thinke,
To eate such kind of things which with you stinke,
As *Ravens, Crowes, Kytes, Otters, Foxes, Beares,*
Dogs, Cats, and Soyles, Eaglets, Hawks, Hounds, & Hares: *
Yet we have *Partriges*, and store of *Deare*,
And that (I thinke) with you is pretty cheere.
Yet let me tell you, Sir, what I love best,
10 Its a *Poore-John*† thats cleane, and neatly drest:
There's not a meat found in the Land, or Seas,
Can Stomacks better please, or lesse displease,
It is a fish of profit, and of pleasure,
Ile write more of it, when I have more leisure:
These and much more are here the ancient store:
Since we came hither, we have added more.

———————

* Dogs and Cats are fishes so call'd, and Hounds a kind of Fowle
† Cald in French *Poure Gens*, in English corruptly *Poore John,*
  being the principall Fish brought out of this Countrie.

                                                        (1628)

HENRY KELSEY
1667?–1724

Probably born near London, Henry Kelsey was apprenticed in 1684 to the Hudson's Bay Company, where he served for forty years. His most memorable feat was his journey of 1690-92 westward from York Factory [Manitoba] across the prairies. His journal of that trip, dated 1693 but not published until 1929, opens with an unusual (and unpunctuated) rhyming prologue.

Henry Kelsey his Book being ye Gift of
James Hubbud in the year of our Lord 1693

Now Reader Read for I am well assur'd
Thou dost not know the hardships I endur'd
In this same desert where Ever y^t I have been
Nor wilt thou me believe without y^t thou had seen
The Emynent Dangers that did often me attend
But still I lived in hopes y^t once it would amend
And makes me free from hunger & from Cold
Likewise many other things wch I cannot here unfold
For many times I have often been oppresst
10 With fears & Cares y^t I could not take my rest
Because I was alone & no friend could find
And once y^t in my travels I was left behind
Which struck fear & terror into me
But still I was resolved this same Country for to see
Although through many dangers I did pass
Hoped still to undergo y^m at the Last
Now Considering y^t it was my dismal fate
for to repent I thought it now to late
Trusting still unto my masters Consideration
20 Hoping they will Except of this my small Relation
Which here I have pend & still will Justifie
Concerning of those Indians & their Country

22

If this wont do farewell to all as I may say
And for my living i'll seek some other way
In sixteen hundred & ninety'th year
I set forth as plainly may appear
Through Gods assistance for to understand
The natives language & to see their land
And for my masters interest I did soon
30 Sett from yᵉ house yᵉ twealth of June
Then up yᵉ River I with heavy heart
Did take my way & from all English part
To live amongst yᵉ Natives of this place
If god permits me for one two years space
The Inland Country of Good report hath been
By Indians but by English yet not seen
Therefore I on my Journey did not stay
But making all yᵉ hast I could upon our way
Gott on yᵉ borders of yᵉ stone Indian Country
40 I took possession on yᵉ tenth Instant July
And for my masters I speaking for yᵐ all
This neck of land I deerings point did call
Distance from hence by Judgement at yᵉ lest
From yᵉ house six hundred miles southwest
Through Rivers wᶜʰ run strong with falls
thirty three Carriages five lakes in all
The ground begins for to be dry with wood
Poplo & birch with ash thats very good
For the Natives of that place wᶜʰ knows
50 No use of Better than their wooden Bows
According to yᵉ use & custom of this place
In September I brought those Natives to a peace
But I had no sooner from those Natives turnd my back
Some of the home Indians came upon their track
And for old grudges & their minds to fill
Came up with them Six tents of wᶜʰ they kill'd
This ill news kept secrett was from me

Nor none of those home Indians did I see
Untill that they their murder all had done
60 And the Chief acter was he y^ts called ye Sun
So far I have spoken concerning of the spoil
And now will give acco^t. of that same Country soile
Which hither part is very thick of wood
Affords small nutts wth little cherryes very good
Thus it continues till you leave ye woods behind
And then you have beast of severall kind
The one is a black a Buffillo great
Another is an outgrown Bear wch is good meat
His skin to gett I have used all ye ways I can
70 He is mans food & he makes food of man
His hide they would not me it preserve
But said it was a god & they should Starve
This plain affords nothing but Beast & grass
And over it in three days time we past
getting unto ye woods on the other side
It being about forty sixe miles wide
This wood is poplo ridges with small ponds of water
there is beavour in abundance but no Otter
with plains & ridges in the Country throughout
80 Their Enemies many whom they cannot rout
But now of late they hunt their Enemies
And with our English guns do make y^m flie
At deerings point after the frost
I set up their a Certain Cross
In token of my being there
Cut out on it ye date of year
And Likewise for to veryfie the same
added to it my master sir Edward deerings name
So having not more to trouble you wth all I am
90 Sir your most obedient & faithfull Servt. at Command

                                 HENRY KELSEY
                                         [1693]

DONNCHA RUA MAC CONMARA

c. 1716–1810

Born in County Clare, Ireland, and educated in Rome, Donncha Rua Mac Conmara taught in Ireland and influenced Irish bardic circles before and after visiting Newfoundland between 1745 and 1770. To the reputed delight of Irish cod fishery workers in a St. John's tavern, his skill in counterpointing Irish and English enabled him to recite pro-Jacobite, pro-Irish verse with impunity in the presence of English sailors. His poetry was later gathered in John O'Daly's *The Poets and Poetry of Munster* (1849) and *The Adventures of Donnchadh Ruadh Mac Con-Mara, A Slave of Adversity* (1853).

Donncha Rua i dTalamh an Éisc
[Donncha Rua in Newfoundland]

As I was walking one evening fair,
Agus mé go déanach a mBaile Sheáin;
>   *(And I lately in St. John's town)*
I met a gang of English blades,
Agus iad á dtraochadh ag neart a namhad:
>   *(Who had been cowed by opponent's might:)*
I boozed and drank both late and early,
With these courageous men of war;
Is gur bhinne liom na Sasanaigh ag rith ar éigean,
10 Is gan de Ghaeil ann ach fíorbheagán.
>   *(A sweet sight was this fleeing English crew,*
>   *As their Irish victors numbered so few.)*

I spent my fortune by being freakish,
Drinking, raking, and playing cards;
Cé nach raibh airgead agam ná gréithre,
Ná rud sa saol ach ní gan aird.
>   *(Although my pockets had been shallow*
>   *And my possessions few.)*

Then I turned a jolly tradesman,
20 By work and labour I lived abroad;
A's bíodh ar m'fhallaing gur mór an bhréag sin,
Is gur beag den saothar do thit lem' láimh.
> *(May the Lord forgive the deception*
> *I had scarce fondness for toil and exertion.)*

Newfoundland is a fine plantation;
It will be my station before I die;
Is mo chrá go mb'fhearr liom a bheith in Éirinn,
Ag díol gáirtéirí ná ag dul faoin gcoill.
> *(O, to be back in Ireland*
30 > *Selling garters rather than roaming wild.)*
Here you may find a virtuous lady,
A smiling fair one to please your mind:
An paca staganna is measa tréithe!
Go mbeire mo shaol ar bheith as a radharc.
> *(The worst old nags you would ever see,*
> *I'd give my life, from them to be free.)*

I'll join in fellowship with "Jack-of-all-trades,"
The last of August could I but see:
'S tá a fhios ag Coisdeala, 's is máistir báid é,
40 Gur b'olc an lámh mé ar muir ná ar tír.
> *(Well does Costello, the boat's master, know*
> *That I'm little use on land or sea.)*
If fortune smiles then, I'll be her darling,
But if she scorns my company,
Déanfad bun os toll in airde,
'S is fada ón áit seo a bheidh mé arís.
> *(I'll go carousing from dusk to dawn,*
> *And it's far from here I'll be anon.)*

Come drink a health, boys, to Royal George,
50 Our chief commander, nár ordaigh Críost:
      (no servant of Christ)
Agus bíodh bhur n-achainíocha chum Muire Mháthair
É féin is a gharda a leagadh síos.
      (Beseech the Blessed Mother on high,
      To overcome this wretched crew)
We'll fear no cannon nor war's alarms,
While noble George will be our guide:
Is, a Chríost, go bhfeice mé an bhrúid á carnadh,
Ag an Mac seo ar fán uainn thall sa Fhrainc.
60   *(O Christ, may I see the demon trounced*
      By thy true son in exile yonder in France.)

                     [174–]

ANONYMOUS

1745

Reputedly written by a British officer stationed at the Bay of Bulls, Newfoundland, this poem refers to Nathaniel Brooks, the naval officer in charge of the Bay of Bulls in 1745, and to the seasonal summer huts, or "tilts," built by Newfoundland fishermen. These were sufficiently smoky to generate the later Newfoundland idiom, "smoking like a tilt." Both the classical form of the poem and the probable reference to the Book of Tobit in the Apocrypha suggest the superior education of the poet.

Nathaniel's Tilt

Not hardened bricks in mouldering flame prepared,
Nor Parian marble the proud fabric reared;
No lofty turrets reaching to the sky,
Reproached the new-found soil with luxury;
But poles and dirt, boxes of slaughtered cod,
The sides composed – the roof was rinds and sod.
At either end – his worship else had choked –
A headless hogshead for a chimney smoked;
Wild through the front seven shattered windows stared,
10 With paper some, and some with rags, repaired;
Four sturdy poles, o'erlaid with twigs of birch,
Projecting from the entrance, formed a porch
Profuse of odours; – here the house-wife good
Her platter washed, and here the hog's trough stood.
More odorous still before the sunny pile
Livers of fish lay rotting into oil.
Less stunk that liver which near Toby's bed
The angel burned, when the choked devil fled,
Oh, Toby! hadst thou here first met thy bride,
20 E'en then, perchance, the devil himself had died,
Yet, here, o'er cods and men Nathaniel rules
The seat imperial of the Bay of Bulls.   [1745]

ANONYMOUS
1750

In 1749, Halifax was founded by the British on the coast of Nova Scotia to offset the threat posed by the fortress of Louisbourg on the French-held island now known as Cape Breton. Throughout the year 1749-50 *The Gentleman's Magazine* of London encouraged settlement and investment in the new town. Its campaign included the publication of letters, a town plan, drawings of plant and animal life, and "Nova Scotia. A New Ballad," to be sung to the tune of "King John and the Abbot of Canterbury."

Nova Scotia. A New Ballad

Let's away to *New Scotland*, where Plenty sits queen
O'er as happy a country as ever was seen;
And blesses her subjects, both little and great,
With each a good house, and a pretty estate.
      Derry down, etc.

There's wood, and there's water, there's wild fowl and
                                 tame;
In the forest good ven'son, good fish in the stream;
Good grass for our cattle, good land for our plough
Good wheat to be reap'd, and good barley to mow.
10   *Derry down, etc.*

No landlords are there the poor tenants to teaze,
No lawyers to bully, nor stewards to seize:
But each honest fellow's a landlord, and dares
To spend on himself the whole fruit of his cares.
      Derry down, etc.

They've no duties on candles, no taxes on malt,
Nor do they, as we do, pay sauce for their salt:
But all is as free as in those times of old,
When poets assure us the age was of gold.
20   *Derry down, etc.*

(1750)

JOSEPH STANSBURY

1740–1809

Born in London, England, but living in Philadelphia at the outbreak of hostilities in 1775, Joseph Stansbury was a leading Tory satirist during the American Revolution. An unhappy Loyalist exile in Shelburne, Nova Scotia, in 1783, he returned to the United States where he resided in Philadelphia and, after 1793, in New York. His poetry appeared in *The Loyal Verses of Joseph Stansbury and Doctor Jonathan Odell* (1860).

To Cordelia

Believe me, Love, this vagrant life
   O'er Nova Scotia's wilds to roam,
While far from children, friends, or wife,
   Or place that I can call a home
Delights not me; – another way
My treasures, pleasures, wishes lay.

In piercing, wet, and wintry skies,
   Where man would seem in vain to toil
I see, where'er I turn my eyes,
10   Luxuriant pasture, trees and soil.
Uncharm'd I see: – another way
My fondest hopes and wishes lay.

Oh could I through the future see
   Enough to form a settled plan,
To feed my infant train and thee
   And fill the rank and style of man:
I'd cheerful be the livelong day;
Since all my wishes point that way.

But when I see a sordid shed
20   Of birchen bark, procured with care,
Design'd to shield the aged head
      Which British mercy placed there –
'Tis too, too much: I cannot stay,
But turn with streaming eyes away.

Oh! how your heart would bleed to view
      Six pretty prattlers like your own,
Expos'd to every wind that blew;
      Condemn'd in such a hut to moan.
Could this be borne, Cordelia, say?
30 Contented in your cottage stay.

'Tis true, that in this climate rude,
      The mind resolv'd may happy be;
And may, with toil and solitude,
      Live independent and be free.
So the lone hermit yields to slow decay:
Unfriended lives – unheeded glides away.

If so far humbled that no pride remains,
      But moot indifference which way flows the stream;
Resign'd to penury, its cares and pains;
40   And hope has left you like a painted dream;
Then here, Cordelia, bend your pensive way,
And close the evening of Life's wretched day.

                                        [c. 1783]

DEBORAH HOW COTTNAM
("PORTIA")
1728–1806

Raised and educated on Grassy Island off Canso, Nova Scotia, Deborah How Cottnam settled in Salem, Massachusetts, with her military husband after being held as a civilian prisoner of war at Louisbourg in 1744. After her return to the Maritimes in 1775 as a Loyalist refugee, she established schools for girls in Halifax and Saint John during the 1780s and 1790s before moving to Windsor, Nova Scotia. Circulating her pseudonymous poetry privately, as did many eighteenth-century women, she was later cited by her great-granddaughter, the poet Griselda Tonge, as an inspiration.

On Being Asked What Recollection Was

What Recollection is – Oh! wouldst thou know?
'Tis the soul's highest privilege below:
A kind indulgence, by our Maker given –
The mind's perfection, and the stamp of Heaven;
In this, alone, the strength of reason lies –
It makes us happy, and it makes us wise.

What does not man to Recollection owe?
What various joys from calm reflection flow? –
What but this power – this faculty divine,
10 Can Time recall, and make it once more thine? –
By this unaided, mortals could no more
Review the past, explore the future hour.

What poignant pangs would rend the feeling heart,
Doomed with the lover and the friend to part –
If with the object, Memory, too, should fail –
And dark oblivion draw her sable veil
O'er every pleasing scene of former love,
Our present bliss, our future hopes above?

Who could survive a friend's departed breath,
20 If all were blank before, and after death?
What smoothes the bed of pain, and brow of care,
If happy Recollection dwell not there?
'Tis this alone bids virtuous hopes arise,
And makes the awakening penitent grow wise.

When joys tumultuous rush upon the soul,
Or grief or rage its faculties controul,
'Tis this bids tyrannizing passion cool –
Calms and resigns the mind to reason's rule;
'Tis this secures the blooming artless maid,
30 When false delusive flattery would invade –
This guards the heart 'gainst treachery and surprize,
And teaches to bestow on worth the prize.

The pleasing retrospect of blameless youth –
Boundless benevolence – unblemish'd truth –
Are joys whose full extent Eliza knows,
When sweet Reflection in her bosom glows.
Hark! Recollection whispers while I write –
Condemns the rash attempt, the adventurous flight,
To paint those beauties – or that Power define
Which loudly speaks our origin divine;
To explain what baffles all descriptive arts –
40 The *Deity* implanted in our hearts;
Struck and convinced, I drop the onequal task,
Nor further dare though *my Eliza ask*.

[178?]

A piece for a Sampler

Observe in time, ye growing Fair!
How transient Youth, & Beauty are;
These gayest Charms! how quickly gone!
How often blighted in their dawn!
Attend then, to your better part,
Attain each useful, pleasing, Art;
Expand your Genius in its prime,
Your mind inform, improve your time;
New pleasures, each, new days shall give,
10 And Virtue's bloom, shall time out-live.

[c. 1793]

HENRY ALLINE

1748–1784

Born in Newport, Rhode Island, and raised in the strict
religious precepts of Congregationalism, Henry Alline
immigrated with his parents to Falmouth, Nova Scotia, in
1760 as a New England "Planter." Following a joyous
conversion in March 1775, he preached throughout the
Maritimes, charismatically teaching through songs and
sermons his "New Light" doctrine of personal grace. His
beliefs, expressed in *Hymns and Spiritual Songs* (Boston,
1786) and in his autobiography, *The Life and Journal of the
Rev. Mr. Henry Alline* (1806), drew the wrath of such tradi-
tional Anglican clerics as the Reverend Jacob Bailey.

from *Hymns and Spiritual Songs*

Book I, Hymn LII
The conduct of most sailors

I

While sailors blest with wind and tide,
Do safely o'er the ocean ride,
Chearful they spend their hours in mirth:
But when the raging tempests blow,
And yawning graves invade below,
They tremble on the verge of death.

II

Then to their knees the wretches fly
To seek a friend; they mourn and cry,
Confess their sins, and help implore;
10 And while distress'd to heav'n they vow
If GOD will help, and save them now
They'll tread their sinful ways no more.

III

But when he stills the foaming main,
And calms the furious winds again,
Soon they forget the vows they made;
"Come on, they say, ye merry souls,
"We'll drown our grief with jolly bowls;
"Good luck has all our fears allay'd."

IV

O poor returns for grace so great
20 To wretches on the brink of fate!
Good Lord forgive th'unhappy crew;
O may they now by grace reform,
Before the great and dreadful storm
Prove their eternal overthrow.

(1786)

Book III, Hymn VI
Sion comforted, or religion reviving

I

Dark was the day, our fears were great,
　　And mournful was our captive song,
When wandering our captive state,
　　And all our threat'ning foes were strong.

II

Sing us a song of Sion now,
　　They laughing in derision said;
Our harps were hung, our hopes were low,
　　And all our souls a prey was made.

III

'Twas hard to speak of Sion then,
10   And hard to think our GOD would fail;
How could we bear that cruel men
      Should triumph, and at last prevail!

IV

Then did the pow'rs of hell blaspheme,
      Because our broken walls were low,
Saying *"Where is your boasted fame?*
      "And where's your mighty Saviour now?"

V

But in the midst of all our grief,
      Our GOD made known deliv'ring power;
His arm appear'd for our relief,
20   And brought the long-desired hour.

VI

Soon he expel'd the gloomy shade,
      Our hopes, and strength, and joys restor'd;
The lambs which from his fold had stray'd,
      He call'd, and fed around his board.

VII

'Tis now we'll sing the Victor's song,
      And laud our heavenly Captain's name;
Eternal praise to him belongs,
      While all our foes are cloth'd with shame.

VIII

All glory be to Sion's King,
30   Whose love redeem'd us from our wo!
Let saints above his praises sing,
      And we with humbler notes below.

(1786)

JACOB BAILEY
1731–1808

Born in Rowley, Massachusetts, and educated at Harvard
University, the Reverend Jacob Bailey became Anglican
rector of Cornwallis, Nova Scotia, and later Annapolis
Royal, after being driven from his Church of England par-
ish in Maine at the outbreak of the American Revolution.
One of the most trenchant of the Tory verse satirists dur-
ing the war, he continued in Nova Scotia to attack Ameri-
can-style republicanism and evangelism, including the
"New Light" movement of Henry Alline. His poetry circu-
lated privately, and his journals and some poems were col-
lected posthumously in *The Frontier Missionary* (1853).

[Verse Against the New Lights]

Behold the gifted teacher rise
and roll to heaven his half shut eyes
In every feature of his face
see stiffness sanctity and grace
like whipping post erect he stands
and stretches out his waving hands
then with a slow and gentle voice
begins to make a languid noise
strives with a thousand airs to move
10 to melt and thaw your hearts to love
but when he fails by softning arts
to mollify your frozen hearts
observe him spring with eager jump
and on the table fiercely thump
with double fist he beats the air
pours out his soul in wrathful prayer
then seized with furious agitation
screams forth a frightful exhortation
And with a sharp and hideous yell

20 sends all your carnal folks to Hell
    Now to excite your fear and wonder
    tries the big jarring voice of thunder
    like wounded Serpent in the vale
    he writhes, his body and his tail
    strives by each motion to express
    the Agonies of deep distress
    Then groans, and scolds and roars aloud
    till dread and frenzy fire the crowd
    The madness spreads with rapid power
30 confusion reigns and wild uproar
    a consort grand of joyful tones
    mingl'd with sighs and rueful moans
    Some heaven extol with rapturous air
    while others rave in black dispair
    a blendid groupe of different voices
    confound and stund us with their noises
    Thus in some far and lonely site
    amidst the deepest glooms of night
    where roll the slow and sullen floods
40 ore hung with rocks and dusky woods
    I've heard the wolves terrific howl
    the doleful Music of the owl
    The frogs in hoarser murmers croak
    while from the top of some tall oak
    with notes more piercing soft and shrill
    resounds the sprightly whi'poorwill
    these give the ears a wondrous greeting
    not much unlike a pious meeting

    Here blue-eyed Jenny plays her part
50 inured to every saint like art
    she works and heaves from head to heel
    with pangs of puritanic zeal
    now in a fit of deep distress

the holy maid turns prophetess
and to our light and knowledge brings
a multitude of secret things
and as Enthusiasm advances
falls into extacies and trances
herself with decency resigns
60 to these impulses, and reclines
on Jemmy Trimm, a favourite youth
a chosen vessel of the truth
who as she sinks into his arms
feels thro' his veins her powerful charms
grown warm with throbs of strong devotion
he finds his blood in high commotion
and fir'd with love of this dear Sister
is now unable to resist her.

[178–]

ANNE HECHT
(*fl.* 1786)

Written on birchbark by bridesmaid Anne Hecht, this poem was typical of marriage-poem conventions brought into early English Canada by British and American settlers. The bride in this instance was Mehetible Calef (1768-1860), an eighteen-year-old Loyalist exile in Saint John, New Brunswick, who in 1786 married Captain David Mowat, a Loyalist twenty years her senior.

Advice to Mrs. Mowat

Dear Hetty –
           Since the single state
You've left to choose yourself a mate,
Since metamorphosed to a wife,
And bliss or woe insured for life,
A friendly muse the way should show
To gain the bliss and miss the woe.
But first of all I must suppose
You've with mature reflection chose.
10 And thus premised I think you may
Here find to married bliss the way.
Small is the province of a wife
And narrow is her sphere in life,
Within that sphere to walk aright
Should be her principal delight.
To grace the home with prudent care
And properly to spend and spare,
To make her husband bless the day
He gave his liberty away,
20 To train the tender infant's mind,
These are the tasks to wives assigned.
Then never think domestic care
Beneath the notice of the fair.

But matters every day inspect
That naught be wasted by neglect.
Be frugal (plenty round you seen)
And always keep the golden mean.
Let decent neatness round you shine
Be always clean but seldom fine.
30 If once fair decency be fled
Love soon deserts the genial bed.
Not nice your house, though neat and clean
In all things there's a proper mean.
Some of our sex mistake in this;
Too anxious some – some too remiss.
The early days of married life
Are oft o'er cast with childish strife
Then let it be your chiefest care
To keep that hour bright and fair;
40 Then is the time, by gentlest art
To fix his empire in your heart.
For should it by neglect expire
No art again can light the fire.
To charm his reason dress your mind
Till love shall be with friendship joined.
Raised on that basis t'will endure
From time and death itself secure.
Be sure you ne'er for power contend
Or try with tears to gain your end
50 Sometimes the tears that dim your eyes
From pride and obstancy arise.
Heaven gave to man unquestioned sway.
Then Heaven and man at once obey.
Let sullen looks your brow ne'er cloud
Be always cheerful, never loud.
Let trifles never discompose
Your temper, features or repose.
Abroad for happiness ne'er roam
True happiness resides at home.

60 Still make your partner easy there
   Man finds abroad sufficient care.
   If every thing at home be right
   He'll always enter with delight.
   Your presence he'll prefer to all,
   That cheats the world does pleasure call.
   With cheerful chat his cares beguile
   And always greet him with a smile,
   Never with woe his thoughts engage
   Nor ever meet his rage with rage.
70 With all our sex's softening art
   Recall lost reason to his heart.
   Thus calm the tempest in his breast
   And sweetly soothe his soul to rest.
   Be sure you ne'er arraign his sense,
   Few husbands pardon that offence,
   T'will discord raise, disgust it breeds
   And hatred certainly succeeds.
   Then shun, O shun that hated self,
   Still think him wiser than yourself.
80 And if you otherwise believe
   Ne'er let him such a thought perceive.
   When cares invade your partner's heart
   Bear you a sympathetic part.
   . . . . [illegible] . . . .
   From morn till noon, from noon till night
   To see him pleased your chief delight.
   And now, methinks, I hear you cry;
   Shall she presume – Oh vanity!
   To lay down rules for wedded life
90 Who never was herself a wife?
   I've done nor longer will presume
   To trespass on time that's not your own.
                                    ANNE HECHT
                                      [1786]

ROGER VIETS

1738–1811

Born in Simsbury, Connecticut, and educated at Yale,
Roger Viets became an Anglican rector in 1763. After being
imprisoned in the Simsbury salt mine for his Tory sym-
pathies during the American Revolution, he immigrated
to Nova Scotia in 1786. As Loyalist rector of Trinity Church
in Digby, Nova Scotia, he issued a number of sermons and
Annapolis-Royal (1788), the first poem to be published in
pamphlet form in what would become Canada.

Annapolis-Royal

The King of Rivers, solemn, calm and slow,
Flows tow'rd the Sea, yet scarce is seen to flow;
On each fair Bank, the verdant Lands are seen,
In gayest Cloathing of perpetual Green:
On ev'ry Side, the Prospect brings to Sight
The Fields, the Flow'rs, and ev'ry fresh Delight:
His lovely Banks, most beauteously are grac'd
With Nature's sweet Variety of Taste.
Herbs, Fruits and Grass, with intermingled Trees
10 The Prospect lengthen, and the Joys increase:
The lofty Mountains rise in ev'ry View,
Creation's Glory, and it's Beauty too.
To higher Grounds, the raptur'd View extends,
Whilst in the Cloud-top'd Cliffs the Landscape ends.

Fair Scenes! to which, should Angels turn their Sight;
Angels might stand astonish'd with Delight.
Majestic Groves in ev'ry View arise,
And greet with Wonder the Beholder's Eyes.

In gentle Windings, where this River glides,
20 And Herbage thick it's Current almost hides;
Where sweet Meanders lead his pleasant Course,

Where Trees and Plants and Fruits themselves disclose;
Where never-fading Groves of fragrant Fir,
And beauteous Pine perfume the ambient Air;
The Air, at once, both Health and Fragrance yields,
Like sweet Arabian or Elysian Fields.

    As this delightful Stream glides tow'rd the Sea, ⎫
Thou Royal Settlement! he washes Thee;   ⎬
Thou Village, blest of Heav'n, and dear to me. ⎭
30 Nam'd from a pious Sov'reign, now at Rest,
The last of STUART'S Line, of QUEENS the best.

    Amidst the rural Joys, the Town is seen,
Enclos'd with Woods and Hills, forever green:
The Streets, the Buildings, Gardens, all concert
To please the Eye, to gratify the Heart.
But none of these so pleasing, or so fair,
As those bright Maidens, who inhabit there.

    Your potent Charms, fair Nymphs, my Verse inspire,
Your Charms supply the chaste, poetic Fire.
40 Could these my Strains, but live, when I'm no more,
On future Fame's bright Wings, your Names should soar.

    Where this romantic Village lifts her Head,
Betwixt the Royal Port and humble Mead;
The decent Mansions, deck'd with mod'rate Cost,
Of honest Thrift, and gen'rous Owners boast;
There Skill and Industry their Sons employ,
In Works of Peace, Integrity and Joy;
Their Lives in social, harmless Bliss, they spend,
Then to the Grave, in honor'd Age descend:
50 The hoary Sire and aged Matron see
Their prosp'rous Offspring, to the fourth Degree:
With Grief sincere, the blooming Offspring close
Their Parent's Eyes, and pay their Debt of Woes;
Then hast to honest, joyous Marriage Bands,

A newborn Race is rear'd by careful Hands:
Thro' num'rous Ages thus they'll happy move
In active Bus'ness, and in chastest Love.

The Nymphs and Swains appear in Streets and
                                    Bowers,
As Morning fresh, as lovely as the Flowers.
60 As bright as Phoebus, Ruler of the Day,
Prudent as Pallas, and as Flora gay.

A Spire majestic rears it's solemn Vane,
Where Praises, Pray'r and true Devotion reign;
Where Truth and Peace and Charity abound,
Where God is sought, and heav'nly Blessings found.
The gen'rous Flock reward their Pastor's Care,
His Pray'rs, his Wants, his Happiness they share.
Retir'd from worldly Care, from Noise and Strife,
In sacred Thoughts and Deeds, he spends his Life;
70 To mod'rate Bounds, his Wishes he confines,
All Views of Grandeur, Pow'r and Wealth resigns;
With Pomp and Pride can chearfully dispense,
Dead to the World, and empty Joys of Sense

The Symphony of heav'nly Song he hears,⎫
Celestial Concord vibrates on his Ears,   ⎬
Which emulates the Music of the Spheres. ⎭
The Band of active Youths and Virgins fair,
Rank'd in due Order, by their Teacher's Care,
The Sight of all Beholders gratify,
80 Sweet to the Soul, and pleasing to the Eye.

But when their Voices sound, in Songs of Praise,
When they to God's high Throne their Anthems raise,
By those harmonious Sounds such Rapture's giv'n,
Their loud Hosannas waft the Soul to Heav'n:
The fourfold Parts, in one bright Center meet,
To form the blessed Harmony complete.

Lov'd by the Good, esteemed by the Wise,
To gracious Heav'n, a pleasing Sacrifice.
Each Note, each Part, each Voice, each Word conspire
90 T'inflame all pious Hearts with holy Fire;
Each one, in Fancy seems among the Throng
Of Angels, chanting Heav'ns eternal Song.

Hail Music, Foretaste of celestial Joy!
That always satiat'st, yet canst never cloy:
Each pure, refin'd, extatic Pleasure's thine,
Thou rapt'rous Science! Harmony divine!

May each kind Wish of ev'ry virtuous Heart
Be giv'n to all, who teach, or learn thine Art:
May all the Wise, and all the Good unite,
100 With all the Habitants of Life and Light,
To treat the Sons of Music with Respect,
Their Progress to encourage and protect.
May each Musician, and Musician's Friend
Attain to Hymns divine, which never end.

(1788)

JONATHAN ODELL

1737–1818

Born in Newark, New Jersey, and educated at the College of
New Jersey (now Princeton University), Jonathan Odell
was a Church of England cleric before becoming a leading
Tory satirist, chaplain, and sometime espionage agent in
the American Revolution. Appointed Provincial Secretary
of New Brunswick in 1784 for his Loyalist service, he con-
tinued to write poetry and prose until his death in Frederic-
ton. Selected poems were published in *The Loyal Verses of
Joseph Stansbury and Doctor Jonathan Odell* (1860).

Our thirty-ninth Wedding day

6th May 1810

    Twice nineteen years, dear Nancy, on this day
Complete their Circle, since the smiling May
Beheld us, at the altar, kneel and join
In holy rites and Vows which made thee mine.
Then, like the reddening East, without a cloud,
Bright was my dawn of joy. To Heaven I bowed
In thankful exultation, well assured
That all my heart could covet was secured.

    But ah, how soon this dawn of joy, so bright,
10 Was followed by a dark and stormy Night!
The howling tempest, in a fatal hour,
Drove me, an Exile from our nuptial Bower,
To seek for refuge in the tented field,
Till democratic Tyranny should yield.
Thus, torn asunder, we, from year to year,
Endured the alternate Strife of hope and fear,
Till, from Suspence deliver'd by defeat,
I hither came, and found a safe retreat.

    Here, join'd by Thee and thy young playful train,
20 I was o'erpaid for years of toil and pain.

We had renounced our native *hostile* Shore,
And met, I trust, *till death to part no more.*
But now, approaching fast the verge of life,
With what emotions do I see a Wife
And children, smiling with affection dear,
And think *how sure* that parting and *how near*!

The solemn thought I wish not to restrain.
Though painful, 'tis a salutary pain.
Then let this Verse in your remembrance live;
30 That when from life releas'd, I still may give
Some token of my love, may whisper still
Some fault to shun, some duty to fulfill;
May prompt your Sympathy some pain to share,
Or warn you of some pleasures to beware;
Remind you that the arrow's silent flight,
Unseen alike at Noon or dead of Night,
Should cause no perturbation or dismay,
But teach you to enjoy the *passing day*
With dutiful tranquility of mind,
40 Active and diligent, but still *resign'd.*
For *our Redeemer liveth*, and we know,
How or whenever parted here below,
His faithful Servants, in the Realm above,
Shall meet again as Heirs of his eternal Love.

[1810]

The Comet of 1811

Of things new and rare, if you wish for a Sample,
Here is one that surpasses all former example.
For who, in these *Regions of Frost*, ever saw
December display so *prodigious* a *thaw*!
After having been used many days as a Road,
And borne, like a Turn-pike, full many a load,
Our *River*, escaping from *Winter's* arrest,

Has drown'd half our Cattle, and starved half the rest.
And *Winter*, mean-time, has himself taken Wing,
10 And the breath of *December* reminds us of *Spring*.
But Oh, look around you and see, far and wide,
What havock is made by this merciless tide!
Can you tell us the cause, or assign any reason
For such a portentous unnatural Season?
Don't you think it *miraculous*? – Oh no – far from it –
'Tis all from that *frizzle-pate vagabond Comet*,
Who, squeezing his tail, like a Sponge, as he pass'd,
Has drenched us with rain "from the Skirt of his blast,"
And left us, not *wading*, like Crows on the plain,
20 At the death of *Rochvaldus*, in *blood* of the slain,
But *wadling* in *Mud*, as we stroll along shore,
And the loss of our Beef and our Mutton deplore.

[1811]

The Battle of Queen's Town, Upper Canada

Again, with confidence elate,
    The invading foe has found
A captive's unexpected fate
    On our Canadian Ground.
Triumphant, as before, though still
    Outnumber'd by the foe,
Our chiefs again have shown how Skill
    Can deal the unerring blow.

Again we boast – but with a Sigh!
10   A brilliant Day's career;
For *Brock* demands from every eye
    The tribute of a tear.
Devoted to this Country's cause,
    The Soldier's debt he paid;
From Age to Age, with just applause,
    His name shall be convey'd.

(1812)

GRISELDA TONGE

c. 1803–1825

Born and educated in Windsor, Nova Scotia, Griselda
Tonge acknowledged the influence of her great-grand-
mother, poet Deborah How Cottnam ["Portia"], on her
own writing. Tonge died of a fever in Demerara while visit-
ing her father and brother. Praised by former *Blackwood's*
critic, James Irving, for her handling of the Spenserian
stanza, she was mythologized by Joseph Howe as "the
highly gifted songstress of Acadia" for her poems pub-
lished in newspaper and broadsheet form.

To My Dear Grandmother,

on her 80th Birth Day

How oft from honored Portia's * polished lyre
In tones harmonious this loved theme has flowed;
Each strain, while breathing all the poet's fire,
The feeling heart and fertile fancy showed;
Oftimes in childhood my young mind has glowed
While dwelling on her sweet descriptive lay –
Oh, that on me the power had been bestowed!
A tribute fitting for the theme to pay,
With joy I'd touch each string to welcome in this day.

10 But thou wilt not despise the humbler song
 Though genius decks it not; – though rude and wild
 Its numbers are; – ah! surely no, for long
 Thy kindness I have proved: while yet a child,
 Pleased I have sought the Muse, and oft beguiled
 With her low plaintive tones the passing hour;
 On the young effort thou hast sweetly smiled,

---

* The adopted Poetical name of the Writer's Great
 Grandmother [Deborah How Cottnam].

And reared my mind, even as an opening flower,
Watching with anxious love each new expanding power.

Oh! more than parent! friend unequalled! how
20 Can I my love for thee express! or say
With what a fervent, what a hallowed glow,
I hail thy mental beauty through decay!
While I thy venerable form survey,
Though eighty lengthened years have scatter'd snow
Upon thy honored head; though sorrow's seal
Is stamped with heavy pressure on thy brow,
Thine is an angel's mind, and oh! I feel
It gives an angel's look, which age can never steal!

Thy soul has long been ripening for its God,
30 And when he calls it I should not repine;
But nature still must mourn, and o'er they sod
I know no tears will faster fall than mine:
I know the bitter anguish that will twine
Around my heart strings: – but the thought is pain;
I will not think that I must soon resign
What I can never find on earth again –
Oh, that blessed prize has not been lent in vain!

For I do hope thy firm but mild controul,
Thy precepts and example may have shone
40 With rays of brightness o'er my youthful soul,
Which will my pathway light when thou art gone;
And when before thy Father's mercy throne
Thou join'st with myriads in the holy song,
If it may be, wilt thou on me look down,
And watch my faultering footsteps while along,
This busy maze I pass, and warn me still from wrong?

                                        [1824] (1825)

OLIVER GOLDSMITH

1794–1861

Born in St. Andrews, New Brunswick, the son of Loyalists and the grand-nephew and namesake of the well-known Irish writer, Oliver Goldsmith, the Canadian Oliver Goldsmith entered the commissariat service of the British army in 1810. He served in Halifax, Saint John, Hong Kong, and Newfoundland before retiring to Britain in the mid-1850s. Written in response to his great-uncle's *The Deserted Village* (1770), *The Rising Village* was first published in Britain in 1825, and republished in revised form in Saint John in 1834 as *The Rising Village with Other Poems*.

The Rising Village

Thou dear companion of my early years,
Partner of all my boyish hopes and fears,
To whom I oft addressed the youthful strain,
And sought no other praise than thine to gain;
Who oft hast bid me emulate his fame
Whose genius formed the glory of our name;
Say, when thou canst, in manhood's ripened age,
With judgment scan the more aspiring page,
Wilt thou accept this tribute of my lay,
10 By far too small thy fondness to repay?
Say, dearest Brother, wilt thou now excuse
This bolder flight of my adventurous muse?

   If, then, adown your cheek a tear should flow
For Auburn's Village, and its speechless woe;
If, while you weep, you think the "lowly train"
Their early joys can never more regain,
Come, turn with me where happier prospects rise,
Beneath the sternness of Acadian skies.
   And thou, dear spirit! whose harmonious lay
20 Didst lovely Auburn's piercing woes display,

Do thou to thy fond relative impart
Some portion of thy sweet poetic art;
Like thine, Oh! let my verse as gently flow,
While truth and virtue in my numbers glow:
And guide my pen with thy bewitching hand,
To paint the Rising Village of the land.

    How chaste and splendid are the scenes that lie
Beneath the circle of Britannia's sky!
What charming prospects there arrest the view,
30 How bright, how varied, and how boundless too!
Cities and plains extending far and wide,
The merchant's glory, and the farmer's pride.
Majestic palaces in pomp display
The wealth and splendour of the regal sway;
While the low hamlet and the shepherd's cot,
In peace and freedom mark the peasant's lot.
There nature's vernal bloom adorns the field,
And Autumn's fruits their rich luxuriance yield.
There men, in busy crowds, with men combine,
40 That arts may flourish, and fair science shine;
And thence, to distant climes their labours send,
As o'er the world their widening views extend.
Compar'd with scenes like these, how lone and drear
Did once Acadia's woods and wilds appear;
Where wandering savages, and beasts of prey,
Displayed, by turns, the fury of their sway.
What noble courage must their hearts have fired,
How great the ardour which their souls inspired,
Who leaving far behind their native plain,
50 Have sought a home beyond the Western main;
And braved the perils of the stormy seas,
In search of wealth, of freedom, and of ease!
Oh! none can tell but they who sadly share
The bosom's anguish, and its wild despair,
What dire distress awaits the hardy bands,

That venture first on bleak and desert lands.
How great the pain, the danger, and the toil,
Which mark the first rude culture of the soil.
When, looking round, the lonely settler sees
60 His home amid a wilderness of trees:
How sinks his heart in those deep solitudes,
Where not a voice upon his ear intrudes;
Where solemn silence all the waste pervades,
Heightening the horror of its gloomy shades;
Save where the sturdy woodman's strokes resound,
That strew the fallen forest on the ground.
See! from their heights the lofty pines descend,
And crackling, down their pond'rous lengths extend.
Soon from their boughs the curling flames arise,
70 Mount into air, and redden all the skies;
And where the forest once its foliage spread,
The golden corn triumphant waves its head. *

How blest did nature's ruggedness appear
The only source of trouble or of fear;
How happy, did no hardship meet his view,
No other care his anxious steps pursue;
But, while his labour gains a short repose,
And hope presents a solace for his woes,
New ills arise, new fears his peace annoy,
80 And other dangers all his hopes destroy.
Behold the savage tribes in wildest strain,

---

* *The golden corn triumphant waves its head.* The process of
clearing land, though simple, is attended with a great deal of
labour. The trees are all felled, so as to lie in the same
direction; and after the fire has passed over them in that state,
whatever may be left is collected into heaps, and reduced to
ashes. The grain is then sown between the stumps of the trees,
which remain, until the lapse of time, from ten to fifteen years,
reduces them to decay.

Approach with death and terror in their train;
No longer silence o'er the forest reigns,
No longer stillness now her power retains;
But hideous yells announce the murderous band,
Whose bloody footsteps desolate the land;
He hears them oft in sternest mood maintain,
Their right to rule the mountain and the plain;
He hears them doom the *white man's* instant death,
90 Shrinks from the sentence, while he gasps for breath,
Then, rousing with one effort all his might,
Darts from his hut, and saves himself by flight.
Yet, what a refuge! Here a host of foes,
On every side, his trembling steps oppose;
Here savage beasts around his cottage howl,
As through the gloomy wood they nightly prowl,
Till morning comes, and then is heard no more
The shouts of man, or beast's appalling roar;
The wandering Indian turns another way,
100 And brutes avoid the first approach of day.
    Yet, tho' these threat'ning dangers round him roll,
Perplex his thoughts, and agitate his soul,
By patient firmness and industrious toil,
He still retains possession of the soil;
Around his dwelling scattered huts extend,
Whilst every hut affords another friend.
And now, behold! his bold aggressors fly,
To seek their prey beneath some other sky;
Resign the haunts they can maintain no more,
110 And safety in far distant wilds explore.
His perils vanished, and his fears o'ercome,
Sweet hope portrays a happy peaceful home.
On every side fair prospects charm his eyes,
And future joys in every thought arise.
His humble cot, built from the neighbouring trees,
Affords protection from each chilling breeze;

His rising crops, with rich luxuriance crowned,
In waving softness shed their freshness round;
By nature nourished, by her bounty blest,
120 He looks to Heaven, and lulls his cares to rest.
    The arts of culture now extend their sway,
And many a charm of rural life display.
Where once the pine upreared its lofty head,
The settlers' humble cottages are spread;
Where the broad firs once sheltered from the storm,
By slow degrees a neighbourhood they form;
And, as its bounds, each circling year, increase
In social life, prosperity, and peace,
New prospects rise, new objects too appear,
130 To add more comfort to its lowly sphere.
Where some rude sign or post the spot betrays,
The tavern first its useful front displays.
Here, oft the weary traveller at the close
Of evening, finds a snug and safe repose.
The passing stranger here, a welcome guest,
From all his toil enjoys a peaceful rest;
Unless the host, solicitous to please,
With care officious mar his hope of ease,
With flippant questions to no end confined,
140 Exhaust his patience, and perplex his mind.
    Yet, let no one condemn with thoughtless haste,
The hardy settler of the dreary waste,
Who, far removed from every busy throng,
And social pleasures that to life belong,
Whene'er a stranger comes within his reach,
Will sigh to learn whatever he can teach.
To this, must be ascribed in great degree,
That ceaseless, idle curiosity,
Which over all the Western world prevails,
150 And every breast, or more or less, assails;
Till, by indulgence, so o'erpowering grown,

It seeks to know all business but its own.
Here, oft when winter's dreary terrors reign,
And cold, and snow, and storm, pervade the plain,
Around the birch-wood blaze the settlers draw,
"To tell of all they felt, and all they saw."
When, thus in peace are met a happy few,
Sweet are the social pleasures that ensue.
What lively joy each honest bosom feels,
160 As o'er the past events his memory steals,
And to the listeners paints the dire distress,
That marked his progress in the wilderness;
The danger, trouble, hardship, toil, and strife,
Which chased each effort of his struggling life.

    In some lone spot of consecrated ground,
Whose silence spreads a holy gloom around,
The village church in unadorned array,
Now lifts its turret to the opening day.
How sweet to see the villagers repair
170 In groups to pay their adoration there;
To view, in homespun dress, each sacred morn,
The old and young its hallowed seats adorn,
While, grateful for each blessing God has given,
In pious strains, they waft their thanks to Heaven.
    Oh, heaven-born faith! sure solace of our woes,
How lost is he who ne'er thy influence knows,
How cold the heart thy charity ne'er fires,
How dead the soul thy spirit ne'er inspires!
When troubles vex and agitate the mind,
180 By gracious Heaven for wisest ends designed,
When dangers threaten, or when fears invade,
Man flies to thee for comfort and for aid;
The soul, impelled by thy all-powerful laws,
Seeks safety, only, in a Great First Cause!
If, then, amid the busy scene of life,
Its joy and pleasure, care, distrust, and strife;

Man, to his God for help and succour fly,
And on his mighty power to save, rely;
If, then, his thoughts can force him to confess
190 His errors, wants, and utter helplessness;
How strong must be those feelings which impart
A sense of all his weakness to the heart,
Where not a friend in solitude is nigh,
His home the wild, his canopy the sky;
And, far removed from every human arm,
His God alone can shelter him from harm.

    While now the Rising Village claims a name,
Its limits still increase, and still its fame.
The wandering Pedlar, who undaunted traced
200 His lonely footsteps o'er the silent waste;
Who traversed once the cold and snow-clad plain,
Reckless of danger, trouble, or of pain,
To find a market for his little wares,
The source of all his hopes, and all his cares,
Established here, his settled home maintains,
And soon a merchant's higher title gains.
Around his store, on spacious shelves arrayed,
Behold his great and various stock in trade.
Here, nails and blankets, side by side, are seen,
210 There, horses' collars, and a large tureen;
Buttons and tumblers, fish-hooks, spoons and knives,
Shawls for young damsels, flannel for old wives;
Woolcards and stockings, hats for men and boys,
Mill-saws and fenders, silks, and children's toys;
All useful things, and joined with many more,
Compose the well-assorted country store. *

    The half-bred Doctor next then settles down,

----

* *Compose the well-assorted country store.* Every shop in
  America, whether in city or village, in which the most trifling
  articles are sold, is dignified with the title of a store.

And hopes the village soon will prove a town.
No rival here disputes his doubtful skill,
220 He cures, by chance, or ends each human ill;
By turns he physics, or his patient bleeds,
Uncertain in what case each best succeeds.
And if, from friends untimely snatched away,
Some beauty fall a victim to decay;
If some fine youth, his parents' fond delight,
Be early hurried to the shades of night,
Death bears the blame, 'tis his envenomed dart
That strikes the suffering mortal to the heart.
　　Beneath the shelter of a log-built shed
230 The country school-house next erects its head.
No "man severe," with learning's bright display,
Here leads the opening blossoms into day;
No master here, in every art refined,
Through fields of science guides the aspiring mind;
But some poor wanderer of the human race,
Unequal to the task, supplies his place,
Whose greatest source of knowledge or of skill
Consists in reading, and in writing ill;
Whose efforts can no higher merit claim,
240 Than spreading Dilworth's great scholastic fame.
No modest youths surround his awful chair,
His frowns to deprecate, or smiles to share,
But all the terrors of his lawful sway
The proud despise, the fearless disobey;
The rugged urchins spurn at all control,
Which cramps the movements of the free-born soul,
Till, in their own conceit so wise they've grown,
They think their knowledge far exceeds his own.
　　As thus the village each successive year
250 Presents new prospects, and extends its sphere,
While all around its smiling charms expand,
And rural beauties decorate the land.

The humble tenants, who were taught to know,
By years of suffering, all the weight of woe;
Who felt each hardship nature could endure,
Such pains as time alone could ease or cure,
Relieved from want, in sportive pleasures find
A balm to soften and relax the mind;
And now, forgetful of their former care,
260 Enjoy each sport, and every pastime share.
Beneath some spreading tree's expanded shade
Here many a manly youth and gentle maid,
With festive dances or with sprightly song
The summer's evening hours in joy prolong,
And as the young their simple sports renew,
The aged witness, and approve them too.
And when the Summer's bloomy charms are fled,
When Autumn's fallen leaves around are spread,
When Winter rules the sad inverted year,
270 And ice and snow alternately appear,
Sports not less welcome lightly they essay,
To chase the long and tedious hours away.
Here, ranged in joyous groups around the fire,
Gambols and freaks each honest heart inspire;
And if some venturous youth obtain a kiss,
The game's reward, and summit of its bliss,
Applauding shouts the victor's prize proclaim,
And every tongue augments his well-earned fame;
While all the modest fair one's blushes tell
280 Success had crowned his fondest hopes too well.
Dear humble sports, Oh! long may you impart
A guileless pleasure to the youthful heart,
Still may your joys from year to year increase,
And fill each breast with happiness and peace.
    Yet, tho' these simple pleasures crown the year,
Relieve its cares, and every bosom cheer,
As life's gay scenes in quick succession rise,

To lure the heart and captivate the eyes;
Soon vice steals on, in thoughtless pleasure's train,
290 And spreads her miseries o'er the village plain.
Her baneful arts some happy home invade,
Some bashful lover, or some tender maid;
Until, at length, repressed by no control,
They sink, debase, and overwhelm the soul.
How many aching breasts now live to know
The shame, the anguish, misery and woe,
That heedless passions, by no laws confined,
Entail forever on the human mind.
Oh, Virtue! that thy powerful charms could bind
300 Each rising impulse of the erring mind.
That every heart might own thy sovereign sway,
And every bosom fear to disobey;
No father's heart would then in anguish trace
The sad remembrance of a son's disgrace;
No mother's tears for some dear child undone
Would then in streams of poignant sorrow run,
Nor could my verse the hapless story tell
Of one poor maid who loved – and loved too well.
    Among the youths that graced their native plain,
310 Albert was foremost of the village train;
The hand of nature had profusely shed
Her choicest blessings on his youthful head;
His heart seemed generous, noble, kind, and free,
Just bursting into manhood's energy.
Flora was fair, and blooming as that flower
Which spreads its blossom to the April shower; *

---

* *Which spreads its blossom to the April shower*; The May-flower
(*Epigaea repens*) is indigenous to the wilds of Acadia, and is in
bloom from the middle of April to the end of May. Its leaves
are white, faintly tinged with red, and it possesses a delightful
fragrance.

Her gentle manners and unstudied grace
Still added lustre to her beaming face,
While every look, by purity refined,
320 Displayed the lovelier beauties of her mind.
    Sweet was the hour, and peaceful was the scene
When Albert first met Flora on the green;
Her modest looks, in youthful bloom displayed,
Then touched his heart, and there a conquest made.
Nor long he sighed, by love and rapture fired,
He soon declared the passion she inspired.
In silence, blushing sweetly, Flora heard
His vows of love and constancy preferred;
And, as his soft and tender suit he pressed,
330 The maid, at length, a mutual flame confessed.
    Love now had shed, with visions light as air,
His golden prospects on this happy pair;
Those moments soon rolled rapidly away,
Those hours of joy and bliss that gently play
Around young hearts, ere yet they learn to know
Life's care or trouble, or to feel its woe.
The day was fixed, the bridal dress was made,
And time alone their happiness delayed,
The anxious moment that, in joy begun,
340 Would join their fond and faithful hearts in one.
'Twas now at evening's hour, about the time
When in Acadia's cold and northern clime
The setting sun, with pale and cheerless glow,
Extends his beams o'er trackless fields of snow,
That Flora felt her throbbing heart oppressed
By thoughts, till then, a stranger to her breast.
Albert had promised that his bosom's pride
That very morning should become his bride;
Yet morn had come and passed; and not one vow
350 Of his had e'er been broken until now.
But, hark! a hurried step advances near,

'Tis Albert's breaks upon her listening ear;
Albert's, ah, no! a ruder footstep bore,
With eager haste, a letter to the door;
Flora received it, and could scarce conceal
Her rapture, as she kissed her lover's seal.
Yet, anxious tears were gathered in her eye,
As on the note it rested wistfully;
Her trembling hands unclosed the folded page,
360 That soon she hoped would every fear assuage,
And while intently o'er the lines she ran,
In broken half breathed tones she thus began:
    "Dear Flora, I have left my native plain,
And fate forbids that we shall meet again:
'Twere vain to tell, nor can I now impart
The sudden motive to this change of heart.
The vows so oft repeated to thine ear
As tales of cruel falsehood must appear.
Forgive the hand that deals this treacherous blow,
370 Forget the heart that can afflict this woe;
Farewell! and think no more of Albert's name,
His weakness pity, now involved in shame."
    Ah! who can paint her features as, amazed,
In breathless agony, she stood and gazed!
Oh, Albert, cruel Albert! she exclaimed,
Albert was all her faltering accents named.
A deadly feeling seized upon her frame,
Her pulse throbb'd quick, her colour went and came;
A darting pain shot through her frenzied head,
380 And from that fatal hour her reason fled!
    The sun had set; his lingering beams of light
From western hills had vanished into night.
The northern blast along the valley rolled,
Keen was that blast, and piercing was the cold,
When, urged by frenzy, and by love inspired,
For what but madness could her breast have fired!

Flora, with one slight mantle round her waved,
Forsook her home, and all the tempest braved.
Her lover's falsehood wrung her gentle breast,
390 His broken vows her tortured mind possessed;
Heedless of danger, on she bent her way
Through drifts of snow, where Albert's dwelling lay,
With frantic haste her tottering steps pursued
Amid the long night's darkness unsubdued;
Until, benumbed, her fair and fragile form
Yielded beneath the fury of the storm;
Exhausted nature could no further go,
And, senseless, down she sank amid the snow.

   Now as the morn had streaked the eastern sky
400 With dawning light, a passing stranger's eye,
By chance directed, glanced upon the spot
Where lay the lovely sufferer: To his cot
The peasant bore her, and with anxious care
Tried every art, till hope became despair.
With kind solicitude his tender wife
Long vainly strove to call her back to life;
At length her gentle bosom throbs again,
Her torpid limbs their wonted power obtain;
The loitering current now begins to flow,
410 And hapless Flora wakes once more to woe:
But all their friendly efforts could not find
A balm to heal the anguish of her mind.

   Come hither, wretch, and see what thou hast done,
Behold the heart thou hast so falsely won,
Behold it, wounded, broken, crushed and riven,
By thy unmanly arts to ruin driven;
Hear Flora calling on thy much loved name,
Which, e'en in madness, she forbears to blame.
Not all thy sighs and tears can now restore
420 One hour of pleasure that she knew before;
Not all thy prayers can now remove the pain,

That floats and revels o'er her maddened brain.
Oh, shame of manhood! that could thus betray
A maiden's hopes, and lead her heart away;
Oh, shame of manhood! that could blast her joy,
And one so fair, so lovely, could destroy.

    Yet, think not oft such tales of real woe
Degrade the land, and round the village flow.
Here virtue's charms appear in bright array,
430 And all their pleasing influence display;
Here modest youths, impressed in beauty's train,
Or captive led by love's endearing chain,
And fairest girls whom vows have ne'er betrayed,
Vows that are broken oft as soon as made,
Unite their hopes, and join their lives in one,
In bliss pursue them, as at first begun.
Then, as life's current onward gently flows,
With scarce one fault to ruffle its repose,
With minds prepared, they sink in peace to rest,
440 To meet on high the spirits of the blest.

    While time thus rolls his rapid years away,
The Village rises gently into day.
How sweet it is, at first approach of morn,
Before the silvery dew has left the lawn,
When warring winds are sleeping yet on high,
Or breathe as softly as the bosom's sigh,
To gain some easy hill's ascending height,
Where all the landscape brightens with delight,
And boundless prospects stretched on every side,
450 Proclaim the country's industry and pride.
Here the broad marsh extends its open plain,
Until its limits touch the distant main;
There verdant meads along the uplands spring,
And grateful odours to the breezes fling;
Here crops of grain in rich luxuriance rise,

And wave their golden riches to the skies;
There smiling orchards interrupt the scene,
Or gardens bounded by some fence of green;
The farmer's cottage, bosomed 'mong the trees,
460 Whose spreading branches shelter from the breeze;
The winding stream that turns the busy mill,
Whose clacking echos o'er the distant hill;
The neat white church, beside whose walls are spread
The grass-clod hillocks of the sacred dead,
Where rude cut stones or painted tablets tell,
In laboured verse, how youth and beauty fell;
How worth and hope were hurried to the grave,
And torn from those who had no power to save.
    Or, when the Summer's dry and sultry sun
470 Adown the West his fiery course has run;
When o'er the vale his parting rays of light
Just linger, ere they vanish into night,
How sweet to wander round the wood-bound lake,
Whose glassy stillness scarce the zephyrs wake;
How sweet to hear the murmuring of the rill,
As down it gurgles from the distant hill;
The note of Whip-poor-Will how sweet to hear, *
When sadly slow it breaks upon the ear,
And tells each night, to all the silent vale,
480 The hopeless sorrows of its mournful tale.
Dear lovely spot! Oh may such charms as these,
Sweet tranquil charms, that cannot fail to please,
Forever reign around thee, and impart

---

* *The note of Whip-poor-Will how sweet to hear.* The Whip-poor-
Will (*Caprimulgus vociferus*) is a native of America. On a
summer's evening the wild and mournful cadence of its note is
heard at a great distance; and the traveller listens with delight
to the repeated tale of its sorrows.

Joy, peace, and comfort to each native heart.
    Happy Acadia! though around thy shore *
Is heard the stormy wind's terrific roar;
Though round thee Winter binds his icy chain,
And his rude tempests sweep along thy plain,
Still Summer comes, and decorates thy land
490 With fruits and flowers from her luxuriant hand;
Still Autumn's gifts repay the labourer's toil
With richest products from thy fertile soil;
With bounteous store his varied wants supply,
And scarce the plants of other suns deny.
How pleasing, and how glowing with delight
Are now thy budding hopes! How sweetly bright
They rise to view! How full of joy appear
The expectations of each future year!
Not fifty Summers yet have blessed thy clime,
500 How short a period in the page of time!
Since savage tribes, with terror in their train,
Rushed o'er thy fields, and ravaged all thy plain.
But some few years have rolled in haste away
Since, through thy vales, the fearless beast of prey,
With dismal yell and loud appalling cry,
Proclaimed his midnight reign of terror nigh.
And now how changed the scene! the first, afar,
Have fled to wilds beneath the northern star;
The last has learned to shun man's dreaded eye,
510 And, in his turn, to distant regions fly.
While the poor peasant, whose laborious care
Scarce from the soil could wring his scanty fare;

---

* *Happy Acadia! though around thy shore.* The Provinces of Nova
Scotia and New Brunswick now comprehend that part of
British North America, which was formerly denominated
Acadia, or L'Acadie, by the French, and Nova Scotia by the
English.

Now in the peaceful arts of culture skilled,
Sees his wide barn with ample treasures filled;
Now finds his dwelling, as the year goes round,
Beyond his hopes, with joy and plenty crowned.
    Nor culture's arts, a nation's noblest friend,
Alone o'er Scotia's fields their power extend;
From all her shores, with every gentle gale,
520 Commerce expands her free and swelling sail;
And all the land, luxuriant, rich, and gay,
Exulting owns the splendour of their sway.
These are thy blessings, Scotia, and for these,
For wealth, for freedom, happiness, and ease,
Thy grateful thanks to Britain's care are due,
Her power protects, her smiles past hopes renew,
Her valour guards thee, and her councils guide,
Then, may thy parent ever be thy pride!
    Happy Britannia! though thy history's page
530 In darkest ignorance shrouds thine infant age,
Though long thy childhood's years in error strayed,
And long in superstition's bands delayed;
Matur'd and strong, thou shin'st in manhood's prime,
The first and brightest star of Europe's clime.
The nurse of science, and the seat of arts,
The home of fairest forms and gentlest hearts;
The land of heroes, generous, free, and brave,
The noblest conquerors of the field and wave;
Thy flag, on every sea and shore unfurled,
540 Has spread thy glory, and thy thunder hurled.
When, o'er the earth, a tyrant would have thrown
His iron chain, and called the world his own,
Thine arm preserved it, in its darkest hour,
Destroyed his hopes, and crushed his dreaded power,
To sinking nations life and freedom gave,
'Twas thine to conquer, as 'twas thine to save.
    Then blest Acadia! ever may thy name,

Like hers, be graven on the rolls of fame;
May all thy sons, like hers, be brave and free,
550 Possessors of her laws and liberty;
Heirs of her splendour, science, power, and skill,
And through succeeding years her children still.
And as the sun, with gentle dawning ray,
From night's dull bosom wakes, and leads the day,
His course majestic keeps, till in the height
He glows one blaze of pure exhaustless light;
So may thy years increase, thy glories rise,
To be the wonder of the Western skies;
And bliss and peace encircle all thy shore,
560 Till empires rise and sink, on earth, no more.

(1825)

ANONYMOUS

1829

The "Canadian Boat-Song" first appeared in September 1829 in the *Noctes Ambrosianae* section of *Blackwood's Magazine*. Described as a translation from the Gaelic of emigrant oarsmen working on the St. Lawrence, it was purportedly sent from Upper Canada by an acquaintance of "Christopher North." Although many putative authors have been proposed, including John Galt, William ("Tiger") Dunlop, Dr. David Macbeth Moir, and even Sir Walter Scott, its origin remains a literary mystery.

Canadian Boat-Song

(from the Gaelic)

Listen to me, as when ye heard our father
    Sing long ago the song of other shores –
Listen to me, and then in chorus gather
    All your deep voices, as ye pull your oars:
             CHORUS
    Fair these broad meads – these hoary woods are grand;
    But we are exiles from our fathers' land.

From the lone shieling of the misty island
    Mountains divide us, and the waste of seas –
Yet still the blood is strong, the heart is Highland,
10   And we in dreams behold the Hebrides:
    Fair these broad meads – these hoary woods are grand;
    But we are exiles from our fathers' land.

We ne'er shall tread the fancy-haunted valley,
    Where 'tween the dark hills creeps the small clear
                             stream,
In arms around the patriarch banner rally,
    Nor see the moon on royal tombstones gleam:

Fair these broad meads – these hoary woods are grand;
But we are exiles from our fathers' land.

When the bold kindred, in the time long-vanish'd,
20   Conquer'd the soil and fortified the keep, –
No seer foretold the children would be banish'd,
    That a degenerate Lord might boast his sheep:
    Fair these broad meads – these hoary woods are grand;
    But we are exiles from our fathers' land.

Come foreign rage – let Discord burst in slaughter!
    O then for clansman true, and stern claymore –
The hearts that would have given their blood like water,
    Beat heavily beyond the Atlantic roar:
    Fair these broad meads – these hoary woods are grand;
30   *But we are exiles from our fathers' land.*

(1829)

ANONYMOUS
1838

This poem, from the Rebellion of 1837-38, describes the confrontation at Montgomery's tavern in Toronto on the night of December 7-8, 1837, between two hundred farmers led by William Lyon Mackenzie and twelve hundred Government troops. It appeared in August 1838 in *Mackenzie's Gazette*, which Mackenzie published in exile from New York.

The Fight at Montgomery's

(For *Mackenzie's Gazette*)

They have met – that small band, resolved to be free,
As the fierce winds of Heaven that course over the sea –
They have met, in bright hope, with no presage of fear,
Tho' the bugle and drum of the foeman they hear:
Some seize the dread rifle, some wield the tall pike,
For God and their country – for Freedom they strike,
No proud ensign of glory bespeaks their renown,
Yet the scorn of defiance now darkens their frown.
See the foeman advancing, and now sounds afar
10 The clang and the shout of disastrous war.
Yes! onward they come like the mountain's wild flood,
And the lion's dark talons are dappled in blood.
O, God of my country! they turn now to fly –
Hark! the Eagle of Liberty screams in the sky!
Where, where are the thousands that morn should have
found
In battle array on that dew-covered ground?
The few that were there, now wildly have flown,
Did fear stay the others? * * * * * *

Some in the dungeon – some on swelling flood,
20 Some seek the shelter of the pathless wood,
And some in exile – 'neath a foreign sky,
Curse the sad hour they madly turned to fly.
Firmer their tyrants o'er the oozy main
Bind on their shackles – forge the triple chain,
Till other days they still must sadly bear
The withering curse that marks a *Despot's care.*

(1838)

M. ETHELIND SAWTELL

fl. 1840–1851

Born on the Island of Guernsey, Margaret Ethelind Clarke
came to Canada as the wife of Luther Sawtell, who became
lieutenant in a voluntary militia organization, the Sorel
Rifle Corps. After her husband died in 1839, she published
her volume of poems, *The Mourner's Tribute* (Montreal,
1840), to raise money for her support. Between 1848 and
1851 she contributed poems to several Montreal periodi-
cals under the name of Kittson, following her marriage to
Robert H. Kittson, a Sorel businessman.

Achievements of a Volunteer Corps

Whose wish of being called into "active service"
was never gratified.

Brave Volunteers! brave Volunteers!
    Of exploits never known,
"Advance!" with three loud hearty cheers,
    Your valorous deeds to own.

What have you won for England's fame,
    Since England's pay you touch?
Not aught, I think, to raise your name
    In her annals very much.

"O! yes, O! yes – on one cold night,
10   We were a little band,
And wandering forth without moon-light,
    Desired some stumps to stand! –

Yes, in the dark, took them for foes,
    And thought it very fine
To bid them stand, unless they rose,
    To give the countersign.

That's one brave act, we think, to show
   That we were not afraid –
In a lone wood to challenge so,
20   Without a stronger aid!

Another gallant deed achieved
   Was up at Contrècoeur:
Expecting heads to have been cleaved
   Was nothing to allure.

But bravely there we struggled too,
   And really cleared the barge!
So that our deeds, though very few,
   Deserve your praise at large."

                              (1840)

The Indian's Refusal

An Indian, on being asked if he would sell the burial-place
of his ancestors, replied, "Shall I say to the bones of my
fathers, 'Arise – and get into a strange land?'"

Shall I say to the bones of my fathers, "Arise –
   To the land of the stranger begone?"
Shall the bright gold have power to scatter their dust,
   That the white man may reign here alone?
Yes, here, where the warriors have long laid in peace,
   In their soul-haunted valley they rest;
And to them shall I say, "Now arise – now depart –
   I have bartered the earth o'er your breast"?
And beneath this sepulchral, this tall ancient tree,
10   Where often the quiver hath hung,
And the bow hath been bent from beneath its dark shade,
   As the moose from the forest hath sprung,
And the young caraboo, in its swift, fleetest course,
   From their barbed arrows never could flee.
No. The white man may cherish his glittering gold;

But the graves of my fathers are free;
Where the eagle's long plume in the scalp-lock hath been
   By the hands of the warriors undone;
From the green prairie hills, or the dark solemn woods
20   Where the blood track their pathway hath won.
Here often around hath the death-song been raised,
   And lighted the funeral pile,
Where the chiefs of the nations in tortures were bent,
   Their sufferings to meet with a smile.
And here, too, they oft have the calumet wreathed,
   In token of peace and of rest,
And the ivy's tough clasp and the bright creeping moss
   By the conqueror's footsteps been pressed.
Though the Delaware bands from their ambush are gone,
30   And their strength from the forest is fled –
Though the war-cry is hushed, yet the voices arise
   Which for ages have been with the dead.
No. The free winds of heaven, and dews of the morn,
   With the Great Spirit watch o'er their sleep;
And while the Missouri's proud river shall flow,
   Its waves by their green mounds shall sweep.
Then cherish, pale stranger – go cherish thy g[round]
   For their resting-place here yet shall be.
Whilst the word of the Indian is steadfast and s[ound]
40   The bones of the dead shall be free.

                           (1840)

DOUGLAS HUYGHUE
("EUGENE")
1816–1891

Born in Charlottetown, Prince Edward Island, and raised and educated in Saint John, New Brunswick, Douglas Huyghue was a writer and artist whose sympathy with Native peoples in Canada informed his two novels, *Argimou, A Legend of the Micmac* (1847) and *Nomads of the West; or, Ellen Clayton* (1850). His poetry and prose appeared in the Saint John *Amaranth*, the Halifax *Morning Post*, and *Bentley's Miscellany* (London). After immigrating to Australia in 1852, he worked as a government clerk in Ballarat, where he recorded his historically significant eyewitness experience of the Eureka uprising of 1854 in "The Ballarat Riots" (unpublished) and a series of illustrations.

The Miner's Tale

I remind me, 'twas like the mighty rush
Of roaring winds, as through the distant *drift*
That sound came rumbling on; and each man lean'd
Upon his spade – awe-struck and still – each cheek
Blanched in the sickly lamplight; 'twas but
A moment, then cries and yells of warning
Through the vaults, and a man came flying past
With wild shout of agony – "the waters!" –
Aye, all died! The youth in his golden prime,
10 And the old time-worn miner in his age;
The warm heart and the sunny brow, the eye
Of passion and the breast of guile, grew chill
And rigid 'neath that life-devouring flood; –
They perished all!

        Six of us there were,
And we gained a ledge of rock above
The whelming wave, and scann'd each face to see

What friends were there. The horror of our doom
Then withered up our souls, searing as
20 A lightning flash, its depths; to be entomb'd
In rocks of adamant – foodless – hopeless,
O God! 'twas a wild thought; so wild, that some
Grew mad, and cursed and laughed with mirth
Which was a mockery; and some lay down
And covered up their heads in speechless woe,
So silent, that they seemed bereft of thought
And life in their deep misery. But one
There was, a boy – a young and gentle boy; –
The sad, bright tears were flowing down his cheek,
30 As with clasp'd hands, and knee upon the rock,
He breath'd a prayer to heaven, mingled
With his mother's name; I could not look upon
His holy grief; the strong man crush'd and bow'd,
The maniac in his rage, were nothing
To the prayer and tears of that pure child!
Then hunger came and gnaw'd within us, like
An undying worm, and the shrunk skin upon
Each spectral face, look'd hideously
In the expiring lamp. It could not last.
40 Some sprang into the flood with blasphemy,
But others were too weak, and could not move
Their fleshless limbs, save when a spasm shook them;
These died hard, and when their cries were hushed
There were none left but the poor starving boy,
Whose moans grew fainter as his blue eyes clos'd.
I know not how it was – I could not die;
Like sapless autumn leaves they fell around,
Yet still I lingered on, with burning throat,
And swell'd and speechless tongue, craving strength
50 To tear the half-eat shoe with hungry jaws,
And teeth that chatter'd with a hollow sound
In racking pain; yet still I did not die,

But grew delirious, and then, methought,
A gabbering demon sat before me,
Feasting on a bone – a human bone,
And as he tore the flesh with wolfish fangs
He laugh'd with hellish glee, and I laugh'd too,
He seem'd so merry; but the sound I made
Scar'd me into sense, and then I wonder'd
60 Where I was, it seemed so dark and still,
And stretching forth my hand I touch'd a face –
A shrivell'd bony face – and shuddering,
Remember'd all; then numbness crept upon
My nerveless limbs, and thought and feeling merg'd
In listless lethargy.

             Yet still I breath'd,
A bootless thing within that dreadful grave,
Enclosed in solid stone; – a living man
Imprison'd in the bowels of the earth
70 With the rank dead for his companions.
What time elapsed I knew not, but a voice,
Making strange music in that lonely place,
Re-echoed through the cavern; a light
Gleamed before my eye-balls and I look'd,
And lo! a miner bent him over me,
But started when he saw my famish'd face;
The waters had subsided – I alone,
Of those ill-fated mortals yet surviv'd
To tell this tale!

                      (1842)

GEORGE WILLIAM GILLESPIE

d. 1847

Before his emigration to Canada, George W. Gillespie
published *Poems and Songs* (1827) in his native Scotland. In
Toronto, where he died, some of his verses appeared in
local newspapers two years before the production of his
book, *Miscellaneous Poems* (1843).

The Canadian Dominie's Lament

I dwine in my cruive a' the lang winter night,
And never beams round me ae blink o' delight;
I gaunt and I brood a' the weary night lang,
And carena for reading, for music nor sang;
I sigh for Toronto, o' company fain,
And wish frae my heart I were in it again.
A Dominie's life, lone, secluded, I find
Is ane winna souther exact wi' my mind;
I find 'tis an effort that strikes me aft mute,
10 To teach young ideas the method to shoot;
The bairns are a fash, their capacities dull,
Opposed towards letters seems each stupid skull;
My lugs a' day lang are confused wi' their din,
To paik them their parents consider it sin;
My salary's dubious, my labours are sure,
The prospect before me's an unco bare muir;
My pupils are stubborn, not easily tamed,
For their misdemeanours by parents I'm blamed,
Who often are boorish, unsocial, and prone
20 To think there are few like themselves and their own.
My back should I turn, while preparing to eat,
The cat breaks a dish, and the dog steals my meat;
Things a' out o' keeping, confusion grows rife,
For lack o' right sorting, for want o' a wife.

My post I'll abandon and hie to the bush,
There I'll work as a chopper, and sing like a thrush,
Though the bear should molest, and the wolf round me
                                                prowl,
For this is a life only fit for an owl.

                                        (1843)

Lines on Canada

Yes! lovely the land of the poplar and pine,
Where the maple trees flourish, and wild shoots the vine:
Where the sun-flower prolific is every where seen,
The holy-hock, shumac, and bright scarlet-bean.
Oh! rich is the foliage the woods that array,
And charming the plumage their inmates display,
That sweet little wanderer, the humming-bird bright,
Here to flaunt in the sun's fervid beam takes delight;
His home for a period he makes of these bowers,
10 Fond sipping the fragrance and sweets of the flowers.
How charmed in the silence of noon I have strayed,
And the woodpecker's beautiful plumage surveyed;
Whil'st Echo his strokes through the woods made
                                                resound,
And the chipmunk familiar, frisk'd playful around,
While the walnuts prolific, adorning the trees,
Ripe, rapped to the ground at the kiss of each breeze:
And, oh! what for grandeur in season may vie
With the beautiful tints of a Canada sky.
Italia! they tell us, so lauded by Fame,
20 In the lays of the poets, can put in her claim;
The hues of Aurora, the clear sky of noon,
The shades of the evening, and then when the moon
Majestical mounts from the verge of the lake,
And the bright constellations all splendid awake:
With the serpentine form of the near milky way,

The mind may retain, but no words can convey,
More varied than hues of the forests are seen,
More sweet than the flowers that enamel the green:
The fair Upper Canada proudly may boast
30 From Scotia, from Erin, and Anglian coast.
How blest were this land would dissensions all cease,
And again come with smiles the sweet cherub of peace:
The strokes of the woodman, as wont, blythe resound
To the plough-boy's gay whistle, while tilling the ground;
The tears of the matron be dried, I've seen flow,
Bereft of her mate, or her sons plunged in woe.
Hence! hateful rebellion, and dire civil war,
Heaven hold from this Province your horrors afar!

(1843)

Canadian Woodsman's Farewell
to His Log House

Farewell! my wife and children dear,
    Loved partners of my joys and woes;
My snug log-house, adieu, awhile,
    Rear'd where the widening clearance shews;
My sturdy steeds, domestic cow,
    Whose tinkling bell, when homeward-bound,
Oft charm'd the stilly hour of eve, –
    The bugle breathes a different sound.

It calls to quash wild discord's din,
10   To quell rebellion late begun,
To save from foreign power and yoke
    The soil our fathers' valor won.
Be ours the task thence to repel
    The inroads of these sons of spoil,
Our mustering word – integrity, –
    And plaudits of our Parent Isle.

(1843)

GEORGE COPWAY
(KAH-GE-GA-GAH-BOWH)
1818–1869

Born near the mouth of the Trent River, George Copway experienced a youthful conversion to Methodism, becomming a missionary and later an ordained minister. His prose works include some samples of his own verse as well as several translations of traditional Native songs. In addition to assisting with the translation of two books of the Bible into Ojibway, he wrote several books in English, among them his autobiography *The Life, History, and Travels of Kah-ge-ga-gah-bowh* (first published in 1847 and subsequently reissued under several different titles), *The Traditional History and Characteristic Sketches of the Ojibway Nation* (1850), and a narrative poem, *The Ojibway Conquest* (1850).

[Once More I See My Fathers' Land]

Once more I see my fathers' land
    Upon the beach, where oceans roar;
Where whitened bones bestrew the sand,
    Of some brave warrior of yore.
The *groves*, where once my fathers roamed –
    The *rivers*, where the beaver dwelt –
The *lakes*, where angry waters foamed –
    Their *charms*, with my fathers, have fled.

O! tell me, ye "Palefaces," tell,
10   Where have my proud ancestors gone?
Whose smoke curled up from every dale,
    To what land have their free spirits flown?
Whose wigwam stood where cities rise;
    On whose war-paths the steam-horse flies;

And ships, like mon-e-doos in disguise,
  Approach the shore in endless files.

                              (1847)

[War Song] (trans.)

"On that day when our heroes lay low – lay low –
On that day when our heroes lay low,
I fought by their side, and thought, ere I died,
Just vengeance to take on the foe – the foe –
Just vengeance to take on the foe.

"On that day when our chieftains lay dead – lay dead –
On that day when our chieftains lay dead,
I fought hand to hand, at the head of my band,
And *here, on my breast,* have I bled – have I bled –
10 And here, on my breast, have I bled.

"Our chiefs shall return no more – no more –
Our chiefs shall return no more –
And their brothers in war, who can't show scar for scar,
Like women their fates shall deplore – shall deplore –
Like women their fates shall deplore.

"Five winters in hunting we'll spend – we'll spend –
Five winters in hunting we'll spend –
Then, our youths grown to men, to the war lead again,
And our days like our fathers we'll end – we'll end –
20 And our days like our fathers we'll end."

                              (1847)

[War Song] (trans.)

I

I will haste to the land of the foe,
With warriors clad with the bow.

II

I will drink the blood of their very heart;
I will change their joy into sorrow's smart;
Their braves, their sires will I defy,
And a nation's vengeance satisfy.

III

They are in their homes, now happy and free;
No frowning cloud o'er their camp they see;
Yet the youngest of mine shall see the tall
10   Braves, scattered, wandering, and fall.

(1850)

CHARLES SANGSTER

1822–1893

Born in Kingston, Upper Canada, Charles Sangster knew only a rudimentary education before embarking on a lifetime of hard work, which included a period of journalism and a position with the Post Office. During the 1850s and 1860s, when he published *The St. Lawrence and the Saguenay, and Other Poems* (1856) and *Hesperus, and Other Poems and Lyrics* (1860), he was one of Canada's most admired poets.

On Queenston Heights

Eleven: Welcome to the Sabbath bells!
A blessing and a welcome! At this hour
One prays for me at home, two hundred miles
From where I lounge along the grassy knoll,
Far up upon this classic hill. The air
Hath a delicious feeling, as it breathes
Its autumn breath upon me; air so calm,
One cannot feel the beat of Nature's pulse.
No, not a throb. The heav'nly influences,
10 Hearing that maiden's prayer, lean down and move
My being with their answerings of love.
The myriad-tinted leaves have gravely paused
To listen to the spheral whisperings –
The unvoiced harmonies that few can hear
Or feel, much less interpret faithfully;
And the swift waters of the dizzy gorge,
Stunned with their recent plunge against the crags
That hide Niagara's iris-circled feet,
And lashed to very madness as they wound
20 Their circling way past rocks and fretted banks,
Melt into calm in the blue lake beyond,
As starlight melts into the distant sea.

Those ancient willows have a solemn droop;
You scarce can see the dwelling they adorn:
Behind them rest the grain-denuded fields.
Here, to my left, an unpretending town;
There, to my right, another; like two friends,
Each thanking heaven for the Sabbath-pause,
And the brief respite from man's curse of toil.
30 The church bells, pealing now and then a note,
Swell the bless'd paean with their silver tongues.
The very tombstones yonder, near the church,
Look whiter for the eloquent repose.

A few short paces through the cedar trees,
Where the pert chipmunks chatter, and the birds
Select and melodize their sweetest notes,
And I have gained the level. Toward the lake,
Faint cloudlike points of land are dimly seen
Blending with old Ontario, and the gorge
40 Hurries its whirling current past the banks
That glass their fair proportions in the stream.

Here is the Monument. Immortal BROCK,
Whose ashes lie beneath it, not more still
Than is the plain to-day. What have we gained,
But a mere breath of fame, for all the blood
That flowed profusely on this stirring field?
'Tis true, a Victory; through which we still
Fling forth the meteor banner to the breeze,
And have a blood-sealed claim upon the soil.
50 'Twere better than Defeat, a thousand times.
And we have rightly learned to bless the name
Of the Old Land, whose courage won the day –
We, the descendants of her Victor-sires.
But dearer than a hundred victories,
With their swift agony, the earnest Calm,
That, like a blessing from the lips of God,

Rests on the classic plain, o'er which my feet
Tread lightly, in remembrance of the dead –
My Brothers all, Vanquished and Victors both.
60 And yet my heart leaps up, poor human heart!
As I lean proudly, with a human pride,
Against this pillar to a great man's name.
Yet I would rather earn that maiden's prayer,
Than all the fame of the immortal dead.

There may be furrows still upon the field,
Ploughed up by the wild hurricane of war
On that eventful day. Here, certainly,
An angry missile grooved this honored rock.
Though nearly half a century has pass'd,
70 The fissure still is here, and here the rust
Left by the iron messenger of death,
As it sped forward like an angry fate,
Sending, perchance, ten human souls to hell.

There, there was pain. Here, where the wondrous skill
Of the mechanic, with this iron web
Has spanned the chasm, the pulse beats hopefully,
And thoughts of peace sit dove-like in the mind.
Heav'n bridge those people's hearts, and make them one!

(1856)

from *Sonnets, Written in the Orillia Woods*

IV

The birds are singing merrily, and here
A squirrel claims the lordship of the woods,
And scolds me for intruding. At my feet
The tireless ants all silently proclaim
The dignity of labour. In my ear
The bee hums drowsily; from sweet to sweet
Careering, like a lover weak in aim.

I hear faint music in the solitudes;
A dreamlike melody that whispers peace
10   Imbues the calmy forest, and sweet rills
Of tender feeling murmur through my brain,
Like ripplings of pure water down the hills
That slumber in the moonlight. Cease, oh, cease!
Some day my weary heart will coin these into pain.

VIII

Above where I am sitting, o'er these stones,
The ocean waves once heaved their mighty forms;
And vengeful tempests and appalling storms
Wrung from the stricken sea portentous moans,
That rent stupendous icebergs, whose huge heights
Crashed down in fragments through the startled
                                                                    nights.
Change, change, eternal change in all but God!
Mysterious nature! thrice mysterious state
Of body, soul, and spirit! Man is awed,
10   But triumphs in his littleness. A mote,
He specks the eye of the age and turns to dust,
And is the sport of centuries. We note
More surely nature's ever-changing fate;
Her fossil records tell how she performs her trust.

XIII

I've almost grown a portion of this place;
I seem familiar with each mossy stone;
Even the nimble chipmunk passes on,
And looks, but never scolds me. Birds have flown
And almost touched my hand; and I can trace
The wild bees to their hives. I've never known
So sweet a pause from labour. But the tone
Of a past sorrow, like a mournful rill
Threading the heart of some melodious hill,

10   Or the complainings of the whippoorwill,
Passes through every thought, and hope, and aim.
It has its uses; for it cools the flame
Of ardent love that burns my being up –
Love, life's celestial pearl, diffused through all its cup.

(1859)

Midnight Sonnet

1874-'75

As in the depths of some old forest home
The dead trees lie and cumber all the ground,
Ev'n so my thoughts, with not a wing to roam,
Where erst they travelled without stint or bound,
Lie strewn promiscuous. Through all my mind
I seem to stumble over the dead past,
As if there were no present to be twined
In sweet memorial chaplets round the brow
Of some dear fancy, though not doomed to last
10 Beyond the heart-beats of the passing Now.
Yet searching through the rubbish, I perceive
The sharp green blades just peering through the ground,
Fern fancies, as it were, round which to weave
Some yet unheard-of gleams of fine inspired sound.

[1875]

ALEXANDER McLACHLAN

1818–1896

A native of Johnstone, Scotland, Alexander McLachlan was strongly influenced by Glasgow radicalism before his immigration to Upper Canada in 1840. After a series of unsuccessful farming ventures, he settled near Guelph, where he worked as a tailor, lecturer, and immigration agent. In 1877 he moved to a farm near Orangeville. His first volume, *The Spirit of Love, and Other Poems* (1846), was followed by *The Emigrant and Other Poems* (1861), *Poems and Songs* (1874), and *The Poetical Works of Alexander McLachlan* (1900).

We Live in a Rickety House

We live in a rickety house,
    In a dirty dismal street,
Where the naked hide from day,
    And thieves and drunkards meet.

And pious folks, with their tracts,
    When our dens they enter in,
They point to our shirtless backs,
    As the fruits of beer and gin.

And they quote us texts, to prove
10   That our hearts are hard as stone;
And they feed us with the fact,
    That the fault is all our own.

And the parson comes and prays –
    He's very concerned 'bout our souls;
But he never asks, in the coldest days,
    How we may be off for coals,

It will be long ere the poor
    Will learn their grog to shun;

While it's raiment, food and fire,
    And religion all in one.

I wonder some pious folks
    Can look us straight in the face,
For our ignorance and crime
20   Are the Church's shame and disgrace.

We live in a rickety house,
    In a dirty dismal street,
Where the naked hide from day,
    And thieves and drunkards meet.
                                        (1861)

The Anglo-Saxon

The Anglo-Saxon leads the van,
    And never lags behind,
For was not he ordain'd to be
    The leader of mankind?
He carries very little sail,
    Makes very little show,
But gains the haven without fail,
    Whatever winds may blow.

He runs his plough in every land,
10   He sails on every sea,
All prospers where he has a hand,
    For king of men is he.
He plants himself on Afric's sand,
    And 'mong Spitzbergen's snows,
For he takes root in any land,
    And blossoms like the rose.

Into the wilderness he goes,
    He loves the wild and free,
The forests stagger 'neath his blows,

20   A sturdy man is he.
    To have a homestead of his own,
        The giants down he'll bring –
    His shanty's sacred as a throne,
        And there he'll reign a king.

    For let him plant him where he may,
        On this you may depend,
    As sure as worth will have the sway,
        He's ruler in the end.
    For he believes in thrift, and knows
30   The money-making art,
    But tho' in riches great he grows,
        They harden not his heart.

    He never knows when he is beat;
        To knock him down is vain,
    He's sure to get upon his feet,
        And into it again.
    If you're resolved to be his foe,
        You'll find him rather tough,
    But he'll not strike another blow
40   Whene'er you call "enough."

    His is a nature true as steel,
        Where many virtues blend,
    A head to think, a heart to feel,
        A soul to comprehend.
    I love to look upon his face,
        Whate'er be his degree,
    An honour to the human race,
        The king of men is he.

                                (1874)

Young Canada Or
Jack's as Good as His Master

I love this land of forest grand!
   The land where labour's free;
Let others roam away from home,
   Be this the land for me!
Where no one moils, and strains and toils
   That snobs may thrive the faster;
And all are free, as men should be,
   And Jack's as good's his master!

Where none are slaves, that lordly knaves
10   May idle all the year;
For rank and caste are of the past, –
   They'll never flourish here!
And Jew or Turk if he'll but work,
   Need never fear disaster;
He reaps the crop he sowed in hope,
   For Jack's as good's his master.

Our aristocracy of toil
   Have made us what you see –
The nobles of the forge and soil,
20   With ne'er a pedigree!
It makes one feel himself a man,
   His very blood leaps faster,
Where wit or worth's preferred to birth,
   And Jack's as good's his master!

Here's to the land of forests grand!
   The land where labour's free;
Let others roam away from home,
   Be this the land for me!
For here 'tis plain, the heart and brain,
30   The very soul grow vaster!

Where men are free, as they should be,
And Jack's as good's his master!
                    (1874)

The Man Who Rose From Nothing

Around the world the fame is blown
Of fighting heroes, dead and gone;
But we've a hero of our own –
    The man who rose from nothing.

He's a magician great and grand;
The forests fled at his command;
And here he said, "let cities stand!" –
    The man who rose from nothing.

And in our legislative hall
10 He towering stands alone, like Saul,
"A head and shoulders over all," –
    The man who rose from nothing.

His efforts he will ne'er relax,
Has faith in figures and in facts,
And always calls an axe an axe, –
    The man who rose from nothing.

The gentleman in word and deed;
And short and simple is his creed;
"Fear God and help the soul in need!" –
20   The man who rose from nothing.

In other lands he's hardly known,
For he's a product of our own;
Could grace a shanty or a throne, –
    The man who rose from nothing.

Here's to the land of lakes and pines,
On which the sun of freedom shines,

Because we meet on all our lines
   The man who rose from nothing.
            (1874)

Cartha Again

Oh, why did I leave thee! Oh, why did I part
Frae thee, lovely Cartha, thou stream of my heart?
Oh, why did I leave thee, and wander awa'
Frae the hame o' my childhood, Gleniffer an' a'?
The thocht o' thee aye mak's my bosom o'erflow
Wi' a langing that nane save the weary can know;
And a' Fortunes favours are empty and vain,
If I'm ne'er to return to thee, Cartha again.

When I hear the soft tone o' my ain Lowlan' tongue,
10 Ance mair I'm a laddie the gowans among;
I see thee still winding the green valley through,
And the Highland hills towering afar in the blue;
But the lintie, the laverock, the blackbird an' a',
Are a' singing – "Laddie ye've lang been awa'."
Nae wonder I sit doun an' mak' my sad mane –
"Am I ne'er to behold thee, sweet Cartha, again?"

When I hear the sweet lilt o' some auld Scottish sang,
O how my bluid leaps as it gallops alang!
The thumps o' my heart gar my bosom a' stoun,
20 My heid it grows dizzie, an' rins roun' an' roun',
My very heartstrings tug as if they would crack,
And burst a' the bonds that are keepin' me back;
But then comes the thocht – here I'm doom'd to remain,
And ne'er to return to thee, Cartha, again!

In a grave o' the forest, when life's journey's past,
Unknown and unhonoured, they'll lay me at last;
Aboon me nae blue-bell nor gowan shall wave,
Nor nae robin come to sing ower my grave.

But surely! ah surely! the love o' this heart
30 For thee, lovely Cartha, can never depart;
But free frae a' sorrow, a' sadness and pain,
My spirit shall haunt thee, dear Cartha, again.

(1874)

PAMELIA VINING YULE

1826–1897

Born on a farm in New York State, Pamelia Vining came to Canada in 1860 to teach at the Canadian Literary Institute, a Baptist school in Woodstock, Ontario. Although her teaching career ended with her marriage to Reverend James C. Yule in 1866, she remained active as a writer and contributed articles to Baptist publications. In addition to her collection of poetry, *Poems of the Heart and Home* (1881), she published several temperance novels.

The Beech-Nut Gatherer

All over the earth like a mantle,
    Golden, and green, and grey,
Crimson, and scarlet, and yellow,
    The Autumn foliage lay; –
The sun of the Indian Summer
    Laughed at the bare old trees
As they shook their leafless branches
    In the soft October breeze.

Gorgeous was every hill-side,
10   And gorgeous every nook,
And the dry, old log was gorgeous,
    Spanning the little brook;
Its holiday robes, the forest
    Had suddenly cast to earth,
And, as yet, seemed scarce to miss them,
    In its plenitude of mirth.

I walked where the leaves the softest,
    The brightest, and goldenest lay;
And I thought of a forest hill-side,
20   And an Indian Summer day, –
Of an eager, little child-face

O'er the fallen leaves that bent,
    As she gathered her cup of beech-nuts
        With innocent content.

I thought of the small, brown fingers
    Gleaning them one by one,
With the partridge drumming near her
    In the forest bare and dun,
And the jet-black squirrel, winking
30   His saucy, jealous eye
At those tiny, pilfering fingers,
    From his sly nook up on high.

Ah, barefooted little maiden!
    With thy bonnetless, sun-burnt brow,
Thou glean'st no more on the hill-side –
    Where art thou gleaning now?
I knew by the lifted glances
    Of thy dark, imperious eye,
That the tall trees bending o'er thee
40   Would not shelter thee by and by.

The cottage by the brookside,
    With its mossy roof is gone; –
The cattle have left the uplands,
    The young lambs left the lawn; –
Gone are thy blue-eyed sister,
    And thy brother's laughing brow;
And the beech-nuts lie ungathered
    On the lonely hill-side now.

What have the returning seasons
50   Brought to thy heart since then,
In thy long and weary wand'rings
    In the paths of busy men? –
Has the Angel of grief, or of gladness,
    Set his seal upon thy brow?

Maiden, joyous or tearful,
   Where art thou gleaning now?
       (1862)

The Drunkard's Child

A little child stood moaning
   At the hour of midnight lone,
And no human ear was list'ning
   To the feebly wailing tone;
The cold, keen blast of winter
   With funeral wail swept by,
And the blinding snow fell darkly
   Through the murky, wintry sky.

Ah! desolate and wretched
10   Was the drunkard's outcast child,
Driven forth amidst the horrors
   Of that night of tempests wild.
The babe so fondly cherished
   Once 'neath a parent's eye,
Now laid her down in anguish
   Midst the drifting snows to die!

"Papa! – papa!" – she murmured,
   "The night is cold and drear,
And I'm freezing! – Oh, I'm freezing!
20   In the storm and darkness here; –
My naked feet are stiff'ning,
   And my little hands are numb, –
Papa, can I not come to thee,
   And warm myself at home?

Mamma! mamma!" – more wildly,
   The little suff'rer cried –
Forgetting, in her anguish,
   How her stricken mother died –

"Oh, take me to your bosom,
30   And warm me on your breast,
Then lay me down and kiss me,
    In my little bed to rest!"

Poor child! – the sleep that gathers
    Thy stiffened eyelids o'er,
Will know no weary waking
    To a life of anguish more.
Sleep on! – the snows may gather
    O'er thy cold and pulseless form –
Thou art resting, calmly resting,
40   In the wild, dark, midnight storm!

                 (1863)

ROSANNA ELEANOR MULLINS LEPROHON

1829–1879

Born in Montreal and educated at the Convent of the Congregation, Rosanna Mullins published many poems and serialized novels in magazines and newspapers before her 1851 marriage to Dr. Jean-Lukin Leprohon, a descendant of an old Québec family. Despite the births of thirteen children and the responsibilities of a middle-class matron, she maintained a steady output of poetry and fiction, including her best-known novel, *Antoinette de Mirecourt; or, Secret Marrying and Secret Sorrowing* (1864). In 1881, her poems were collected posthumously in *The Poetical Works of Mrs. Leprohon.*

Husband and Wife

The world had chafed his spirit proud
   By its wearing, crushing strife,
The censure of the thoughtless crowd
   Had touched a blameless life;
Like the dove of old, from the water's foam,
He wearily turned to the ark of home.

Hopes he had cherished with joyous heart,
   Had toiled for many a day,
With body and spirit, and patient art,
10   Like mists had melted away;
And o'er day-dreams vanished, o'er fond hopes flown,
He sat him down to mourn alone.

No, not alone, for soft fingers rest
   On his hot and aching brow,
Back the damp hair is tenderly pressed
   While a sweet voice whispers low:
"Thy joys have I shared, O my husband true,
And shall I not share thy sorrows too?"

Vain task to resist the loving gaze
20   That so fondly meets his own,
Revealing a heart that cares for praise
    From him and him alone;
And though censure and grief upon him pall,
Unto to her, at least, he is all in all.

What though false friends should turn aside,
    Or chill with icy look;
What though he meet the pitying pride,
    The proud heart ill can brook;
There are depths of love in one gentle heart,
30 Whose faith with death alone will part.

Aye! well may thy brow relax its gloom,
    For a talisman hast thou
'Gainst hopes that are blighted in their bloom,
    'Gainst scornful look or brow –
Her heart is a high and a holy throne
Where monarch supreme thou reignest alone.

Kindly return her tender gaze,
    Press closely that little hand,
Whisper fond words and soothing praise –
40   They are ever at thy command;
It is all the harvest she asks to reap
In return for love as the ocean deep.

                (1862)

Given and Taken

The snow-flakes were softly falling
   Adown on the landscape white,
When the violet eyes of my first-born
   Opened unto the light;
And I thought as I pressed him to me,
   With loving, rapturous thrill,
He was pure and fair as the snow-flakes
   That lay on the landscape still.

I smiled when they spoke of the weary
10   Length of the winter's night,
Of the days so short and so dreary,
   Of the sun's cold cheerless light –
I listened, but in their murmurs
   Nor by word nor thought took part,
For the smiles of my gentle darling
   Brought light to my home and heart.

Oh! quickly the joyous springtime
   Came back to our ice-bound earth,
Filling meadows and woods with sunshine,
20   And hearts with gladsome mirth,
But, ah! on earth's dawning beauty
   There rested a gloomy shade,
For our tiny household blossom
   Began to droop and fade.

And I, shuddering, felt that the frailest
   Of the flowers in the old woods dim
Had a surer hold on existence
   Than I dared to hope for him.
In the flush of the summer's beauty
30   On a sunny, golden day,
When flowers gemmed dell and upland,
   My darling passed away.

Now I chafed at the brilliant sunshine
    That flooded my lonely room,
Now I wearied of bounteous Nature,
    So full of life and bloom;
I regretted the wintry hours
    With the snow-flakes falling fast,
And the little form of my nursling
40   With his arms around me cast.

They laid his tiny garment
    In an attic chamber high,
His coral, his empty cradle,
    That they might not meet my eye;
And his name was never uttered,
    What e'er each heart might feel,
For they wished the wound in my bosom
    Might have time to close and heal.

It has done so, thanks to that Power
50   That has been my earthly stay,
And should you talk of my darling,
    I could listen now all day,
For I know that each passing minute
    Brings me nearer life's last shore,
And nearer that glorious Kingdom
    Where we both shall meet once more!

(1863)

CHARLES HEAVYSEGE

1816–1876

A self-educated carpenter and cabinet-maker, Charles Heavysege emigrated from England to Montreal in 1853. After working briefly as a reporter for the *Montreal Transcript*, he joined the staff of the *Montreal Daily Witness*. Although he wrote a novel, *The Advocate* (1865), his reputation rests on his poetic dramas, *The Revolt of Tartarus* (1855), *Saul* (1857), and *Count Filippo* (1860), and his long narrative poem, *Jephtha's Daughter* (1865).

sonnets from Jephtha's Daughter

II

Up from the deep Annihilation came,
And shook the shore of nature with his frame:
Vulcan, nor Polyphemus of one eye,
For size or strength could with the monster vie;
Who, landed, round his sullen eyeballs rolled,
While dripped the ooze from limbs of mighty mould.
But who the bard that shall in song express
(For he was clad) the more than Anarch's dress?
All round about him hanging were decays,
10 And ever-dropping remnants of the past; –
But how shall I recite my great amaze
As down the abyss I saw him coolly cast
Slowly, but constantly, some lofty name,
Men thought secure in bright, eternal fame?

VII

Open, my heart, thy ruddy valves;
It is thy master calls;
Let me go down, and, curious, trace
Thy labyrinthine halls.
Open, O heart, and let me view
The secrets of thy den;
Myself unto myself now show
With introspective ken.
Expose thyself, thou covered nest
10   Of passions, and be seen;
Stir up thy brood, that in unrest
Are ever piping keen.
Ah! what a motley multitude.
Magnanimous and mean!

X

The day was lingering in the pale north-west,
And night was hanging o'er my head, –
Night where a myriad stars were spread;
While down in the east, where the light was least,
Seemed the home of the quiet dead.
And, as I gazed on the field sublime,
To watch the bright, pulsating stars,
Adown the deep where the angels sleep
Came drawn the golden chime
10   Of those great spheres that sound the years
For the horologe of time.
Millenniums numberless they told,
Millenniums a millionfold
From the ancient hour of prime.

(1865)

JAMES ANDERSON

1842–1923

Scottish-born James Anderson, who followed the lure of
gold to British Columbia in 1863, became known as the
"poet laureate" of the Cariboo. His rhymes appeared in the
Barkerville newspaper, the *Cariboo Sentinel*, which in
1868 printed his collection, *Sawney's Letters, or Cariboo
Rhymes*. In 1871 Anderson left Canada; he died in England
in 1923.

The Prospector's Shanty

See yonder shanty on the hill,
'Tis but an humble biggin',
Some ten by six within the wa's –
Your head may touch the riggin' –
The door stands open to the south,
The fire, outside the door;
The logs are chinket close wi' fog –
And nocht but mud the floor –
A knife an' fork, a pewter plate,
10 An' cup o' the same metal,
A teaspoon an' a sugar bowl,
A frying pan an' kettle;

The bakin' board hangs on the wa',
Its purposes are twa-fold –
For mixing bread wi' yeast or dough,
Or panning oot the braw gold!
A log or twa in place o' stools,
A bed withoot a hangin',
Are feckly a' the furnishin's
20 This little house belangin';

The laird and tenant o' this sty,
I canna name it finer,
Lives free an' easy as a lord,
Tho' but an "honest miner."

               (1868)

Song of the Mine

Drift! Drift! Drift!
From the early morn till night.
Drift! Drift! Drift!
From twilight till broad-day light,
With pick, and crow-bar and sledge,
Breaking a hard gravel face;
In slum, and water and mud,
Working with face-board and brace;
Main set, false set, and main set –
10 Repeated, shift after shift –
Day after day the same song –
The same wearisome Song of the Drift.

Run! Run! Run!
Rush to the shaft the rich pay!
Backward and forward in haste –
Watching the track by the way –
Run! Run! Run!
In a kind of nervous dread,
Fearing that "cap" that oft makes
20 A batt'ring ram of your head;
This "curve," – that badly built "switch,"
Look out! you know what they are.
Run! Run! thro' all the long day,
Sings this hasty Song of the Car.

Hoist! Hoist! Hoist!
No music there is in that sound!
Hoist! hoist! HOIST ! –
Impatient voice underground!
You may wish your arm a crank
30 Attached to a water wheel!
With no aching bones at night,
Nor a weary frame to feel –
'Tis vain! Hoist! Hoist away! Hoist! –
The dirt comes heavy and moist,
And thirty buckets an hour
"Foot" to the tune of Hoist! Hoist!

Wash! Wash! Wash!
And rattle the rocks around,
Is the song the Dump-box sings,
40 So cheery the whole week round;
And on Sunday "clean me up,"
And gather the precious "pay."
"Better the day – better the deed,"
Should read, better the deed – the day!
Now say, what have you "wash'd up?"
Small wages – well, never repine –
You know, we'll do better next week!
And so ended the Song of the Mine.

                                        (1868)

JOHN ARTHUR PHILLIPS
1842–1907

Born in Liverpool, England, John Arthur Phillips came to
North America in 1865. He was a journalist working in
Montreal when he wrote "The Factory Girl," which
appeared in the *Ontario Workman* in April 1873 and also in
his first book, *Thompson's Turkey, and Other Christmas
Tales, Poems, etc.* (1873). While rising in the journalistic
world to become president of the Ottawa Press Gallery in
1896, he published at least three more collections of
poems, stories, and sketches.

The Factory Girl

She wasn't the least bit pretty,
And only the least bit gay;
And she walked with a firm elastic tread,
In a business-like kind of way.
Her dress was of coarse, brown woollen,
Plainly but neatly made,
Trimmed with some common ribbon
Or cheaper kind of braid;
And a hat with a broken feather,
10 And shawl of a modest plaid.

Her face seemed worn and weary,
And traced with lines of care,
As her nut-brown tresses blew aside
In the keen December air;
Yet she was not old, scarce twenty,
And her form was full and sleek,
But her heavy eye, and tired step,
Seemed of wearisome toil to speak;
She worked as a common factory girl
20 For two dollars and a half a week.

Ten hours a day of labor
In a close, ill-lighted room;
Machinery's buzz for music,
Waste gas for sweet perfume;
Hot stifling vapors in summer,
Chill draughts on a winter's day,
No pause for rest or pleasure
On pain of being sent away;
So ran her civilized serfdom –
30 *Four cents* an hour the pay.

"A fair day's work," say the masters,
And "a fair day's pay," say the men;
There's a strike – a rise in wages,
What effect to the poor girl then?
A harder struggle than ever
The honest path to keep;
And so sink a little lower,
Some humbler home to seek;
For living is dearer – her wages,
40 Two dollars and a half a week.

A man gets thrice the money,
But then "a man's a man,
And a woman surely can't expect
To earn as much as he can."
Of his hire the laborer's worthy,
Be that laborer who it may;
If a woman can do a man's work
She should have a man's full pay,
Not to be left to starve – or sin –
50 On forty cents a day.

Two dollars and a half to live on,
Or starve on, if you will;
Two dollars and a half to dress on,

And a hungry mouth to fill;
Two dollars and a half to lodge on
In some wretched hole or den,
Where crowds are huddled together,
Girls, and women, and men;
If she sins to escape her bondage
60 Is there room for wonder then.

(1873)

ANONYMOUS
1873

"A Popular Creed" was published anonymously in
the *Ontario Workman* in 1873.

A Popular Creed

Dimes and dollars, dollars and dimes!
An empty pocket is the worst of crimes!
If a man's down give him a thrust –
Trample the beggar into the dust!
Presumptuous poverty's quite appalling,
Knock him over, kick him for falling:
If a man is up, eh! lift him higher!
Your soul's for sale and he's the buyer!
    Dimes and dollars, dollars and dimes,
10   An empty pocket is the worst of crimes!

I know a poor but worthy youth,
Whose hopes are built on a maiden's truth,
But a maiden will break her vows with ease,
For a wooer comes whose claims are these,
A hollow heart and an empty head,
A face well tinged with whiskey red,
A soul well trained in villany's school –.
And cash, sweet cash – he knows the rule:
    Dimes and dollars, dollars and dimes!
20   An empty pocket is the worst of crimes!

I know a bold but honest man,
Who strives to live on an honest plan,
But poor is he, and poor will be,
A scorned and hated wretch is he;
At home he meets a starving wife,
Abroad he leads a leper's life –

They struggle against fearful odds!
Who will not bow to the people's gods!
   Dimes and dollars, dollars and dimes!
30   An empty pocket is the worst of crimes!

So get ye wealthy, no matter how,
"No questions" asked of the rich I trow,
Steal by night and steal by day,
(Doing it in a legal way),
Join the church and never forsake her,
Learn to cant and insult your Maker,
Be a hypocrite, liar, knave and fool,
But don't be poor – remember the rule:
   Dimes and dollars, dollars and dimes!
40   An empty pocket is the worst of crimes!
                  (1873)

JAMES McINTYRE
1827–1906

Scottish-born James McIntyre emigrated to Canada West in the early 1840s. By 1858 he had established himself as an undertaker and furniture manufacturer in Ingersoll, Ontario, where he began to publish his rhymes on various topics of local interest. Collected into two volumes, *Musings on the Banks of the Canadian Thames* (1884) and *Poems of James McIntyre* (1889), his verses owe their reputation largely to W.A. Deacon's critique in *The Four Jameses* (1927).

Ode on the Mammoth Cheese

We have seen thee, queen of cheese,
Lying quietly at your ease,
Gently fanned by evening breeze,
Thy fair form no flies dare seize.

All gaily dressed soon you'll go
To the great Provincial show,
To be admired by many a beau
In the city of Toronto.

Cows numerous as a swarm of bees,
10   Or as the leaves upon the trees,
It did require to make thee please,
And stand unrivalled, queen of cheese.

May you not receive a scar as
We have heard that Mr. Harris
Intends to send you off as far as
The great world's show at Paris.

Of the youth beware of these,
For some of them might rudely squeeze
And bite your cheek, then songs or glees
20 We could not sing, oh! queen of cheese.

We'rt thou suspended from balloon,
You'd cast a shade even at noon,
Folks would think it was the moon
About to fall and crush them soon.

                              (1884)

AGNES MAULE MACHAR
("FIDELIS")
1837–1927

Born in Kingston, Ontario, her home for her entire life, Agnes Maule Machar was an active figure in late nineteenth-century literary circles and ameliorist movements. Her novels and her many articles published in Canada's leading journals advocated temperance, labour reform, and women's rights. Some of her poetry was collected in *Lays of the "True North," and Other Canadian Poems* (1899, 1902).

Quebec to Ontario

A Plea for the Life of Riel, September, 1885

You have the land our fathers bought
    With blood, and toil, and pain,
De Monts' and Cartier's earnest thought –
    The life-blood of Champlain.

From fair Acadia's rock-bound strand
    To wide Ontario's shore,
Where Norman swords fought hand to hand
    The Iroquois of yore,

And those great western wilds afar,
10   Where wandering Indians roam,
And where the hardy voyageur
    First reared his cabin home; –

All, all is yours ; from east to west
    The British banner streams,
But in a conquered people's breast
    Will live its early dreams!

So, when your rich men grudge our poor,
   Homes on their native plains,
The blood of the old voyageur
20   Leaps boiling in our veins.

And one whose heart was fired at sight
   Of suffering and wrong
Took arms, in evil hour, to fight,
   For weakness – with the strong.

His wild scheme failed; how could it stand
   Against such fatal odds?
And brave hearts sleep in yon far land
   Beneath the prairie sods!

He stands a traitor at the bar
30   Of your cold modern laws,
And yet, to him who woke the war,
   It seemed a patriot cause!

Nay, more, perchance, the sore distress
   That stirred the bitter fray,
Through *that*, has pierced to ears that else
   Had still been deaf to-day; –

While he who sought his people's weal,
   Who loved his nation well,
The prisoner of your fire and steel,
40   Lies doomed in felon's cell!

Pity the captive in your hand,
   Pity the conquered race;
You – strong, victorious in the land –
   Grant us the victor's grace!

[1885]

Rondeau

Straight to her goal, from eve to day,
Untired, she cleaves her watery way;
    She may not change her course, for fear
    Of hidden rocks, or tempests near; –
Nought lures her from her course to stray!

The sparkling moonbeams dance and play
Above her wake, – she will not stay,
    But still, through light and darkness, steer
        Straight to her goal.

10 Even so, my heart, – may'st thou obey
    'Mid darkening clouds, or passion's play, –
        The compass true that guides thee here, –
        Maintain thy course, serene and clear,
    'Neath summer sun or winter grey,
        Straight to thy goal.

                                        (1891)

Our Lads to the Front!

Embarkation of the Canadian Contingent for South
Africa; – Quebec, October 31, 1899.

Ring out the British cheer,
    Swell forth its loud acclaim, –
The "true North" sends her children dear
    To fight in Britain's name!

They go, as went the knights of old,
    O'er seas and arid plains to fare; –
Not for the love of fame or gold,
    But for the British hearts they bear!
They hear the mother land, afar,
10   Calling her children, – scattered wide; –

They haste, – as wakes the note of war, –
　　To face the conflict at her side!

We follow on, with thoughts and prayer
　　In the rich-freighted vessel's wake,
Through northern chill and tropic air, –
　　O winds, blow softly, for her sake!
She bears the hopes of hearts that bleed
　　With parting pain, – with haunting fears;
Her devious course in safety speed,
20　　Thou Who must guide, where duty steers!

What years of peace essayed to do
　　Sorrow and danger swift complete, –
Fuse our great Empire through and through
　　Till, with one throb, its pulses beat.
One prayer is breathed o'er sea and land
　　From Queen and peasant, cot and hall,
From snow-capped hills, to sunbaked strand,
　　God guard our soldiers – one and all!

O God of Justice, Truth, and Right,
30　　Who seest as no mortal may, –
Whose hand can guide through passion's night –
　　To dawning of a glorious day –
Grant victory as thou deemest best,
　　Turn hate to love, – bid slaughter cease,
Lay sword in sheath and lance in rest,
　　And bring our warriors home in peace!

　　　Ring out the British cheer!
　　　　Swell forth its loud acclaim!
　　　The "true North" sends her children dear
40　　　　To fight in Britain's name!

　　　　　　　　　　　　[1899]

CHARLES MAIR

1838–1927

Born in Lanark, Upper Canada, Charles Mair studied at Queen's University, and was one of the founders of the "Canada First" movement in 1868. Captured by Louis Riel in the 1870 Red River Rebellion, he later returned to the West to assist in the defeat of Riel in 1885. Appointed to the Federal Immigration Service in the West in 1898, he retired to Victoria in 1921. His first book, *Dreamland and Other Poems* (1868), was followed by a verse drama, *Tecumseh* (1886), and other writings.

"The Song" from "The Last Bison"

Hear me, ye smokeless skies and grass-green earth,
   Since by your sufferance still I breathe and live!
Through you fond Nature gave me birth,
   And food and freedom – all she had to give.
Enough! I grew, and with my kindred ranged
Their realm stupendous, changeless and unchanged,
     Save by the toll of nations primitive,
Who throve on us, and loved our life-stream's roar,
And lived beside its wave, and camped upon its shore.

10 They loved us, and they wasted not. They slew,
   With pious hand, but for their daily need;
Not wantonly, but as the due
   Of stern necessity which Life doth breed.
Yea, even as earth gave us herbage meet,
So yielded we, in turn, our substance sweet
     To quit the claims of hunger, not of greed.
So stood it with us that what either did
Could not be on the earth forgone, nor Heaven forbid.

And, so, companioned in the blameless strife
20   Enjoined upon all creatures, small and great,
    Our ways were venial, and our life
      Ended in fair fulfilment of our fate.
No gold to them by sordid hands was passed;
No greedy herdsman housed us from the blast;
        Ours was the liberty of regions rife
In winter's snow, in summer's fruits and flowers –
Ours were the virgin prairies, and their rapture ours!

So fared it with us both; yea, thus it stood
    In all our wanderings from place to place,
30 Until the red man mixed his blood
    With paler currents. Then arose a race –
The reckless hunters of the plains – who vied
In wanton slaughter for the tongue and hide,
      To satisfy vain ends and longings base.
This grew; and yet we flourished, and our name
Prospered until the pale destroyer's concourse came.

Then fell a double terror on the plains,
    The swift inspreading of destruction dire –
Strange men, who ravaged our domains
40   On every hand, and ringed us round with fire;
Pale enemies, who slew with equal mirth
The harmless or the hurtful things of earth,
      In dead fruition of their mad desire:
The ministers of mischief and of might,
Who yearn for havoc as the world's supreme delight.

So waned the myriads which had waxed before
    When subject to the simple needs of men.
As yields to eating seas the shore,
    So yielded our vast multitude, and then –

50 It scattered! Meagre bands, in wild dismay,
　Were parted and, for shelter, fled away
　　　　　To barren wastes, to mountain gorge and glen.
　A respite brief from stern pursuit and care,
　For still the spoiler sought, and still he slew us there.

Hear me, thou grass-green earth, ye smokeless skies,
　Since by your sufferance still I breathe and live!
The charity which man denies
　Ye still would tender to the fugitive!
I feel your mercy in my veins – at length
60 My heart revives, and strengthens with your strength –
　　　　　Too late, too late, the courage ye would give!
　Naught can avail these wounds, this failing breath,
　This frame which feels, at last, the wily touch of death.

Here must the last of all his kindred fall;
　Yet, midst these gathering shadows, ere I die –
Responsive to an inward call,
　My spirit fain would rise and prophesy.
I see our spoilers build their cities great
Upon our plains – I see their rich estate:
70　　　　The centuries in dim procession fly!
Long ages roll, and then at length is bared
The time when they who spared not are no longer
　　　　　　　　　　　　　　　spared.

Once more my vision sweeps the prairies wide,
　But now no peopled cities greet the sight;
All perished, now, their pomp and pride:
　In solitude the wild wind takes delight.
Naught but the vacant wilderness is seen,
And grassy mounds, where cities once had been.
　　　　　The earth smiles as of yore, the skies are bright,
80 Wild cattle graze and bellow on the plain,
　And savage nations roam o'er native wilds again!
　　　　　　　　　　　　　　[1890]

Part Two

Continuations

ISABELLA VALANCY CRAWFORD
1850–1887

Believed to have been born in Dublin on Christmas Day, 1850, Isabella Valancy Crawford came to Canada as a young child with her emigrant family. She is known to have lived in several towns in Canada West before settling in Toronto in 1876, where she died of heart disease in 1887. Although her only book, *Old Spookses' Pass, Malcolm's Katie, and Other Poems* (1884), met with little economic or critical success, she is now considered to be one of the most important poets of nineteenth-century Canada.

"Love Me, Love My Dog"

He had a falcon on his wrist,
    A hound beside his knee:
A jewelled rapier at his thigh,
    Quoth he, "which may she be?
My chieftain cried, 'Bear forth, my page,
    This ring to Lady Clare,
Thou'lt know her by her sunny eyes,
    And golden lengths of hair;'
But here are lovely damsels, three,
10   In glitt'ring coif and veil;
And all have sunny locks and eyes –
    To which unfold the tale?"

Out spake the first, "O pretty page,
    Thou hast a wealthy lord:
I love to see the jewels rare
    Which deck thy slender sword!"
She smil'd, she wav'd her yellow locks,
    Rich damask glow'd her cheek.
He bent his supple knee, and thought –
20   "She's not the maid I seek."
The second had a cheek of rose,

A throat as white as milk;
A jewell'd tire upon her brow,
    A robe and veil of silk.

"O pretty page hold back the hound,
    Uncouth is he and bold:
His rough caress will tear my veil:
    My fringe of glitt'ring gold."
She frown'd, she pouted ruby lips:
30   The page he did not speak:
He bent his curly head and thought
    "She's not the maid I seek."

The third, with cobweb locks of light,
    And cheeks like summer dawn,
Dropped on her knee beside the hound,
    Upon the shaven lawn.
She kiss'd his sinewy throat, she strok'd
    His bristly rings of hair:
"Ho," thought the page, "she loves his hound,
40   So this is Lady Clare!"

                                        (1880)

March

Shall Thor with his hammer
    Beat on the mountain,
As on an anvil,
    A shackle and fetter?

Shall the lame Vulcan
    Shout as he swingeth
God-like his hammer,
    And forge thee a fetter?

Shall Jove, the Thunderer,
10   Twine his swift lightnings

With his loud thunders,
   And forge thee a shackle?

"No," shouts the Titan,
   The young lion-throated;
"Thor, Vulcan, nor Jove
   Cannot shackle and bind me."

Tell what will bind thee,
   Thou young world-shaker,
Up vault our oceans,
20   Down fall our forests.

Ship-masts and pillars
   Stagger and tremble,
Like reeds by the margins
   Of swift running waters.

Men's hearts at thy roaring
   Quiver like harebells
Smitten by hailstones,
   Smitten and shaken.

"O sages and wise men!
30   O bird-hearted tremblers!
Come, I will show ye
   A shackle to bind me.

I, the lion-throated,
   The shaker of mountains!
I, the invincible,
   Lasher of oceans!

Past the horizon,
   Its ring of pale azure
Past the horizon,
40   Where scurry the white clouds,

There are buds and small flowers –
　　Flowers like snow-flakes,
Blossoms like rain-drops,
　　So small and tremulous.

These in a fetter
　　Shall shackle and bind me,
Shall weigh down my shouting
　　With their delicate perfume!"

But who this frail fetter
50　　Shall forge on an anvil,
With hammer of feather
　　And anvil of velvet?

"Past the horizon,
　　In the palm of a valley,
Her feet in the grasses,
　　There is a maiden.

She smiles on the flowers,
　　They widen and redden;
She weeps on the flowers,
60　　They grow up and kiss her.

She breathes in their bosoms,
　　They breathe back in odours;
Inarticulate homage,
　　Dumb adoration.

She shall wreathe them in shackles,
　　Shall weave them in fetters;
In chains shall she braid them,
　　And me shall she fetter.

I, the invincible;
70　　March, the earth-shaker;

> March, the sea-lifter;
>> March, the sky-render;
>
> March, the lion-throated.
>> April the weaver
> Of delicate blossoms,
>> And moulder of red buds –
>
> Shall, at the horizon,
>> Its ring of pale azure,
> Its scurry of white clouds,
> 80   Meet in the sunlight."

(1881)

Love's Forget-Me-Not

When Spring in sunny woodland lay,
  And gilded buds were sparely set
On oak tree and the thorny may,
  I gave my love a violet.
"O Love," she said, and kissed my mouth
  With one light, tender maiden kiss,
"There are no rich blooms in the south
  So fair to me as this!"

When Summer reared her haughty crest,
10   We paused beneath the ruddy stars;
I placed a rose upon her breast,
  Plucked from the modest casement bars.
"O Love," she said, and kissed my mouth –
  Heart, heart, rememb'rest thou the bliss? –
"In east or west, in north or south,
  I know no rose but this!"

When Autumn raised the purple fruit
  In clusters to his bearded lips,
I laid a heartsease on the lute

20   That sang beneath her finger-tips.
"O Love," she said – and fair her eyes
    Smiled thro' the dusk upon the lea –
"No heartsease glows beneath the skies
    But this thou givest me!"

When Winter wept at shaking doors,
    And holly trimmed his ermine vest,
And wild winds maddened on the moors,
    I laid a flower upon her breast.
"Dear Heart," I whispered to the clay,
30   Which stilly smiled yet answered not,
"Bear thou to Heaven itself away
    True love's Forget-me-not!"

(1882)

The Dark Stag

A startl'd stag, the blue-gray night
    Leaps down beyond black pines,
Behind – a length of yellow light –
    The hunter's arrow shines;
His moccasins are stained with red,
    He bends upon his knee,
From cov'ring peaks his shafts are sped,
The blue mists plume his mighty head
    Well may the swift night flee!

10 The pale, pale moon, a snow-white doe,
    Bounds by his dappl'd flank:
They beat the stars down as they go,
    Like wood-bells growing rank.
The winds lift dew-laps from the ground,
    Leap from the quaking reeds;
Their hoarse bays shake the forests round,
With keen cries, on the track they bound,
    Swift, swift the dark stag speeds!

Away! his white doe, far behind,
20   Lies wounded on the plain,
Yells at his flank the nimblest wind,
    His large tears fall in rain
Like lily pads, small clouds grow white
    About his darkling way,
From his bald nest upon the height,
The red-ey'd eagle sees his flight.
He falters, turns, the antler'd night,
    The dark stag stands at bay.

His feet are in the waves of space:
30   His antlers broad and dun,
He lowers – he turns his velvet face
    To front the hunter sun.
He stamps the lilied clouds, and high
    His branches fill the west.
The lean stork sails across the sky,
The shy loon shrieks to see him die,
    The winds leap at his breast.

Roar the rent lakes as thro' the wave,
    Their silver warriors plunge;
40 As vaults from core of crystal cave
    The strong fierce maskelonge.
Red torches of the sumach glare,
    Fall's council fires are lit,
The bittern, squaw-like, scolds the air,
The wild duck splashes loudly where
    The rustling rice spears knit.

Shaft after shaft the red sun speeds,
    Rent the stag's dappl'd side,
His breast, fang'd by the shrill winds, bleeds –
50   He staggers on the tide.
He feels the hungry waves of space,

Rush at him high and blue:
Its white spray smites his dusky face,
Swifter the sun's fierce arrows race
    And pierce his stout heart thro'.

His antlers fall – once more he spurns
    The hoarse hounds of the day,
His blood upon the crisp blue burns,
    Reddens the mounting spray.
60 His branches smite the wave – with cries
    The loud winds pause and flag –
He sinks in space – red glow the skies
The brown earth crimsons as he dies –
    The strong and dusky stag!

                        (1883)

The Canoe

My masters twain made me a bed
Of pine-boughs resinous, and cedar;
Of moss, a soft and gentle breeder
Of dreams of rest; and me they spread
With furry skins, and laughing said,
"Now she shall lay her polish'd sides,
As queens do rest, or dainty brides,
Our slender lady of the tides!"

My masters twain their camp-soul lit,
10 Streamed incense from the hissing cones,
Large, crimson flashes grew and whirl'd
Thin, golden nerves of sly light curl'd
Round the dun camp, and rose faint zones,
Half way about each grim bole knit,
Like a shy child that would bedeck
With its soft clasp a Brave's red neck;
Yet sees the rough shield on his breast,

The awful plumes shake on his crest,
And fearful drops his timid face,
20 Nor dares complete the sweet embrace.

Into the hollow hearts of brakes,
Yet warm from sides of does and stags,
Pass'd to the crisp dark river flags,
Sinuous, red as copper snakes,
Sharp-headed serpents, made of light,
Glided and hid themselves in night.
My masters twain, the slaughter'd deer
Hung on fork'd boughs – with thongs of leather.
Bound were his stiff, slim feet together –
30 His eyes like dead stars cold and drear;
The wand'ring firelight drew near
And laid its wide palm, red and anxious,
On the sharp splendor of his branches;
On the white foam grown hard and sere
          On flank and shoulder.
Death – hard as breast of granite boulder,
          And under his lashes
Peer'd thro' his eyes at his life's grey ashes.

My masters twain sang songs that wove
40 (As they burnish'd hunting blade and rifle)
A golden thread with a cobweb trifle –
Loud of the chase, and low of love.

"O Love, art thou a silver fish?
Shy of the line and shy of gaffing,
Which we do follow, fierce, yet laughing,
Casting at thee the light-wing'd wish,
And at the last shall we bring thee up
From the crystal darkness under the cup
          Of lily folden,
50   On broad leaves golden?

"O Love! art thou a silver deer,
Swift thy starr'd feet as wing of swallow,
While we with rushing arrows follow;
And at the last shall we draw near,
And over thy velvet neck cast thongs –
Woven of roses, of stars, of songs?
    New chains all moulden
    Of rare gems olden!"

They hung the slaughter'd fish like swords
60 On saplings slender – like scimitars
Bright, and ruddied from new-dead wars,
Blaz'd in the light – the scaly hordes.

They pil'd up boughs beneath the trees,
Of cedar-web and green fir tassel;
Low did the pointed pine tops rustle,
The camp fire blush'd to the tender breeze.

The hounds laid dew-laps on the ground,
With needles of pine sweet, soft and rusty –
Dream'd of the dead stag stout and lusty;
70 A bat by the red flames wove its round.

The darkness built its wigwam walls
Close round the camp, and at its curtain
Press'd shapes, thin woven and uncertain,
As white locks of tall waterfalls.

                    (1884)

The Hidden Room

    I marvel if my heart,
    Hath any room apart,
Built secretly its mystic walls within;
    With subtly warded key
    Ne'er yielded unto me –
Where even I have surely never been.

Ah, surely I know all
The bright and cheerful hall
With the fire ever red upon its hearth;
10   My friends dwell with me there,
Nor comes the step of Care
To sadden down its music and its mirth.

Full well I know as mine,
The little cloister'd shrine
No foot but mine alone hath ever trod;
There come the shining wings –
The face of one who brings
The pray'rs of men before the throne of God.

And many know full well,
20   The busy, busy cell,
Where I toil at the work I have to do,
Nor is the portal fast,
Where stand phantoms of the past,
Or grow the bitter plants of darksome rue.

I know the dainty spot
(Ah, who doth know it not?)
Where pure young Love his lily-cradle made;
And nestled some sweet springs
With lily-spangled wings –
30 Forget-me-nots upon his bier I laid.

Yet marvel I, my soul,
Know I thy very whole,
Or dost thou hide a chamber still from me?
Is it built upon the wall?
Is it spacious? is it small?
Is it God, or man, or I who holds the key?

(1884)

Malcolm's Katie: A Love Story

PART I

Max plac'd a ring on little Katie's hand,
A silver ring that he had beaten out
From that same sacred coin – first well-priz'd wage
For boyish labour, kept thro' many years.
"See, Kate," he said, "I had no skill to shape
"Two hearts fast bound together, so I grav'd
"Just K. and M., for Katie and for Max."
"But, look; you've run the lines in such a way,
"That M. is part of K., and K. of M.,"
10 Said Katie, smiling. "Did you mean it thus?
"I like it better than the double hearts."
"Well, well," he said, "but womankind is wise!
"Yet tell me, dear, will such a prophecy
"Not hurt you sometimes, when I am away?
"Will you not seek, keen ey'd, for some small break
"In those deep lines, to part the K. and M.
"For you? Nay, Kate, look down amid the globes
"Of those large lilies that our light canoe
"Divides, and see within the polish'd pool
20 "That small, rose face of yours, – so dear, so fair, –
"A seed of love to cleave into a rock,
"And bourgeon thence until the granite splits
"Before its subtle strength. I being gone –
"Poor soldier of the axe – to bloodless fields
"(Inglorious battles, whether lost or won)
"That sixteen-summer'd heart of yours may say:
"'I but was budding, and I did not know
"'My core was crimson and my perfume sweet;
"'I did not know how choice a thing I am;
30 "'I had not seen the sun, and blind I sway'd
"'To a strong wind, and thought because I sway'd,

" "Twas to the wooer of the perfect rose –
" 'That strong, wild wind has swept beyond my ken –
" 'The breeze I love sighs thro' my ruddy leaves.' "
"O, words!" said Katie, blushing, "only words!
"You build them up that I may push them down;
"If hearts are flow'rs, I know that flow'rs can root –
"Bud, blossom, die – all in the same lov'd soil;
"They do so in my garden. I have made
40 "Your heart my garden. If I am a bud
"And only feel unfoldment feebly stir
"Within my leaves, wait patiently; some June,
"I'll blush a full-blown rose, and queen it, dear,
"In your lov'd garden. Tho' I be a bud,
"My roots strike deep, and torn from that dear soil
"Would shriek like mandrakes – those witch things I read
"Of in your quaint old books. Are you content?"
"Yes – crescent-wise – but not to round, full moon.
"Look at yon hill that rounds so gently up
50 "From the wide lake; a lover king it looks,
"In cloth of gold, gone from his bride and queen;
"And yet delay'd, because her silver locks
"Catch in his gilded fringes; his shoulders sweep
"Into blue distance, and his gracious crest,
"Not held too high, is plum'd with maple groves; –
"One of your father's farms. A mighty man,
"Self-hewn from rock, remaining rock through all."
"He loves me, Max," said Katie. "Yes, I know –
"A rock is cup to many a crystal spring.
60 "Well, he is rich; those misty, peak-roof'd barns –
"Leviathans rising from red seas of grain –
"Are full of ingots, shaped like grains of wheat.
"His flocks have golden fleeces, and his herds
"Have monarchs worshipful, as was the calf
"Aaron call'd from the furnace; and his ploughs,

"Like Genii chained, snort o'er his mighty fields.
"He has a voice in Council and in Church –"
"He work'd for all," said Katie, somewhat pain'd.
"Aye, so, dear love, he did; I heard him tell
70 "How the first field upon his farm was ploughed.
"He and his brother Reuben, stalwart lads,
"Yok'd themselves, side by side, to the new plough;
"Their weaker father, in the grey of life
"(But rather the wan age of poverty
"Than many winters), in large, gnarl'd hands
"The plunging handles held; with mighty strains
"They drew the ripping beak through knotted sod,
"Thro' tortuous lanes of blacken'd, smoking stumps;
"And past great flaming brush heaps, sending out
80 "Fierce summers, beating on their swollen brows.
"O, such a battle! had we heard of serfs
"Driven to like hot conflict with the soil,
"Armies had march'd and navies swiftly sail'd
"To burst their gyves. But here's the little point –
"The polish'd di'mond pivot on which spins
"The wheel of Difference – they OWN'D the rugged soil,
"And fought for love – dear love of wealth and pow'r,
"And honest ease and fair esteem of men;
"One's blood heats at it!" "Yet you said such fields
90 "Were all inglorious," Katie, wondering, said.
"Inglorious? Yes; they make no promises
"Of Star or Garter, or the thundering guns
"That tell the earth her warriors are dead.
"Inglorious! Aye, the battle done and won
"Means not – a throne propp'd up with bleaching bones;
"A country sav'd with smoking seas of blood;
"A flag torn from the foe with wounds and death;
"Or Commerce, with her housewife foot upon
"Colossal bridge of slaughter'd savages,

100 "The Cross laid on her brawny shoulder, and
    "In one sly, mighty hand her reeking sword,
    "And in the other all the woven cheats
    "From her dishonest looms. Nay, none of these.
    "It means – four walls, perhaps a lowly roof;
    "Kine in a peaceful posture; modest fields;
    "A man and woman standing hand in hand
    "In hale old age, who, looking o'er the land,
    "Say: 'Thank the Lord, it all is mine and thine!'
    "It means, to such thew'd warriors of the Axe
110 "As your own father; – well, it means, sweet Kate,
    "Outspreading circles of increasing gold,
    "A name of weight; one little daughter heir,
    "Who must not wed the owner of an axe,
    "Who owns naught else but some dim, dusky woods
    "In a far land; two arms indifferent strong –"
    "And Katie's heart," said Katie, with a smile;
    For yet she stood on that smooth, violet plain,
    Where nothing shades the sun; nor quite believed
    Those blue peaks closing in were aught but mist
120 Which the gay sun could scatter with a glance.
    For Max, he late had touch'd their stones, but yet
    He saw them seam'd with gold and precious ores,
    Rich with hill flow'rs and musical with rills.
    "Or that same bud that will be Katie's heart,
    "Against the time your deep, dim woods are clear'd,
    "And I have wrought my father to relent."
    "How will you move him, sweet? Why, he will rage
    "And fume and anger, striding o'er his fields,
    "Until the last-bought king of herds lets down
130 "His lordly front, and rumbling thunder from
    "His polish'd chest, returns his chiding tones.
    "How will you move him, Katie, tell me how?"
    "I'll kiss him and keep still – that way is sure,"

Said Katie, smiling. "I have often tried."
"God speed the kiss," said Max, and Katie sigh'd,
With pray'rful palms close seal'd, "God speed the axe!"

> *O, light canoe, where dost thou glide?*
> *Below thee gleams no silver'd tide,*
> *But concave Heaven's chiefest pride.*

140   *Above thee burns Eve's rosy bar;*
> *Below thee throbs her darling star;*
> *Deep 'neath thy keel her round worlds are!*

> *Above, below, O sweet surprise,*
> *To gladden happy lover's eyes;*
> *No earth, no wave – all jewell'd skies!*

PART II

The South Wind laid his moccasins aside,
Broke his gay calumet of flow'rs, and cast
His useless wampum, beaded with cool dews,
Far from him, northward; his long, ruddy spear
Flung sunward, whence it came, and his soft locks
Of warm, fine haze grew silver as the birch.
His wigwam of green leaves began to shake;
The crackling rice-beds scolded harsh like squaws;
The small ponds pouted up their silver lips;
10 The great lakes ey'd the mountains, whisper'd "Ugh!
"Are ye so tall, O chiefs? Not taller than
"Our plumes can reach," and rose a little way,
As panthers stretch to try their velvet limbs,
And then retreat to purr and bide their time.
At morn the sharp breath of the night arose
From the wide prairies, in deep-struggling seas,
In rolling breakers, bursting to the sky;
In tumbling surfs, all yellow'd faintly thro'
With the low sun – in mad, conflicting crests,
20 Voic'd with low thunder from the hairy throats

Of the mist-buried herds; and for a man
To stand amid the cloudy roll and moil,
The phantom waters breaking overhead,
Shades of vex'd billows bursting on his breast,
Torn caves of mist wall'd with a sudden gold,
Reseal'd as swift as seen – broad, shaggy fronts,
Fire-ey'd and tossing on impatient horns
The wave impalpable – was but to think
A dream of phantoms held him as he stood.

30 The late, last thunders of the summer crash'd,
Where shrieked great eagles, lords of naked cliffs.
The pulseless forest, lock'd and interlock'd
So closely, bough with bough, and leaf with leaf,
So serf'd by its own wealth, that while from high
The Moons of Summer kiss'd its green-gloss'd locks,
And round its knees the merry West Wind danc'd,
And round its ring, compacted emerald,
The South Wind crept on moccasins of flame,
And the red fingers of th' impatient Sun

40 Pluck'd at its outmost fringes – its dim veins
Beat with no life – its deep and dusky heart,
In a deep trance of shadow, felt no throb
To such soft wooing answer: thro' its dream
Brown rivers of deep waters sunless stole;
Small creeks sprang from its mosses, and amaz'd,
Like children in a wigwam curtain'd close
Above the great, dead heart of some red chief,
Slipp'd on soft feet, swift stealing through the gloom,
Eager for light and for the frolic winds.

50 In this shrill Moon the scouts of Winter ran
From the ice-belted north, and whistling shafts
Struck maple and struck sumach – and a blaze
Ran swift from leaf to leaf, from bough to bough;
Till round the forest flash'd a belt of flame
And inward lick'd its tongues of red and gold

To the deep, tranced inmost heart of all.
Rous'd the still heart – but all too late, too late.
Too late, the branches welded fast with leaves,
Toss'd, loosen'd, to the winds – too late the Sun
60 Pour'd his last vigor to the deep, dark cells
Of the dim wood. The keen, two-bladed Moon
Of Falling Leaves roll'd up on crested mists;
And where the lush, rank boughs had foiled the Sun
In his red prime, her pale, sharp fingers crept
After the wind and felt about the moss,
And seem'd to pluck from shrinking twig and stem
The burning leaves – while groan'd the shudd'ring wood.
Who journey'd where the prairies made a pause,
Saw burnish'd ramparts flaming in the sun,
70 With beacon fires, tall on their rustling walls.
And when the vast, horn'd herds at sunset drew
Their sullen masses into one black cloud,
Rolling thund'rous o'er the quick pulsating plain,
They seem'd to sweep between two fierce red suns
Which, hunter-wise, shot at their glaring balls
Keen shafts, with scarlet feathers and gold barbs.
By round, small lakes with thinner forests fring'd,
More jocund woods that sung about the feet
And crept along the shoulders of great cliffs,
80 The warrior stags, with does and tripping fawns,
Like shadows black upon the throbbing mist
Of evening's rose, flash'd thro' the singing woods –
Nor tim'rous, sniff'd the spicy, cone-breath'd air;
For never had the patriarch of the herd
Seen, limn'd against the farthest rim of light
Of the low-dipping sky, the plume or bow
Of the red hunter; nor, when stoop'd to drink,
Had from the rustling rice-beds heard the shaft
Of the still hunter hidden in its spears;
90 His bark canoe close-knotted in its bronze,

His form as stirless as the brooding air,
His dusky eyes, too, fix'd, unwinking, fires;
His bow-string tighten'd till it subtly sang
To the long throbs, and leaping pulse that roll'd
And beat within his knotted, naked breast.
There came a morn. The Moon of Falling Leaves,
With her twin silver blades, had only hung
Above the low-set cedars of the swamp
For one brief quarter, when the Sun arose
100 Lusty with light and full of summer heat,
And, pointing with his arrows at the blue,
Clos'd, wigwam curtains of the sleeping Moon,
Laugh'd with the noise of arching cataracts,
And with the dove-like cooing of the woods,
And with the shrill cry of the diving loon,
And with the wash of saltless, rounded seas,
And mock'd the white Moon of the Falling Leaves.
"Esa! esa! shame upon you, Pale Face!
"Shame upon you, Moon of Evil Witches!
110 "Have you kill'd the happy, laughing Summer?
"Have you slain the mother of the flowers
"With your icy spells of might and magic?
"Have you laid her dead within my arms?
"Wrapp'd her, mocking, in a rainbow blanket?
"Drown'd her in the frost-mist of your anger?
"She is gone a little way before me;
"Gone an arrow's flight beyond my vision;
"She will turn again and come to meet me,
"With the ghosts of all the slain flowers,
120 "In a blue mist round her shining tresses,
"In a blue smoke in her naked forests –
"She will linger, kissing all the branches;
"She will linger, touching all the places,
"Bare and naked, with her golden fingers,
"Saying, 'Sleep, and dream of me, my children;

"'Dream of me, the mystic Indian Summer;
"'I, who, slain by the cold Moon of Terror,
"'Can return across the Path of Spirits,
"'Bearing still my heart of love and fire,
130 "'Looking with my eyes of warmth and splendour,
"'Whisp'ring lowly thro' your sleep of sunshine.
"'I, the laughing Summer, am not turn'd
"'Into dry dust, whirling on the prairies, –
"'Into red clay, crush'd beneath the snowdrifts.
"'I am still the mother of sweet flowers
"'Growing but an arrow's flight beyond you –
"'In the Happy Hunting Ground – the quiver
"'Of great Manitou, where all the arrows
"'He has shot from his great bow of Pow'r,
140 "'With its clear, bright, singing cord of Wisdom,
"'Are re-gather'd, plum'd again and brighten'd,
"'And shot out, re-barb'd with Love and Wisdom;
"'Always shot, and evermore returning.
"'Sleep, my children, smiling in your heart-seeds
"'At the spirit words of Indian Summer!'
"Thus, O Moon of Falling Leaves, I mock you!
"Have you slain my gold-ey'd squaw, the Summer?"
The mighty morn strode laughing up the land,
And Max, the labourer and the lover, stood
150 Within the forest's edge, beside a tree;
The mossy king of all the woody tribes,
Whose clatt'ring branches rattl'd, shuddering,
As the bright axe cleav'd moon-like thro' the air,
Waking strange thunders, rousing echoes link'd
From the full, lion-throated roar, to sighs
Stealing on dove-wings thro' the distant aisles.
Swift fell the axe, swift follow'd roar on roar,
Till the bare woodland bellow'd in its rage,
As the first-slain slow toppl'd to his fall.
160 "O King of Desolation, art thou dead?"

Thought Max, and laughing, heart and lips, leap'd on
The vast, prone trunk. "And have I slain a King?
"Above his ashes will I build my house –
"No slave beneath its pillars, but – a King!"
Max wrought alone, but for a half-breed lad,
With tough, lithe sinews and deep Indian eyes,
Lit with a Gallic sparkle. Max, the lover, found
The labourer's arms grow mightier day by day –
More iron-welded as he slew the trees;

170 And with the constant yearning of his heart
Towards little Kate, part of a world away,
His young soul grew and shew'd a virile front,
Full muscl'd and large statur'd, like his flesh.
Soon the great heaps of brush were builded high,
And, like a victor, Max made pause to clear
His battle-field, high strewn with tangl'd dead.
Then roar'd the crackling mountains, and their fires
Met in high heaven, clasping flame with flame.
The thin winds swept a cosmos of red sparks

180 Across the bleak, midnight sky; and the sun
Walk'd pale behind the resinous, black smoke.
And Max car'd little for the blotted sun,
And nothing for the startl'd, outshone stars;
For Love, once set within a lover's breast,
Has its own Sun – its own peculiar sky,
All one great daffodil – on which do lie
The sun, the moon, the stars – all seen at once,
And never setting; but all shining straight
Into the faces of the trinity, –

190 The one belov'd, the lover, and sweet Love!
It was not all his own, the axe-stirr'd waste.
In these new days men spread about the earth
With wings at heel – and now the settler hears,
While yet his axe rings on the primal woods,
The shrieks of engines rushing o'er the wastes;

Nor parts his kind to hew his fortunes out.
And as one drop glides down the unknown rock
And the bright-threaded stream leaps after it
With welded billions, so the settler finds
200 His solitary footsteps beaten out,
With the quick rush of panting, human waves
Upheav'd by throbs of angry poverty,
And driven by keen blasts of hunger, from
Their native strands – so stern, so dark, so dear!
O, then, to see the troubl'd, groaning waves,
Throb down to peace in kindly, valley beds,
Their turbid bosoms clearing in the calm
Of sun-ey'd Plenty – till the stars and moon,
The blessed sun himself, has leave to shine
210 And laugh in their dark hearts! So shanties grew
Other than his amid the blacken'd stumps;
And children ran with little twigs and leaves
And flung them, shouting, on the forest pyres
Where burn'd the forest kings – and in the glow
Paus'd men and women when the day was done.
There the lean weaver ground anew his axe,
Nor backward look'd upon the vanish'd loom,
But forward to the ploughing of his fields,
And to the rose of Plenty in the cheeks
220 Of wife and children – nor heeded much the pangs
Of the rous'd muscles tuning to new work.
The pallid clerk look'd on his blister'd palms
And sigh'd and smil'd, but girded up his loins
And found new vigour as he felt new hope.
The lab'rer with train'd muscles, grim and grave,
Look'd at the ground and wonder'd in his soul,
What joyous anguish stirr'd his darken'd heart,
At the mere look of the familiar soil,
And found his answer in the words – "*Mine own!*"
230 Then came smooth-coated men, with eager eyes,

And talk'd of steamers on the cliff-bound lakes;
And iron tracks across the prairie lands;
And mills to crush the quartz of wealthy hills;
And mills to saw the great, wide-arm'd trees;
And mills to grind the singing stream of grain;
And with such busy clamour mingled still
The throbbing music of the bold, bright Axe –
The steel tongue of the Present, and the wail
Of falling forests – voices of the Past.

240   Max, social-soul'd, and with his practised thews,
Was happy, boy-like, thinking much of Kate,
And speaking of her to the women-folk,
Who, mostly, happy in new honeymoons
Of hope themselves, were ready still to hear
The thrice-told tale of Katie's sunny eyes
And Katie's yellow hair, and household ways;
And heard so often, "There shall stand our home –
"On yonder slope, with vines about the door!"
That the good wives were almost made to see
250   The snowy walls, deep porches, and the gleam
Of Katie's garments flitting through the rooms;
And the black slope all bristling with burn'd stumps
Was known amongst them all as "Max's House."

> O, Love builds on the azure sea,
>   And Love builds on the golden sand;
> And Love builds on the rose-wing'd cloud,
>   And sometimes Love builds on the land.

> O, if Love build on sparkling sea –
>   And if Love build on golden strand –
250   And if Love build on rosy cloud –
>   To Love these are the solid land.

> O, Love will build his lily walls,
>   And Love his pearly roof will rear, –

On cloud or land, or mist or sea —
Love's solid land is everywhere!

PART III

The great farm house of Malcolm Graem stood
Square shoulder'd and peak roof'd upon a hill,
With many windows looking everywhere;
So that no distant meadow might lie hid,
Nor corn-field hide its gold — nor lowing herd
Browse in far pastures, out of Malcolm's ken.
He lov'd to sit, grim, grey, and somewhat stern,
And thro' the smoke-clouds from his short clay pipe
Look out upon his riches; while his thoughts
10 Swung back and forth between the bleak, stern past,
And the near future, for his life had come
To that close balance, when, a pendulum,
The memory swings between the "Then" and "Now";
His seldom speech ran thus two diff'rent ways:
"When I was but a laddie, thus I did";
Or, "Katie, in the fall I'll see to build
"Such fences or such sheds about the place;
"And next year, please the Lord, another barn."
Katie's gay garden foam'd about the walls,
20 'Leagur'd the prim-cut modern sills, and rush'd
Up the stone walls — and broke on the peak'd roof.
And Katie's lawn was like a poet's sward,
Velvet and sheer and di'monded with dew;
For such as win their wealth most aptly take
Smooth, urban ways and blend them with their own;
And Katie's dainty raiment was as fine
As the smooth, silken petals of the rose;
And her light feet, her nimble mind and voice,
In city schools had learn'd the city's ways,
30 And grafts upon the healthy, lovely vine
They shone, eternal blossoms 'mid the fruit.

For Katie had her sceptre in her hand
And wielded it right queenly there and here,
In dairy, store-room, kitchen – ev'ry spot
Where women's ways were needed on the place.
And Malcolm took her through his mighty fields,
And taught her lore about the change of crops;
And how to see a handsome furrow plough'd;
And how to choose the cattle for the mart;
40 And how to know a fair day's work when done;
And where to plant young orchards; for he said,
"God sent a lassie, but I need a son –
"Bethankit for His mercies all the same."
And Katie, when he said it, thought of Max –
Who had been gone two winters and two springs,
And sigh'd, and thought, "Would he not be your son?"
But all in silence, for she had too much
Of the firm will of Malcolm in her soul
To think of shaking that deep-rooted rock;
50 But hop'd the crystal current of his love
For his one child, increasing day by day,
Might fret with silver lip until it wore
Such channels thro' the rock that some slight stroke
Of circumstance might crumble down the stone.
The wooer, too, had come, Max prophesied;
Reputed wealthy; with the azure eyes
And Saxon-gilded locks – the fair, clear face,
And stalwart form that most women love,
And with the jewels of some virtues set
60 On his broad brow. With fires within his soul
He had the wizard skill to fetter down
To that mere pink, poetic, nameless glow,
That need not fright a flake of snow away –
But, if unloos'd, could melt an adverse rock
Marrow'd with iron, frowning in his way.
And Malcolm balanc'd him by day and night;

And with his grey-ey'd shrewdness partly saw
He was not one for Kate; but let him come,
And in chance moments thought: "Well, let it be –
70 "They make a bonnie pair – he knows the ways
"Of men and things: can hold the gear I give,
"And, if the lassie wills it, let it be."
And then, upstarting from his midnight sleep,
With hair erect and sweat upon his brow
Such as no labor e'er had beaded there;
Would cry aloud, wide-staring thro' the dark –
"Nay, nay; she shall not wed him – rest in peace."
Then fully waking, grimly laugh and say:
"Why did I speak and answer when none spake?"
80 But still lie staring, wakeful, through the shades;
List'ning to the silence, and beating still
The ball of Alfred's merits to and fro –
Saying, between the silent arguments:
"But would the mother like it, could she know?
"I would there was a way to ring a lad
"Like a silver coin, and so find out the true;
"But Kate shall say him 'Nay' or say him 'Yea'
"At her own will." And Katie said him "Nay,"
In all the maiden, speechless, gentle ways
90 A woman has. But Alfred only laugh'd
To his own soul, and said in his wall'd mind:
"O, Kate, were I a lover, I might feel
"Despair flap o'er my hopes with raven wings;
"Because thy love is giv'n to other love.
"And did I love – unless I gain'd thy love,
"I would disdain the golden hair, sweet lips,
"Air-blown form and true violet eyes;
"Nor crave the beauteous lamp without the flame;
"Which in itself would light a charnel house.
100 "Unlov'd and loving, I would find the cure
"Of Love's despair in nursing Love's disdain –

"Disdain of lesser treasure than the whole.
"One cares not much to place against the wheel
"A di'mond lacking flame – nor loves to pluck
"A rose with all its perfume cast abroad
"To the bosom of the gale. Not I, in truth!
"If all man's days are three-score years and ten,
"He needs must waste them not, but nimbly seize
"The bright, consummate blossom that his will
110 "Calls for most loudly. Gone, long gone the days
"When Love within my soul for ever stretch'd
"Fierce hands of flame, and here and there I found
"A blossom fitted for him – all up-fill'd
"With love as with clear dew – they had their hour
"And burn'd to ashes with him, as he droop'd
"In his own ruby fires. No Phœnix he,
"To rise again because of Katie's eyes,
"On dewy wings, from ashes such as his!
"But now, another Passion bids me forth,
120 "To crown him with the fairest I can find,
"And makes me lover – not of Katie's face,
"But of her father's riches! O, high fool,
"Who feels the faintest pulsing of a wish
"And fails to feed it into lordly life!
"So that, when stumbling back to Mother Earth,
"His freezing lip may curl in cold disdain
"Of those poor, blighted fools who starward stare
"For that fruition, nipp'd and scanted here.
"And, while the clay o'ermasters all his blood –
130 "And he can feel the dust knit with his flesh –
"He yet can say to them, 'Be ye content;
"'I tasted perfect fruitage thro' my life,
"'Lighted all lamps of passion, till the oil
"'Fail'd from their wicks; and now, O now, I know
"'There is no Immortality could give
"'Such boon as this – to simply cease to be!

"'*There* lies your Heaven, O ye dreaming slaves,
"'If ye would only live to make it so;
"'Nor paint upon the blue skies lying shades
140 "'Of – *what is not*. Wise, wise and strong the man
"'Who poisons that fond haunter of the mind,
"'Craving for a hereafter with deep draughts
"'Of wild delights – so fiery, fierce, and strong,
"'That when their dregs are deeply, deeply drain'd,
"'What once was blindly crav'd of purblind Chance,
"'Life, life eternal – throbbing thro' all space,
"'Is strongly loath'd – and with his face in dust,
"'Man loves his only Heav'n – six feet of Earth!'
"So, Katie, tho' your blue eyes say me 'Nay,'
150 "My pangs of love for gold must needs be fed,
"And shall be, Katie, if I know my mind."
Events were winds close nestling in the sails
Of Alfred's bark, all blowing him direct
To his wish'd harbour. On a certain day,
All set about with roses and with fire;
One of three days of heat which frequent slip,
Like triple rubies, in between the sweet,
Mild, emerald days of summer, Katie went,
Drawn by a yearning for the ice-pale blooms,
160 Natant and shining – firing all the bay
With angel fires built up of snow and gold.
She found the bay close pack'd with groaning logs,
Prison'd between great arms of close-hing'd wood,
All cut from Malcolm's forests in the west,
And floated hither to his noisy mills;
And all stamp'd with the potent "G." and "M.,"
Which much he lov'd to see upon his goods,
The silent courtiers owning him their king.
Out clear beyond, the rustling ricebeds sang,
170 And the cool lilies starr'd the shadow'd wave.
"This is a day for lily-love," said Kate,

While she made bare the lilies of her feet,
And sang a lily-song that Max had made,
That spoke of lilies – always meaning Kate.

"White Lady of the silver'd lakes,
     Chaste Goddess of the sweet, still shrines,
          The jocund river fitful makes,
     By sudden, deep gloom'd brakes,
     Close shelter'd by close weft and woof of vine,
180   Spilling a shadow gloomy-rich as wine,
     Into the silver throne where thou dost sit,
     Thy silken leaves all dusky round thee knit!

"Mild soul of the unsalted wave!
     White bosom holding golden fire!
Deep as some ocean-hidden cave
     Are fix'd the roots of thy desire,
Thro' limpid currents stealing up,
And rounding to the pearly cup.
          Thou dost desire,
190   With all thy trembling heart of sinless fire,
          But to be fill'd
          With dew distill'd
From clear, fond skies that in their gloom
Hold, floating high, thy sister moon.
Pale chalice of a sweet perfume,
Whiter-breasted than a dove –
To thee the dew is – love!"

Kate bared her little feet, and pois'd herself
On the first log close grating on the shore;
200 And with bright eyes of laughter, and wild hair –
A flying wind of gold – from log to log
Sped, laughing as they wallow'd in her track,
Like brown-scal'd monsters rolling, as her foot
Spurn'd each in turn with its rose-white sole.
A little island, out in middle wave,

With its green shoulder held the great drive brac'd
Between it and the mainland; here it was
The silver lilies drew her with white smiles;
And as she touch'd the last great log of all,
210 It reel'd, upstarting, like a column brac'd
A second on the wave – and when it plung'd
Rolling upon the froth and sudden foam,
Katie had vanish'd, and with angry grind
The vast logs roll'd together, – nor a lock
Of drifting, yellow hair – an upflung hand,
Told where the rich man's chiefest treasure sank
Under his wooden wealth. But Alfred, laid
With pipe and book upon the shady marge
Of the cool isle, saw all, and seeing hurl'd
220 Himself, and hardly knew it, on the logs.
By happy chance a shallow lapp'd the isle
On this green bank; and when his iron arms
Dash'd the bark'd monsters, as frail stems of rice,
A little space apart, the soft, slow tide
But reach'd his chest, and in a flash he saw
Kate's yellow hair, and by it drew her up,
And lifting her aloft, cried out, "O, Kate!"
And once again said, "Katie! is she dead?"
For like the lilies broken by the rough
230 And sudden riot of the armor'd logs,
Kate lay upon his hands; and now the logs
Clos'd in upon him, nipping his great chest,
Nor could he move to push them off again
For Katie in his arms. "And now," he said,
"If none should come, and any wind arise
"To weld these woody monsters 'gainst the isle,
"I shall be crack'd like any broken twig;
"And as it is, I know not if I die,
"For I am hurt – aye, sorely, sorely hurt!"
240 Then look'd on Katie's lily face, and said,

"Dead, dead or living? Why, an even chance.
"O lovely bubble on a troubl'd sea,
"I would not thou shouldst lose thyself again
"In the black ocean whence thy life emerg'd,
"But skyward steal on gales as soft as love,
"And hang in some bright rainbow overhead,
"If only such bright rainbow spann'd the earth."
Then shouted loudly, till the silent air
Rous'd like a frighten'd bird, and on its wings
250 Caught up his cry and bore it to the farm.
There Malcolm, leaping from his noontide sleep,
Upstarted as at midnight, crying out,
"She shall not wed him – rest you, wife, in peace!"
They found him, Alfred, haggard-ey'd and faint,
But holding Katie ever towards the sun,
Unhurt, and waking in the fervent heat.
And now it came that Alfred, being sick
Of his sharp hurts and tended by them both,
With what was like to love, being born of thanks,
260 Had choice of hours most politic to woo,
And used his deed as one might use the sun,
To ripen unmellow'd fruit; and from the core
Of Katie's gratitude hop'd yet to nurse
A flow'r all to his liking – Katie's love.
But Katie's mind was like the plain, broad shield
Of a table di'mond, nor had a score of sides;
And in its shield, so precious and so plain,
Was cut, thro' all its clear depths – Max's name.
And so she said him "Nay" at last, in words
270 Of such true-sounding silver that he knew
He might not win her at the present hour,
But smil'd and thought – "I go, and come again!
"Then shall we see. Our three-score years and ten
"Are mines of treasure, if we hew them deep,
"Nor stop too long in choosing out our tools!"

PART IV

From his far wigwam sprang the strong North Wind
And rush'd with war-cry down the steep ravines,
And wrestl'd with the giants of the woods;
And with his ice-club beat the swelling crests
Of the deep watercourses into death;
And with his chill foot froze the whirling leaves
Of dun and gold and fire in icy banks;
And smote the tall reeds to the harden'd earth;
And sent his whistling arrows o'er the plains,
10 Scatt'ring the ling'ring herds – and sudden paus'd
When he had frozen all the running streams,
And hunted with his war-cry all the things
That breath'd about the woods, or roam'd the bleak
Bare prairies swelling to the mournful sky.
"White squaw," he shouted, troubl'd in his soul,
"I slew the dead, wrestl'd with naked chiefs
"Unplum'd before, scalped of their leafy plumes;
"I bound sick rivers in cold thongs of death,
"And shot my arrows over swooning plains,
20 "Bright with the paint of death – and lean and bare.
"And all the braves of my loud tribe will mock
"And point at me – when our great chief, the Sun,
"Relights his Council fire in the Moon
"Of Budding Leaves: 'Ugh, ugh! he is a brave!
"'He fights with squaws and takes the scalps of babes!'
"And the least wind will blow his calumet –
"Fill'd with the breath of smallest flow'rs – across
"The war-paint on my face, and pointing with
"His small, bright pipe, that never moved a spear
30 "Of bearded rice, cry, 'Ugh! he slays the dead!'
"O, my white squaw, come from thy wigwam grey,
"Spread thy white blanket on the twice-slain dead,
"And hide them, ere the waking of the Sun!"

High grew the snow beneath the low-hung sky,
And all was silent in the Wilderness;
In trance of stillness Nature heard her God
Rebuilding her spent fires, and veil'd her face
While the Great Worker brooded o'er His work.

> "Bite deep and wide, O Axe, the tree,
40 > What doth thy bold voice promise me?"

> "I promise thee all joyous things,
> That furnish forth the lives of kings!

> "For ev'ry silver ringing blow,
> Cities and palaces shall grow!"

> "Bite deep and wide, O Axe, the tree,
> Tell wider prophecies to me."

> "When rust hath gnaw'd me deep and red,
> A nation strong shall lift his head!

> "His crown the very Heav'ns shall smite,
50 > Æons shall build him in his might!"

> "Bite deep and wide, O Axe, the tree;
> Bright Seer, help on thy prophecy!"

Max smote the snow-weigh'd tree and lightly laugh'd.
"See, friend," he cried to one that look'd and smil'd,
"My axe and I – we do immortal tasks –
"We build up nations – this my axe and I!"
"O," said the other with a cold, short smile,
"Nations are not immortal! Is there now
"One nation thron'd upon the sphere of earth,
60 "That walk'd with the first Gods, and saw
"The budding world unfold its slow-leav'd flow'r?
"Nay; it is hardly theirs to leave behind
"Ruins so eloquent that the hoary sage

"Can lay his hand upon their stones, and say:
"'These once were thrones!' The lean, lank lion peals
"His midnight thunders over lone, red plains,
"Long-ridg'd and crested on their dusty waves
"With fires from moons red-hearted as the sun;
"And deep re-thunders all the earth to him.
70 "For, far beneath the flame-fleck'd, shifting sands,
"Below the roots of palms, and under stones
"Of younger ruins, thrones, tow'rs and cities
"Honeycomb the earth. The high, solemn walls
"Of hoary ruins – their foundings all unknown
"(But to the round-ey'd worlds that walk
"In the blank paths of Space and blanker Chance) –
"At whose stones young mountains wonder, and the seas'
"New-silv'ring, deep-set valleys pause and gaze,
"Are rear'd upon old shrines, whose very Gods
80 "Were dreams to the shrine-builders of a time
"They caught in far-off flashes – as the child
"Half thinks he can remember how one came
"And took him in her hand and shew'd him that,
"He thinks, she call'd the sun. Proud ships rear high
"On ancient billows that have torn the roots
"Of cliffs, and bitten at the golden lips
"Of firm, sleek beaches, till they conquer'd all,
"And sow'd the reeling earth with salted waves.
"Wrecks plunge, prow foremost, down still, solemn slopes,
90 "And bring their dead crews to as dead a quay;
"Some city built before that ocean grew,
"By silver drops from many a floating cloud,
"By icebergs bellowing in their throes of death,
"By lesser seas toss'd from their rocking cups,
"And leaping each to each; by dew-drops flung
"From painted sprays, whose weird leaves and flow'rs
"Are moulded for new dwellers on the earth,

"Printed in hearts of mountains and of mines.
"Nations immortal? Where the well-trimm'd lamps
100 "Of long-past ages, when Time seem'd to pause
"On smooth, dust-blotted graves that, like the tombs
"Of monarchs, held dead bones and sparkling gems?
"She saw no glimmer on the hideous ring
"Of the black clouds; no stream of sharp, clear light
"From those great torches, pass'd into the black
"Of deep oblivion. She seem'd to watch, but she
"Forgot her long-dead nations. When she stirr'd
"Her vast limbs in the dawn that forc'd its fire
"Up the black East, and saw the imperious red
110 "Burst over virgin dews and budding flow'rs,
"She still forgot her molder'd thrones and kings,
"Her sages and their torches, and their Gods,
"And said, 'This is my birth – my primal day!'
"She dream'd new Gods, and rear'd them other shrines,
"Planted young nations, smote a feeble flame
"From sunless flint, re-lit the torch of mind;
"Again she hung her cities on the hills,
"Built her rich tow'rs, crown'd her kings again,
"And with the sunlight on her awful wings
120 "Swept round the flow'ry cestus of the earth,
"And said, 'I build for Immortality!'
"Her vast hand rear'd her tow'rs, her shrines, her thrones;
"The ceaseless sweep of her tremendous wings
"Still beat them down and swept their dust abroad;
"Her iron finger wrote on mountain sides
"Her deeds and prowess – and her own soft plume
"Wore down the hills! Again drew darkly on
"A night of deep forgetfulness; once more
"Time seem'd to pause upon forgotten graves –
130 "Once more a young dawn stole into her eyes –
"Again her broad wings stirr'd, and fresh, clear airs,

"Blew the great clouds apart; – again Time said,
"'This is my birth – my deeds and handiwork
"'Shall be immortal.' Thus and so dream on
"Fool'd nations, and thus dream their dullard sons.
"Naught is immortal save immortal – Death!"
Max paus'd and smil'd: "O, preach such gospel, friend,
"To all but lovers who most truly love;
"For *them*, their gold-wrought scripture glibly reads,
140 "All else is mortal but immortal – Love!"
"Fools! fools!" his friend said, "most immortal fools! –
"But pardon, pardon, for, perchance, you love?"
"Yes," said Max, proudly smiling, "thus do I
"Possess the world and feel eternity!"
Dark laughter blacken'd in the other's eyes:
"Eternity! why, did such Iris-arch
"Enring our worm-bored planet, never liv'd
"One woman true enough such tryst to keep!"
"I'd swear by Kate," said Max; and then, "I had
150 "A mother, and my father swore by her."
"By Kate? Ah, that were lusty oath, indeed!
"Some other man will look into her eyes,
"And swear me roundly, 'By true Catherine!'
"As Troilus swore by Cressèd – so they say."
"You never knew my Kate," said Max, and pois'd
His axe again on high. "But let it pass –
"You are too subtle for me; argument
"Have I none to oppose yours with – but this,
"Get you a Kate, and let her sunny eyes
160 "Dispel the doubting darkness in your soul."
"And have not I a Kate? Pause, friend, and see.
"She gave me this faint shadow of herself
"The day I slipp'd the watch-star of our loves –
"A ring – upon her hand – she loves me, too;
"Yet tho' her eyes be suns, no Gods are they
"To give me worlds, or make me feel a tide

"Of strong Eternity set towards my soul;
"And tho' she loves me, yet am I content
"To know she loves me by the hour – the year –
170 "Perchance the second – as all women love."
The bright axe falter'd in the air, and ripp'd
Down the rough bark, and bit the drifted snow,
For Max's arm fell, wither'd in its strength,
'Long by his side. "Your Kate," he said; "your Kate!"
"Yes, mine, while holds her mind that way, my Kate;
"I sav'd her life, and had her love for thanks;
"Her father is Malcolm Graem – Max, my friend,
"You pale! What sickness seizes on your soul?"
Max laugh'd, and swung his bright axe high again:
180 "Stand back a pace – a too far-reaching blow
"Might level your false head with yon prone trunk –
"Stand back and listen while I say, 'You lie!'
"That is my Katie's face upon your breast,
"But 'tis my Katie's love lives in my breast –
"Stand back, I say! my axe is heavy, and
"Might chance to cleave a liar's brittle skull.
"Your Kate! your Kate! your Kate! – hark, how the woods
"Mock at your lie with all their woody tongues.
"O, silence, ye false echoes! Not his Kate
190 "But mine – I'm certain I will have your life!"
All the blue heav'n was dead in Max's eyes;
Doubt-wounded lay Kate's image in his heart,
And could not rise to pluck the sharp spear out.
"Well, strike, mad fool," said Alfred, somewhat pale;
"I have no weapon but these naked hands."
"Aye, but," said Max, "you smote my naked heart!
"O shall I slay him? – Satan, answer me –
"I cannot call on God for answer here.
"O Kate –!"
200 A voice from God came thro' the silent woods
And answer'd him – for suddenly a wind

Caught the great tree-tops, con'd with high-pil'd snow,
And smote them to and fro, while all the air
Was sudden fill'd with busy drifts, and high
White pillars whirl'd amid the naked trunks,
And harsh, loud groans, and smiting, sapless boughs
Made hellish clamour in the quiet place.
With a shrill shriek of tearing fibres, rock'd
The half-hewn tree above his fated head;
210 And, tott'ring, risked the sudden blast, "Which way?"
And, answ'ring its windy arms, crash'd and broke
Thro' other lacing boughs, with one loud roar
Of woody thunder; all its pointed boughs
Pierc'd the deep snow – its round and mighty corpse,
Bark-flay'd and shudd'ring, quiver'd into death.
And Max – as some frail, wither'd reed, the sharp
And piercing branches caught at him, as hands
In a death-throe, and beat him to the earth –
And the dead tree upon its slayer lay.
220 "Yet hear we much of Gods; – if such there be,
"They play at games of chance with thunderbolts,"
Said Alfred, "else on me this doom had come.
"This seals my faith in deep and dark unfaith!
"Now, Katie, are you mine, for Max is dead –
"Or will be soon, imprison'd by those boughs,
"Wounded and torn, sooth'd by the deadly palms
"Of the white, trait'rous frost; and buried then
"Under the snows that fill those vast, grey clouds,
"Low-sweeping on the fretted forest roof.
230 "And Katie shall believe you false – not dead;
"False, false! – and I? O, she shall find me true –
"True as a fabl'd devil to the soul
"He longs for with the heat of all Hell's fires.
"These myths serve well for simile, I see.
"And yet – down, Pity! Knock not at my breast,

"Nor grope about for that dull stone my heart;
"I'll stone thee with it, Pity! Get thee hence,
"Pity, I'll strangle thee with naked hands;
"For thou dost bear upon thy downy breast
240 "Remorse, shap'd like a serpent, and her fangs
"Might dart at me and pierce my marrow thro'.
"Hence, beggar, hence – and keep with fools, I say!
"He bleeds and groans! Well, Max, thy God or mine,
"Blind Chance, here play'd the butcher – 'twas not I.
"Down hands! Ye shall not lift his fall'n head.
"What cords tug at ye? What? Ye'd pluck him up
"And staunch his wounds? There rises in my breast
"A strange, strong giant, throwing wide his arms
"And bursting all the granite of my heart!
250 "How like to quiv'ring flesh a stone may feel!
"Why, it has pangs! I'll none of them. I know
"Life is too short for anguish and for hearts –
"So I wrestle with thee, giant! and my will
"Turns the thumb, and thou shalt take the knife.
"Well done! I'll turn thee on the arena dust,
"And look on thee. What? thou wert Pity's self,
"Stol'n in my breast; and I have slaughter'd thee –
"But hist – where hast thou hidden thy fell snake,
"Fire-fang'd Remorse? Not in my breast, I know,
260 "For all again is chill and empty there,
"And hard and cold – the granite knitted up.
"So lie there, Max – poor fond and simple Max,
"'Tis well thou diest: earth's children should not call
"Such as thee father – let them ever be
"Father'd by rogues and villains, fit to cope
"With the foul dragon Chance, and the black knaves
"Who swarm in loathsome masses in the dust.
"True Max, lie there, and slumber into death."

PART V

Said the high hill, in the morning: "Look on me –
"Behold, sweet earth, sweet sister sky, behold
"The red flames on my peaks, and how my pines
"Are cressets of pure gold; my quarried scars
"Of black crevasse and shadow-fill'd canon,
"Are trac'd in silver mist. Now on my breast
"Hang the soft purple fringes of the night;
"Close to my shoulder droops the weary moon,
"Dove-pale, into the crimson surf the sun
10 "Drives up before his prow; and blackly stands
"On my slim, loftiest peak, an eagle with
"His angry eyes set sunward, while his cry
"Falls fiercely back from all my ruddy heights;
"And his bald eaglets, in their bare, broad nest,
"Shrill pipe their angry echoes: 'Sun, arise,
"'And show me that pale dove, beside her nest,
"'Which I shall strike with piercing beak and tear
"'With iron talons for my hungry young.'"
And that mild dove, secure for yet a space,
20 Half waken'd, turns her ring'd and glossy neck
To watch dawn's ruby pulsing on her breast,
And see the first bright golden motes slip down
The gnarl'd trunks about her leaf-deep nest,
Nor sees nor fears the eagle on the peak.

"Aye, lassie, sing – I'll smoke my pipe the while,
"And let it be a simple, bonnie song,
"Such as an old, plain man can gather in
"His dulling ear, and feel it slipping thro'
"The cold, dark, stony places of his heart."
30 "Yes, sing, sweet Kate," said Alfred in her ear;
"I often heard you singing in my dreams
"When I was far away the winter past."
So Katie on the moonlit window lean'd,

And in the airy silver of her voice
Sang of the tender, blue "Forget-me-not."

"Could every blossom find a voice,
    And sing a strain to me,
I know where I would place my choice,
    Which my delight should be.
40   I would not choose the lily tall,
      The rose from musky grot;
But I would still my minstrel call
      The blue 'Forget-me-not!'

"And I on mossy bank would lie
    Of brooklet, ripp'ling clear;
And she of the sweet azure eye,
    Close at my list'ning ear,
Should sing into my soul a strain
    Might never be forgot –
50   So rich with joy, so rich with pain,
      The blue 'Forget-me-not!'

"Ah, ev'ry blossom hath a tale
    With silent grace to tell,
From rose that reddens to the gale
    To modest heather bell;
But O, the flow'r in ev'ry heart
    That finds a sacred spot
To bloom, with azure leaves apart,
    Is the 'Forget-me-not!'

60   "Love plucks it from the mosses green
      When parting hours are nigh,
And places it Love's palms between,
    With many an ardent sigh;
And bluely up from grassy graves
    In some lov'd churchyard spot,
It glances tenderly and waves,
    The dear 'Forget-me-not!'"

And with the faint, last cadence, stole a glance
At Malcolm's soften'd face – a bird-soft touch
70 Let flutter on the rugged, silver snarls
Of his thick locks, and laid her tender lips
A second on the iron of his hand.
"And did you ever meet," he sudden ask'd
Of Alfred, sitting pallid in the shade,
"Out by yon unco place, a lad – a lad
"Nam'd Maxwell Gordon; tall and straight, and strong;
"About my size, I take it, when a lad?"
And Katie at the sound of Max's name,
First spoken for such a space by Malcolm's lips,
80 Trembl'd and started, and let down her brow,
Hiding its sudden rose on Malcolm's arm.
"Max Gordon? Yes. Was he a friend of yours?"
"No friend of mine, but of the lassie's here –
"How comes he on? I wager he's a drone,
"And never will put honey in the hive."
"No drone," said Alfred, laughing; "when I left,
"He and his axe were quarr'ling with the woods
"And making forests reel – love steels a lover's arm."
O, blush that stole from Katie's swelling heart,
90 And with its hot rose brought the happy dew
Into her hidden eyes. "Aye, aye! is that the way?"
Said Malcolm, smiling. "Who may be his love?"
"In that he is a somewhat simple soul,
"Why, I suppose he loves –" he paused, and Kate
Look'd up with two "Forget-me-nots" for eyes,
With eager jewels in their centres set
Of happy, happy tears, and Alfred's heart
Became a closer marble than before.
"– Why I suppose he loves – his lawful wife."
100 "His wife! his wife!" said Malcolm, in amaze,
And laid his heavy hand on Katie's head;
"Did you two play me false, my little lass?

"Speak and I'll pardon! Katie, lassie, what?"
"He has a wife," said Alfred, "lithe and bronz'd,
"An Indian woman, comelier than her kind;
"And on her knee a child with yellow locks,
"And lake-like eyes of mystic Indian brown.
"And so you knew him? He is doing well."
"False, false!" said Katie, lifting up her head.
110 "O, you know not the Max my father means!"
"He came from yonder farm-house on the slope."
"Some other Max – we speak not of the same."
"He has a red mark on his temple set."
"It matters not – 'tis not the Max we know."
"He wears a turquoise ring slung round his neck."
"And many wear them – they are common stones."
"His mother's ring – her name was Helen Wynde."
"And there be many Helens who have sons."
"O Katie, credit me – it is the man."
120 "O not the man! Why, you have never told
"Us of the true soul that the true Max has:
"The Max we know has such a soul, I know."
"How know you that, my foolish little lass?"
Said Malcolm, a storm of anger bound
Within his heart, like Samson with green withs –
"Belike it is the false young cur we know!"
"No, no," said Katie, simply, and low-voic'd;
"If he were traitor I must needs be false,
"For long ago love melted our two hearts,
130 "And time has moulded those two hearts in one,
"And he is true since I am faithful still."
She rose and parted, trembling as she went,
Feeling the following steel of Alfred's eyes,
And with the icy hand of scorn'd mistrust
Searching about the pulses of her heart –
Feeling for Max's image in her breast.
"To-night she conquers Doubt; to-morrow's noon

    "His following soldiers sap the golden wall,
    "And I shall enter and possess the fort,"
140 Said Alfred, in his mind. "O Katie, child,
    "Wilt thou be Nemesis, with yellow hair,
    "To rend my breast? for I do feel a pulse
    "Stir when I look into thy pure-barb'd eyes –
    "O, am I breeding that false thing, a heart,
    "Making my breast all tender for the fangs
    "Of sharp Remorse to plunge their hot fire in?
    "I am a certain dullard! Let me feel
    "But one faint goad, fine as a needle's point,
    "And it shall be the spur in my soul's side
150 "To urge the madd'ning thing across the jags
    "And cliffs of life, into the soft embrace
    "Of that cold mistress, who is constant too,
    "And never flings her lovers from her arms –
    "Not Death, for she is still a fruitful wife,
    "Her spouse the Dead, and their cold marriage yields
    "A million children, born of mould'ring flesh –
    "So Death and Flesh live on – immortal they!
    "I mean the blank-ey'd queen whose wassail bowl
    "Is brimm'd from Lethe, and whose porch is red
160 "With poppies, as it waits the panting soul –
    "She, she alone is great! No scepter'd slave
    "Bowing to blind, creative giants, she;
    "No forces seize her in their strong, mad hands,
    "Nor say, 'Do this – be that!' Were there a God,
    "His only mocker, she, great Nothingness!
    "And to her, close of kin, yet lover too,
    "Flies this large nothing that we call the soul."

       Doth true Love lonely grow?
             Ah, no! ah, no!
170   *Ah, were it only so –*
       That it alone might show

Its ruddy rose upon its sapful tree,
   Then, then in dewy morn,
   Joy might his brow adorn
With Love's young rose as fair and glad as he.

But with Love's rose doth blow,
        Ah, woe! ah, woe!
Truth with its leaves of snow,
And Pain and Pity grow
With Love's sweet roses on its sapful tree!
   Love's rose buds not alone,
   But still, but still doth own
A thousand blossoms cypress-hued to see!

PART VI

Who curseth Sorrow knows her not at all.
Dark matrix she, from which the human soul
Has its last birth; whence, with its misty thews,
Close-knitted in her blackness, issues out,
Strong for immortal toil up such great heights,
As crown o'er crown rise through Eternity.
Without the loud, deep clamour of her wail,
The iron of her hands, the biting brine
Of her black tears, the Soul but lightly built
Of indeterminate spirit, like a mist
Would lapse to Chaos in soft, gilded dreams,
As mists fade in the gazing of the sun.
Sorrow, dark mother of the soul, arise!
Be crown'd with spheres where thy bless'd children
                        dwell,
Who, but for thee, were not. No lesser seat
Be thine, thou Helper of the Universe,
Than planet on planet pil'd! – thou instrument
Close-clasp'd within the great Creative Hand!

The Land had put his ruddy gauntlet on,
20 Of harvest gold, to dash in Famine's face.
And like a vintage wain, deep dy'd with juice,
The great moon falter'd up the ripe, blue sky,
Drawn by silver stars – like oxen white
And horn'd with rays of light. Down the rich land
Malcolm's small valleys, fill'd with grain, lip-high,
Lay round a lonely hill that fac'd the moon,
And caught the wine-kiss of its ruddy light.
A cusp'd, dark wood caught in its black embrace
The valleys and the hill, and from its wilds,
30 Spic'd with dark cedars, cried the Whip-poor-will.
A crane, belated, sail'd across the moon.
On the bright, small, close-link'd lakes green islets lay,
Dusk knots of tangl'd vines, or maple boughs,
Or tuft'd cedars, boss'd upon the waves.
The gay, enamell'd children of the swamp
Roll'd a low bass to treble, tinkling notes
Of little streamlets leaping from the woods.
Close to old Malcolm's mills, two wooden jaws
Bit up the water on a sloping floor;
40 And here, in season, rush'd the great logs down,
To seek the river winding on its way.
In a green sheen, smooth as a Naiad's locks,
The water roll'd between the shudd'ring jaws –
Then on the river-level roar'd and reel'd –
In ivory-arm'd conflict with itself.
"Look down," said Alfred, "Katie, look and see
"How that but pictures my mad heart to you.
"It tears itself in fighting that mad love
"You swear is hopeless – hopeless – is it so?"
50 "Ah, yes!" said Katie, "ask me not again."
"But Katie, Max is false; no word has come,
"Nor any sign from him for many months,

"And – he is happy with his Indian wife."
She lifted eyes fair as the fresh, grey dawn
With all its dews and promises of sun.
"O, Alfred! – saver of my little life –
"Look in my eyes and read them honestly."
He laugh'd till all the isles and forests laugh'd.
"O simple child! what may the forest flames
60 "See in the woodland ponds but their own fires?
"And have you, Katie, neither fears nor doubts?"
She, with the flow'r-soft pinkness of her palm
Cover'd her sudden tears, then quickly said:
"Fears – never doubts, for true love never doubts."
Then Alfred paus'd a space, as one who holds
A white doe by the throat and searches for
The blade to slay her. "This your answer still –
"You doubt not – doubt not this far love of yours,
"Tho' sworn a false young recreant, Kate, by me?"
70 "He is as true as I am," Katie said;
"And did I seek for stronger simile,
"I could not find such in the universe!"
"And were he dead? What, Katie, were he dead –
"A handful of brown dust, a flame blown out –
"What then would love be strongly true to – Naught?"
"Still true to Love my love would be," she said,
And, faintly smiling, pointed to the stars.
"O fool!" said Alfred, stirr'd – as craters rock
To their own throes – and over his pale lips
80 Roll'd flaming stone, his molten heart. "Then, fool –
"Be true to what thou wilt – for he is dead.
"And there have grown this gilded summer past
"Grasses and buds from his unburied flesh.
"I saw him dead. I heard his last loud cry,
"'O Kate!' ring thro' the woods; in truth I did."
She half raised up a piteous, pleading hand,

Then fell along the mosses at his feet.
"Now will I show I love you, Kate," he said,
"And give you gift of love; you shall not wake
90 "To feel the arrow, feather-deep, within
"Your constant heart. For me, I never meant
"To crawl an hour beyond what time I felt
"The strange, fang'd monster that they call Remorse
"Fold round my waken'd heart. The hour has come;
"And as Love grew, the welded folds of steel
"Slipp'd round in horrid zones. In Love's flaming eyes
"Stared its fell eyeballs, and with Hydra head
"It sank hot fangs in breast, and brow and thigh.
"Come, Kate! O Anguish is a simple knave
100 "Whom hucksters could outwit with small trade lies,
"When thus so easily his smarting thralls
"May flee his knout! Come, come, my little Kate;
"The black porch with its fringe of poppies waits –
"A propylaeum hospitably wide, –
"No lictors with their fasces at its jaws,
"Its floor as kindly to my fire-vein'd feet
"As to thy silver, lilied, sinless ones.
"O you shall slumber soundly, tho' the white,
"Wild waters pluck the crocus of your hair,
110 "And scaly spies stare with round, lightless eyes
"At your small face laid on my stony breast.
"Come, Kate! I must not have you wake, dear heart,
"To hear you cry, perchance, on your dead Max."
He turn'd her still face close upon his breast,
And with his lips upon her soft, ring'd hair,
Leap'd from the bank, low shelving o'er the knot
Of frantic waters at the long slide's foot.
And as the sever'd waters crash'd and smote
Together once again, – within the wave-
120 Stunn'd chamber of his ear there peal'd a cry:
"O Kate! stay, madman; traitor, stay! O Kate!"

Max, gaunt as prairie wolves in famine time,
With long-drawn sickness, reel'd upon the bank –
Katie, new-rescu'd, waking in his arms.
On the white riot of the waters gleam'd,
The face of Alfred, calm, with close-seal'd eyes,
And blood red on his temple where it smote
The mossy timbers of the groaning slide.
"O God!" said Max, as Katie's opening eyes
130 Looked up to his, slow budding to a smile
Of wonder and of bliss, "My Kate, my Kate!"
She saw within his eyes a larger soul
Than that light spirit that before she knew,
And read the meaning of his glance and words.
"Do as you will, my Max. I would not keep
"You back with one light-falling finger-tip!"
And cast herself from his large arms upon
The mosses at his feet, and hid her face
That she might not behold what he would do;
140 Or lest the terror in her shining eyes
Might bind him to her, and prevent his soul
Work out its greatness; and her long, wet hair
Drew, mass'd, about her ears, to shut the sound
Of the vex'd waters from her anguish'd brain.
Max look'd upon her, turning as he look'd.
A moment came a voice in Katie's soul:
"Arise, be not dismay'd, arise and look;
"If he should perish, 'twill be as a God,
"For he would die to save his enemy."
150 But answer'd her torn heart: "I cannot look –
"I cannot look and see him sob and die
"In those pale, angry arms. O, let me rest
"Blind, blind and deaf until the swift-pac'd end.
"My Max! O God – was that his Katie's name?"
Like a pale dove, hawk-hunted, Katie ran,
Her fear's beak in her shoulder; and below,

Where the coil'd waters straighten'd to a stream,
Found Max all bruis'd and bleeding on the bank,
But smiling with man's triumph in his eyes,
160 When he has on fierce Danger's lion neck
Plac'd his right hand and pluck'd the prey away.
And at his feet lay Alfred, still and white,
A willow's shadow tremb'ling on his face.
"There lies the false, fair devil, O my Kate,
"Who would have parted us, but could not, Kate!"
"But could not, Max," said Katie. "Is he dead?"
But, swift perusing Max's strange, dear face,
Close clasp'd against his breast – forgot him straight
And ev'ry other evil thing upon
170 The broad green earth.

PART VII

Again rang out the music of the axe,
And on the slope, as in his happy dreams,
The home of Max with wealth of drooping vines
On the rude walls; and in the trellis'd porch
Sat Katie, smiling o'er the rich, fresh fields;
And by her side sat Malcolm, hale and strong;
Upon his knee a little, smiling child,
Nam'd – Alfred, as the seal of pardon set
Upon the heart of one who sinn'd and woke
10 To sorrow for his sins – and whom they lov'd
With gracious joyousness – nor kept the dusk
Of his past deeds between their hearts and his.
Malcolm had follow'd with his flocks and herds
When Max and Katie, hand in hand, went out
From his old home; and now, with slow, grave smile,
He said to Max, who twisted Katie's hair
About his naked arm, bare from his toil:
"It minds me of old times, this house of yours;
"It stirs my heart to hearken to the axe,

20 "And hear the windy crash of falling trees;
  "Aye, these fresh forests make an old man young."
  "Oh, yes!" said Max, with laughter in his eyes;
  "And I do truly think that Eden bloom'd
  "Deep in the heart of tall, green maple groves,
  "With sudden scents of pine from mountain sides,
  "And prairies with their breasts against the skies.
  "And Eve was only little Katie's height."
  "Hoot, lad! you speak as ev'ry Adam speaks
  "About his bonnie Eve; but what says Kate?"
30 "O Adam had not Max's soul," she said;
  "And these wild woods and plains are fairer far
  "Than Eden's self. O bounteous mothers they!
  "Beck'ning pale starvelings with their fresh, green hands,
  "And with their ashes mellowing the earth,
  "That she may yield her increase willingly.
  "I would not change these wild and rocking woods,
  "Dotted by little homes of unbark'd trees,
  "Where dwell the fleers from the waves of want, –
  "For the smooth sward of selfish Eden bowers,
40 "Nor – Max for Adam, if I knew my mind!"

                      (1884)

WILLIAM WILFRED CAMPBELL
1860?–1918

Probably born near Newmarket, Ontario, William Wilfred Campbell studied, like his father, to become an Anglican minister. Deeply disturbed by the post-Darwinian challenge to traditional orthodoxy, he left the Church in 1891 for a civil service position in Ottawa. He published four volumes of poetry and drama before bringing out his *Collected Poems* in 1905; these were followed by two novels and several books of prose as well as his edition of the first *Oxford Book of Canadian Verse* (1913).

Indian Summer

Along the line of smoky hills
    The crimson forest stands,
And all the day the blue jay calls
    Throughout the autumn lands.

Now by the brook the maple leans
    With all his glory spread,
And all the sumachs on the hills
    Have turned their green to red.

Now by great marshes wrapt in mist,
10   Or past some river's mouth,
Throughout the long, still autumn day
    Wild birds are flying south.

                (1881)

The Winter Lakes

Out in a world of death far to the northward lying,
    Under the sun and the moon, under the dusk and the
                      day;

Under the glimmer of stars and the purple of sunsets
dying,
Wan and waste and white, stretch the great lakes
away.

Never a bud of spring, never a laugh of summer,
Never a dream of love, never a song of bird;
But only the silence and white, the shores that grow
chiller and dumber,
Wherever the ice winds sob, and the griefs of winter
are heard.

Crags that are black and wet out of the grey lake
looming,
10   Under the sunset's flush and the pallid, faint glimmer
of dawn;
Shadowy, ghost-like shores, where midnight surfs are
booming
Thunders of wintry woe over the spaces wan.

Lands that loom like spectres, whited regions of winter,
Wastes of desolate woods, deserts of water and shore;
A world of winter and death, within these regions who
enter,
Lost to summer and life, go to return no more.

Moons that glimmer above, waters that lie white under,
Miles and miles of lake far out under the night;
Foaming crests of waves, surfs that shoreward thunder,
20   Shadowy shapes that flee, haunting the spaces white.

Lonely hidden bays, moon-lit, ice-rimmed, winding,
Fringed by forests and crags, haunted by shadowy
shores;

Hushed from the outward strife, where the mighty surf
                                                    is grinding
    Death and hate on the rocks, as sandward and
                                        landward it roars.
                                    [1885–87] (1889)

August Evening on the Beach, Lake Huron

A lurid flush of sunset sky,
    An angry sketch of gleaming lake,
I will remember till I die
The sound, of pines that sob and sigh,
    Of waves upon the beach that break.

'Twas years ago, and yet it seems,
    O love, but only yesterday
We stood in holy sunset dreams,
While all the day's diaphanous gleams
10   Sobbed into silence bleak and gray.

We scarcely knew, but our two souls
    Like night and day rushed into one;
The stars came out in gleaming shoals:
While, like a far-off bell that tolls,
    Came voices from the wave-dipped sun.

We scarcely knew, but hand in hand,
    With subtle sense, was closer pressed;
As we two walked in that old land
Forever new, whose shining strand
20   Goes gleaming round the world's great breast.

What was it sweet our spirits spoke?
    No outward sound of voice was heard.
But was it bird or angel broke
The silence, till a dream voice woke
    And all the night was music-stirred?

What was it, love, did mantle us,
    Such fire of incense filled our eyes?
The moon-light was not ever thus:
Such star-born music rained on us,
30   We grew so glad and wonder-wise.

But this, O love, was long ago,
    Although it seems but yesterday
The moon rose in her silver glow,
As she will rise on nights of woe,
    On hands uplift, on hearts that pray.

A lurid flush of sunset sky,
    An angry sketch of gleaming lake;
I will remember till I die,
The sound of pines that sob and sigh,
40   Of waves upon the beach that break.
              (1889)

How Spring Came

(To the Lake Region)

No passionate cry came over the desolate places,
    No answering call from iron-bound land to land;
But dawns and sunsets fell on mute, dead faces,
        And noon and night death crept from strand to
                strand.

Till love breathed out across the wasted reaches,
    And dipped in rosy dawns from desolate deeps;
And woke with mystic songs the sullen beaches,
    And flamed to life the pale, mute, death-like sleeps.

Then the warm south, with amorous breath inblowing,
10   Breathed soft o'er breast of wrinkled lake and mere;
And faces white from scorn of the north's snowing,
    Now rosier grew to greet the kindling year.
              (1889)

On the Ledge

I lie out here on a ledge with the surf on the rocks below
                                                    me,
The hazy sunlight above and the whispering forest
                                                behind;
I lie and listen, O lake, to the legends and songs you
                                            throw me,
Out of the murmurous moods of your multitudinous
                                                mind.

I lie and listen a sound like voices of distant thunder,
The roar and throb of your life in your rock wall's
                                        mighty cells;
Then after a softer voice that comes from the beaches
                                                under,
A chiming of waves on rocks, a laughter of silver bells.

A glimmer of bird-like boats, that loom from the far
                                            horizon;
10 That scud and tack and dip under the gray and the blue;
A single gull that floats and skims the waters, and flies
                                                    on
Till she is lost like a dream, in the haze of the distance,
                                                    too.

A steamer that rises a smoke, then after a tall, dark
                                            funnel,
That moves like a shadow across your water and sky's
                                        gray edge;
A dull, hard beat of a wave that diggeth himself a tunnel,
Down in the crevices dark under my limestone ledge.

And here I lie on my ledge, and listen the songs you sing
                                                    me,
Songs of vapor and blue, songs of island and shore;

And strange and glad are the hopes and sweet are the
                    thoughts you bring me,
20 Out of the throbbing depths and wells of your heart's
                    great store.

                       (1889)

The Dread Voyage

Trim the sails the weird stars under –
Past the iron hail and thunder,
Past the mystery and the wonder,
   Sails our fated bark;
Past the myriad voices hailing,
Past the moaning and the wailing,
The far voices failing, failing,
   Drive we to the dark.

Past the headlands grim and sombre,
10 Past the shores of mist and slumber,
Leagues on leagues no man may number,
   Soundings none can mark;
While the olden voices calling,
One by one behind are falling;
Into silence dread, appalling,
   Drift we to the dark.

Far behind, the sad eyes yearning,
Hands that wring for our returning,
Lamps of love yet vainly burning:
20   Past the headlands stark!
Through the wintry snows and sleeting,
On our pallid faces beating,
Through the phantom twilight fleeting,
   Drive we to the dark.

Without knowledge, without warning,
Drive we to no lands of morning;
Far ahead no signals horning
    Hail our nightward bark.
Hopeless, helpless, weird, outdriven,
30 Fateless, friendless, dread, unshriven,
For some race-doom unforgiven,
    Drive we to the dark.

Not one craven or unseemly;
In the flare-light gleaming dimly,
Each ghost-face is watching grimly:
    Past the headlands stark!
Hearts wherein no hope may waken,
Like the clouds of night wind-shaken,
Chartless, anchorless, forsaken,
40   Drift we to the dark.

               [1890–91] (1893)

Morning on the Shore

The lake is blue with morning; and the sky
    Sweet, clear, and burnished as an orient pearl.
  High in its vastness scream and skim and whirl
White gull-flocks where the gleaming beaches die
Into dim distance, where great marshes lie.
    Far in ashore the woods are warm with dreams,
    The dew-wet road in ruddy sunlight gleams,
The sweet, cool earth, the clear blue heaven on high.

Across the morn a carolling school-boy goes,
10 Filling the world with youth to heaven's stair;
    Some chattering squirrel answers from his tree;
But down beyond the headland, where ice-floes
Are great in winter, pleading in mute prayer,
    A dead, drowned face stares up immutably.

                    (1893)

At Even

I sit me moanless in the sombre fields,
The cows come with large udders down the dusk,
One cudless, the other chewing of a husk,
Her eye askance, for that athwart her heels,
Flea-haunted and rib-cavernous, there steals
The yelping farmer-dog. An old hen sits
And blinks her eyes. (Now I must rack my wits
To find a rhyme, while all this landscape reels.)

Yes! I forgot the sky. The stars are out,
10 There being no clouds; and then the pensive maid!
Of course she comes with tin-pail up the lane.
Mosquitoes hum and June bugs are about.
(That line hath "quality" of loftiest grade.)
And I have eased my soul of its sweet pain.
         – John Pensive Bangs,
            in the Great Too-Too Magazine for July
                                          (1893)

The Lazarus of Empire*

The Celt, he is proud in his protest,
    The Scot, he is calm in his place,
For each has a word in the ruling and doom
    Of the empire that honors his race:
And the Englishman, dogged and grim,
    Looks the world in the face as he goes,
And he holds a proud lip, for he sails his own ship,
    And he cares not for rivals nor foes;
But lowest and last, with his areas vast,
10   And horizon so servile and tame,
Sits the poor beggar Colonial
    Who feeds on the crumbs of her fame.

---

* Written before the Boer War

He knows no place in her councils,
    He holds no part in the word
That girdles the world with its thunders
    When the fiat of Britain is heard;
He beats no drums to her battles,
    He gives no triumphs her name,
But lowest and last, with his areas vast,
20   He feeds on the crumbs of her fame.

How long, O how long, the dishonor,
    The servile and suppliant place?
Are we Britons who batten upon her,
    Or degenerate sons of the race?
It is souls that make nations, not numbers,
    As our forefathers proved in the past,
Let us take up the burden of empire,
    Or nail our own flag to the mast.
Doth she care for us, value us, want us,
30   Or are we but pawns in the game;
Where lowest and last, with our areas vast,
    We feed on the crumbs of her fame?

                [1894] (1899)

Bereavement of the Fields

(In Memory of Archibald Lampman,
who died February 10th, 1899)

Soft fall the February snows, and soft
Falls on my heart the snow of wintry pain;
For never more, by wood or field or croft,
Will he we knew walk with his loved again;
No more, with eyes adream and soul aloft,
In those high moods where love and beauty reign,
Greet his familiar fields, his skies without a stain.

Soft fall the February snows, and deep,
Like downy pinions from the moulting breast
10 Of all the mothering sky, round his hushed sleep,
Flutter a million loves upon his rest,
Where once his well-loved flowers were fain to peep,
With adder-tongue and waxen petals prest,
In young spring evenings reddening down the west.

Soft fall the February snows, and hushed
Seems life's loud action, all its strife removed,
Afar, remote, where grief itself seems crushed,
And even hope and sorrow are reproved;
For he whose cheek erstwhile with hope was flushed,
20 And by the gentle haunts of being moved,
Hath gone the way of all he dreamed and loved.

Soft fall the February snows, and lost,
This tender spirit gone with scarce a tear,
Ere, loosened from the dungeons of the frost,
Wakens with yearnings new the enfranchised year,
Late winter-wizened, gloomed, and tempest-tost;
And Hesper's gentle, delicate veils appear,
When dream anew the days of hope and fear.

And Mother Nature, she whose heart is fain,
30 Yea, she who grieves not, neither faints nor fails,
Building the seasons, she will bring again
March with rudening madness of wild gales,
April and her wraiths of tender rain,
And all he loved, – this soul whom memory veils,
Beyond the burden of our strife and pain.

Not his to wake the strident note of song
Nor pierce the deep recesses of the heart,
Those tragic wells, remote, of [m]ight and wrong;
But rather, with those gentler souls apart,
40 He dreamed like his own summer days along,

Filled with the beauty born of his own heart,
Sufficient in the sweetness of his song.

Outside the prison-house of all our tears,
Enfranchised from our sorrow and our wrong,
Beyond the failure of our days and years,
Beyond the burden of our saddest song,
He moves with those whose music filled his ears,
And claimed his gentle spirit from the throng, –
Wordsworth, Arnold, Keats, high masters of his song.

50 Like some rare Pan of those old Grecian days,
Here in our hour of deeper stress reborn,
Unfortunate thrown upon life's evil ways,
His inward ear heard ever that satyr horn
From Nature's lips reverberate night and morn,
And fled from men and all their troubled maze,
Standing apart, with sad, incurious gaze.

And now, untimely cut, like some sweet flower
Plucked in the early summer of its prime,
Before it reached the fullness of its dower,
60 He withers in the morning of our time;
Leaving behind him, like a summer shower,
A fragrance of earth's beauty, and the chime
Of gentle and imperishable rhyme.

Songs in our ears of winds and flowers and buds
And gentle loves and tender memories
Of Nature's sweetest aspects, her pure moods,
Wrought from the inward truth of intimate eyes
And delicate ears of him who harks and broods,
And, nightly pondering, daily grows more wise,
70 And dreams and sees in mighty solitudes.

Soft fall the February snows, and soft
He sleeps in peace upon the breast of her
He loved the truest; where, by wood and croft,
The wintry silence folds in fleecy blur
About his silence, while in glooms aloft
The mighty forest fathers, without stir,
Guard well the rest of him, their rare sweet worshipper.

(1899)

CHARLES G.D. ROBERTS

1860–1943

Born in Douglas, New Brunswick, the son of an Anglican minister and first cousin of Bliss Carman, Charles G.D. Roberts published his first book, *Orion, and Other Poems*, in 1880. A graduate in classics from the University of New Brunswick, he taught for ten years at the University of King's College in Windsor, Nova Scotia, before embarking on a career in New York, London, and Toronto as an editor, journalist, and man of letters. Well known for his innovations in the genre of the realistic animal story, his cultural nationalism, and his contribution to literature, he received a knighthood in 1935. His poetry publications include *In Divers Tones* (1886), *Songs of the Common Day* (1893), *The Iceberg and Other Poems* (1934), and *Selected Poems of Sir Charles G.D. Roberts* (1936).

To Fredericton in May-Time

This morning, full of breezes and perfume,
    Brimful of promise of midsummer weather,
    When bees and birds and I are glad together,
Breathes of the full-leaved season, when soft gloom
Chequers thy streets, and thy close elms assume
    Round roof and spire the semblance of green billows;
    Yet now thy glory is the yellow willows,
The yellow willows, full of bees and bloom.

Under their dusty blossoms blackbirds meet,
10   And robins pipe amid the cedars nigher;
Thro' the still elms I hear the ferry's beat;
    The swallows chirp about the towering spire;
The whole air pulses with its weight of sweet;
    Yet not quite satisfied is my desire!

(1881)

Tantramar Revisited

Summers and summers have come, and gone with the
           flight of the swallow;
Sunshine and thunder have been, storm, and winter,
           and frost;
Many and many a sorrow has all but died from
           remembrance,
Many a dream of joy fall'n in the shadow of pain.
Hands of chance and change have marred, or moulded,
           or broken,
Busy with spirit or flesh, all I most have adored;
Even the bosom of Earth is strewn with heavier
           shadows, –
Only in these green hills, aslant to the sea, no change!
Here where the road that has climbed from the inland
           valleys and woodlands,
10 Dips from the hill-tops down, straight to the base of the
           hills, –
Here, from my vantage-ground, I can see the scattering
           houses,
Stained with time, set warm in orchards, meadows, and
           wheat,
Dotting the broad bright slopes outspread to southward
           and eastward,
Wind-swept all day long, blown by the south-east wind.

Skirting the sunbright uplands stretches a riband of
           meadow,
Shorn of the labouring grass, bulwarked well from the
           sea,
Fenced on its seaward border with long clay dykes from
           the turbid
Surge and flow of the tides vexing the Westmoreland
           shores.

Yonder, toward the left, lie broad the Westmoreland
marshes, –
20 Miles on miles they extend, level, and grassy, and dim,
Clear from the long red sweep of flats to the sky in the
distance,
Save for the outlying heights, green-rampired
Cumberland Point;
Miles on miles outrolled, and the river-channels divide
them, –
Miles on miles of green, barred by the hurtling gusts.

Miles on miles beyond the tawny bay is Minudie.
There are the low blue hills; villages gleam at their feet.
Nearer a white sail shines across the water, and nearer
Still are the slim, grey masts of fishing boats dry on the flats.
Ah, how well I remember those wide red flats, above
tide-mark
30 Pale with scurf of the salt, seamed and baked in the sun!
Well I remember the piles of blocks and ropes, and the
net-reels
Wound with the beaded nets, dripping and dark from
the sea!
Now at this season the nets are unwound; they hang
from the rafters
Over the fresh-stowed hay in upland barns, and the wind
Blows all day through the chinks, with the streaks of
sunlight, and sways them
Softly at will; or they lie heaped in the gloom of a loft.

Now at this season the reels are empty and idle; I see them
Over the lines of the dykes, over the gossiping grass,
Now at this season they swing in the long strong wind,
thro' the lonesome
40 Golden afternoon, shunned by the foraging gulls.
Near about sunset the crane will journey homeward
above them;

Round them, under the moon, all the calm night long,
Winnowing soft grey wings of marsh-owls wander and
                                                wander,
Now to the broad, lit marsh, now to the dusk of the dike.
Soon, thro' their dew-wet frames, in the live keen
                                    freshness of morning,
Out of the teeth of the dawn blows back the awakening
                                                wind.
Then, as the blue day mounts, and the low-shot shafts of
                                        the sunlight
Glance from the tide to the shore, gossamers jewelled
                                            with dew
Sparkle and wave, where late sea-spoiling fathoms of
                                            drift-net
50 Myriad-meshed, uploomed sombrely over the land.

Well I remember it all. The salt, raw scent of the margin;
While, with men at the windlass, groaned each reel, and
                                            the net,
Surging in ponderous lengths, uprose and coiled in its
                                            station;
Then each man to his home, – well I remember it all!

Yet, as I sit and watch, this present peace of the
                                        landscape, –
Stranded boats, these reels empty and idle, the hush,
One grey hawk slow-wheeling above yon cluster of
                                        haystacks, –
More than the old-time stir this stillness welcomes me
                                            home.
Ah, the old-time stir, how once it stung me with
                                            rapture, –
60 Old-time sweetness, the winds freighted with honey and
                                            salt!
Yet will I stay my steps and not go down to the
                                        marshland, –

Muse and recall far off, rather remember than see, –
Lest on too close sight I miss the darling illusion,
Spy at their task even here the hands of chance and
                                                change.

                                                (1883)

The Poet Is Bidden to Manhattan Island

Dear Poet, quit your shady lanes
    And come where more than lanes are shady.
Leave Phyllis to the rustic swains
    And sing some Knickerbocker lady.
O hither haste, and here devise
    Divine *ballades* before unuttered.
Your poet's eyes *must* recognize
    The side on which your bread is buttered!

Dream not I tempt you to forswear
10   One pastoral joy, or rural frolic.
I call you to a city where
    The most urbane are most bucolic.
'Twill charm your poet's eyes to find
    Good husbandmen in brokers burly; –
Their stock is ever on their mind;
    To water it they rise up early.

Things you have sung, but ah, not seen –
    Things proper to the age of Saturn –
Shall greet you here; for we have been
20   Wrought quaintly, on the Arcadian pattern.
Your poet's lips will break in song
    For joy, to see at last appearing
The bulls and bears, a peaceful throng,
    While a lamb leads them – to the shearing!

And metamorphoses, of course,
    You'll mark in plenty, *à la* Proteus:
A bear become a little horse –
    Presumably from too much throat-use!
A thousandfold must go untold;
30   But, should you miss your farm-yard sunny,
And miss your ducks and drakes, behold
    We'll make you ducks and drakes – of money!

Greengrocers here are fairly read.
    And should you set your heart upon them,
We lack not beets – but some are dead,
    While others have policemen on them.
And be the dewfall dear to you,
    Possess your poet's soul in patience!
Your *notes* shall soon be falling dew, –
40   Most mystical of transformations!

Your heart, dear Poet, surely yields;
    And soon you'll leave your uplands flowery,
Forsaking fresh and bowery fields,
    For "pastures new" – upon the Bowery!
You've piped at home, where none could pay,
    Till now, I trust, your wits are riper.
Make no delay, but come this way,
    And pipe for them that pay the piper!
                 [1884] (1886)

An Ode for the Canadian Confederacy

Awake, my country, the hour is great with change!
   Under this gloom which yet obscures the land,
From ice-blue strait and stern Laurentian range
   To where giant peaks our western bounds command,
A deep voice stirs, vibrating in men's ears
   As if their own hearts throbbed that thunder forth,
A sound wherein who hearkens wisely hears
   The voice of the desire of this strong North, –
      This North whose heart of fire
10   Yet knows not its desire
Clearly, but dreams, and murmurs in the dream.
The hour of dreams is done. Lo, on the hills the gleam!

Awake, my country, the hour of dreams is done!
   Doubt not, nor dread the greatness of thy fate.
Tho' faint souls fear the keen confronting sun,
   And fain would bid the morn of splendour wait;
Tho' dreamers, rapt in starry visions, cry
   "Lo, yon thy future, yon thy faith, thy fame!"
And stretch vain hands to stars, thy fame is nigh,
20   Here in Canadian hearth, and home, and name, –
      This name which yet shall grow
      Till all the nations know
Us for a patriot people, heart and hand
Loyal to our native earth, our own Canadian land!

O strong hearts, guarding the birthright of our glory,
   Worth your best blood this heritage that ye guard!
These mighty streams resplendent with our story,
   These iron coasts by rage of seas unjarred, –
What fields of peace these bulwarks well secure!
30   What vales of plenty those calm floods supply!
Shall not our love this rough, sweet land make sure,
   Her bounds preserve inviolate, though we die?

O strong hearts of the North,
Let flame your loyalty forth,
And put the craven and base to an open shame,
Till earth shall know the Child of Nations by her name!
[1885] (1886)

The Potato Harvest

A high bare field, brown from the plough, and borne
    Aslant from sunset; amber wastes of sky
    Washing the ridge; a clamour of crows that fly
In from the wide flats where the spent tides mourn
To yon their rocking roosts in pines wind-torn;
    A line of grey snake-fence that zigzags by
    A pond and cattle; from the homestead nigh
The long deep summonings of the supper horn.

Black on the ridge, against that lonely flush,
10   A cart, and stoop-necked oxen; ranged beside
        Some barrels; and the day-worn harvest-folk,
Here emptying their baskets, jar the hush
    With hollow thunders. Down the dusk hillside
    Lumbers the wain; and day fades out like smoke.
(1886)

Severance

The tide falls, and the night falls,
    And the wind blows in from the sea,
And the bell on the bar it calls and calls,
    And the wild hawk cries from his tree.

The late crane calls to his fellows gone
    In long flight over the sea,
And my heart with the crane flies on and on,
    Seeking its rest and thee.

O Love, the tide returns to the strand,
10   And the crane flies back oversea,
But he brings not my heart from his far-off land
    For he brings not thee to me.

                                        (1889)

The Mowing

This is the voice of high midsummer's heat.
    The rasping vibrant clamour soars and shrills
    O'er all the meadowy range of shadeless hills,
As if a host of giant cicadae beat
The cymbals of their wings with tireless feet,
    Or brazen grasshoppers with triumphing note
    From the long swath proclaimed the fate that smote
The clover and timothy-tops and meadowsweet.

The crying knives glide on; the green swath lies.
10   And all noon long the sun, with chemic ray,
    Seals up each cordial essence in its cell,
That in the dusky stalls, some winter's day,
    The spirit of June, here prisoned by his spell,
May cheer the herds with pasture memories.

                                        (1890)

The Flight of the Geese

I hear the low wind wash the softening snow,
    The low tide loiter down the shore. The night,
    Full filled with April forecast, hath no light.
The salt wave on the sedge-flat pulses slow.
Through the hid furrows lisp in murmurous flow
    The thaw's shy ministers; and hark! The height
    Of heaven grows weird and loud with unseen flight
Of strong hosts prophesying as they go!

High through the drenched and hollow night their
wings
10   Beat northward hard on Winter's trail. The sound
Of their confused and solemn voices, borne
Athwart the dark to their long Arctic morn,
    Comes with a sanction and an awe profound,
A boding of unknown, foreshadowed things.

                  (1890)

The Winter Fields

Winds here, and sleet, and frost that bites like steel.
    The low bleak hill rounds under the low sky.
    Naked of flock and fold the fallows lie,
Thin streaked with meagre drift. The gusts reveal
By fits the dim grey snakes of fence, that steal
    Through the white dusk. The hill-foot poplars sigh,
    While storm and death with winter trample by,
And the iron fields ring sharp, and blind lights reel.
Yet in the lonely ridges, wrenched with pain,
10   Harsh solitary hillocks, bound and dumb,
Grave glebes close-lipped beneath the scourge and chain,
    Lurks hid the germ of ecstasy – the sum
Of life that waits on summer, till the rain
    Whisper in April and the crocus come.

                  (1890)

The Pea-Fields

These are the fields of light, and laughing air,
    And yellow butterflies, and foraging bees,
    And whitish, wayward blossoms winged as these,
And pale green tangles like a seamaid's hair.
Pale, pale the blue, but pure beyond compare,
    And pale the sparkle of the far-off seas

A-shimmer like these fluttering slopes of peas,
And pale the open landscape everywhere.

From fence to fence a perfumed breath exhales
10   O'er the bright pallor of the well-loved fields, –
My fields of Tantramar in summer-time;
    And, scorning the poor feed their pasture yields,
Up from the bushy lots the cattle climb
    To gaze with longing through the grey, mossed rails.

                          (1891)

The Salt Flats

Here clove the keels of centuries ago
    Where now unvisited the flats lie bare.
    Here seethed the sweep of journeying waters, where
No more the tumbling floods of Fundy flow,
And only in the samphire pipes creep slow
    The salty currents of the sap. The air
    Hums desolately with wings that seaward fare,
Over the lonely reaches beating low.

The wastes of hard and meagre weeds are thronged
10 With murmurs of a past that time has wronged;
    And ghosts of many an ancient memory
Dwell by the brackish pools and ditches blind,
In these low-lying pastures of the wind,
    These marshes pale and meadows by the sea.

                          (1891)

Ave!

(An Ode for the Shelley Centenary, 1892)

I

O tranquil meadows, grassy Tantramar,
    Wide marshes ever washed in clearest air,
Whether beneath the sole and spectral star

The dear severity of dawn you wear,
  Or whether in the joy of ample day
    And speechless ecstasy of growing June
You lie and dream the long blue hours away
      Till nightfall comes too soon,
Or whether, naked to the unstarred night,
10 You strike with wondering awe my inward sight, –

II

You know how I have loved you, how my dreams
  Go forth to you with longing, though the years
That turn not back like your returning streams
  And fain would mist the memory with tears,
Though the inexorable years deny
  My feet the fellowship of your deep grass,
O'er which, as o'er another, tenderer sky,
    Cloud phantoms drift and pass, –
You know my confident love, since first, a child,
20 Amid your wastes of green I wandered wild.

III

Inconstant, eager, curious, I roamed;
  And ever your long reaches lured me on;
And ever o'er my feet your grasses foamed,
  And in my eyes your far horizons shone.
But sometimes would you (as a stillness fell
  And on my pulse you laid a soothing palm)
Instruct my ears in your most secret spell;
    And sometimes in the calm
Initiate my young and wondering eyes
30 Until my spirit grew more still and wise.

IV

Purged with high thoughts and infinite desire
  I entered fearless the most holy place,

Received between my lips the secret fire,
   The breath of inspiration on my face.
But not for long these rare illumined hours,
   The deep surprise and rapture not for long.
Again I saw the common, kindly flowers,
     Again I heard the song
Of the glad bobolink, whose lyric throat
40 Pealed like a tangle of small bells afloat.

V

The pounce of mottled marsh-hawk on his prey;
   The flicker of sand-pipers in from sea
In gusty flocks that puffed and fled; the play
   Of field-mice in the vetches, – these to me
Were memorable events. But most availed
   Your strange unquiet waters to engage
My kindred heart's companionship; nor failed
     To grant this heritage, –
That in my veins forever must abide
50 The urge and fluctuation of the tide.

VI

The mystic river whence you take your name,
   River of hubbub, raucous Tantramar,
Untamable and changeable as flame,
   It called me and compelled me from afar,
Shaping my soul with its impetuous stress.
   When in its gaping channel deep withdrawn
Its waves ran crying of the wilderness
     And winds and stars and dawn,
How I companioned them in speed sublime,
60 Led out a vagrant on the hills of Time!

VII

And when the orange flood came roaring in
    From Fundy's tumbling troughs and tide-worn caves,
While red Minudie's flats were drowned with din
    And rough Chignecto's front oppugned the waves,
How blithely with the refluent foam I raced
    Inland along the radiant chasm, exploring
The green solemnity with boisterous haste;
       My pulse of joy outpouring
To visit all the creeks that twist and shine
70 From Beauséjour to utmost Tormentine.

VIII

And after, when the tide was full, and stilled
    A little while the seething and the hiss,
And every tributary channel filled
    To the brim with rosy streams that swelled to kiss
The grass-roots all awash and goose-tongue wild
    And salt-sap rosemary, – then how well content
I was to rest me like a breathless child
       With play-time rapture spent, –
To lapse and loiter till the change should come
80 And the great floods turn seaward, roaring home.

IX

And now, O tranquill marshes, in your vast
    Serenity of vision and of dream,
Wherethrough by every intricate vein have passed
    With joy impetuous and pain supreme
The sharp, fierce tides that chafe the shores of earth
    In endless and controlless ebb and flow,
Strangely akin you seem to him whose birth
       One hundred years ago
With fiery succour to the ranks of song
90 Defied the ancient gates of wrath and wrong.

X

Like yours, O marshes, his compassionate breast,
 Wherein abode all dreams of love and peace,
Was tortured with perpetual unrest.
 Now loud with flood, now languid with release,
Now poignant with the lonely ebb, the strife
 Of tides from the salt sea of human pain
That hiss along the perilous coasts of life
  Beat in his eager brain;
But all about the tumult of his heart
100 Stretched the great calm of his celestial art.

XI

Therefore with no far flight, from Tantramar
 And my still world of ecstasy, to thee,
Shelley, to thee I turn, the avatar
 Of Song, Love, Dream, Desire, and Liberty;
To thee I turn with reverent hands of prayer
 And lips that fain would ease my heart of praise,
Whom chief of all whose brows prophetic wear
  The pure and sacred bays
I worship, and have worshipped since the hour
110 When first I felt thy bright and chainless power.

XII

About thy sheltered cradle in the green
 Untroubled groves of Sussex, brooded forms
That to the mother's eye remained unseen, –
 Terrors and ardours, passionate hopes, and storms
Of fierce retributive fury, such as jarred
 Ancient and sceptred creeds, and cast down kings,
And oft the holy cause of Freedom marred
  With lust of meaner things,
With guiltless blood, and many a frenzied crime
120 Dared in the face of unforgetful Time.

XIII

The star that burns on revolution smote
   Wild heats and change on thine ascendant sphere,
Whose influence thereafter seemed to float
   Through many a strange eclipse of wrath and fear,
Dimming awhile the radiance of thy love.
   But still supreme in thy nativity,
All dark, invidious aspects far above,
     Beamed one clear orb for thee, –
The star whose ministrations just and strong
130 Controlled the tireless flight of Dante's song.

XIV

With how august contrition, and what tears
   Of penitential, unavailing shame,
Thy venerable foster-mother hears
   The sons of song impeach her ancient name,
Because in one rash hour of anger blind
   She thrust thee forth in exile, and thy feet
Too soon to earth's wild outer ways consigned, –
     Far from her well-loved seat,
Far from her studious halls and storied towers
140 And weedy Isis winding through his flowers.

XV

And thou, thenceforth the breathless child of change,
   Thine own Alastor, on an endless quest
Of unimagined loveliness didst range,
   Urged ever by the soul's divine unrest.
Of that high quest and that unrest divine
   Thy first immortal music thou didst make,
Inwrought with fairy Alp, and Reuss, and Rhine,
     And phantom seas that break
In soundless foam along the shores of Time,
150 Prisoned in thine imperishable rhyme.

XVI

Thyself the lark melodious in mid-heaven;
    Thyself the Protean shape of chainless cloud,
Pregnant with elemental fire, and driven
    Through deeps of quivering light, and darkness loud
With tempest, yet beneficent as prayer;
    Thyself the wild west wind, relentless strewing
The withered leaves of custom on the air,
        And through the wreck pursuing
O'er lovelier Arnos, more imperial Romes,
160 Thy radiant visions to their viewless homes.

XVII

And when thy mightiest creation thou
    Wert fain to body forth, – the dauntless form,
The all-enduring, all-forgiving brow
    Of the great Titan, flinchless in the storm
Of pangs unspeakable and nameless hates,
    Yet rent by all the wrongs and woes of men,
And triumphing in his pain, that so their fates
        Might be assuaged, – oh then
Out of that vast compassionate heart of thine
170 Thou wert constrained to shape the dream benign.

XVIII

– O Baths of Caracalla, arches clad
    In such transcendent rhapsodies of green
That one might guess the sprites of spring were glad
    For your majestic ruin, yours the scene,
The illuminating air of sense and thought;
    And yours the enchanted light, O skies of Rome,
Where the giant vision into form was wrought;
        Beneath your blazing dome
The intensest song our language ever knew
180 Beat up exhaustless to the blinding blue! –

XIX

The domes of Pisa and her towers superb,
   The myrtles and the ilexes that sigh
O'er San Giuliano, where no jars disturb
   The lonely aziola's evening cry,
The Serchio's sun-kissed waters, – these conspired
   With Plato's theme occult, with Dante's calm
Rapture of mystic love, and so inspired
     Thy soul's espousal psalm,
A strain of such elect and pure intent
190 It breathes of a diviner element.

XX

Thou on whose lips the word of Love became
   A rapt evangel to assuage all wrong,
Not Love alone, but the austerer name
   Of Death engaged the splendours of thy song.
The luminous grief, the spacious consolation
   Of thy supreme lament, that mourned for him
Too early haled to that still habitation
     Beneath the grass-roots dim, –
Where his faint limbs and pain-o'erwearied heart
200 Of all earth's loveliness became a part,

XXI

But where, thou sayest, himself would not abide, –
   Thy solemn incommunicable joy
Announcing Adonais has not died,
   Attesting death to free but not destroy,
All this was as thy swan-song mystical.
   Even while the note serene was on thy tongue
Thin grew the veil of the Invisible,
     The white sword nearer swung, –
And in the sudden wisdom of thy rest
210 Thou knewest all thou hadst but dimly guessed.

XXII

Lament, Lerici, mourn for the world's loss!
　　Mourn that pure light of song extinct at noon!
Ye waves of Spezzia that shine and toss
　　Repent that sacred flame you quenched too soon!
Mourn, Mediterranean waters, mourn
　　In affluent purple down your golden shore!
Such strains as his, whose voice you stilled in scorn,
　　　　Our ears may greet no more,
Unless at last to that far sphere we climb
220 Where he completes the wonder of his rhyme!

XXIII

How like a cloud she fled, thy fateful bark,
　　From eyes that watched to hearts that waited, till
Up from the ocean roared the tempest dark –
　　And the wild heart Love waited for was still!
Hither and thither in the slow, soft tide,
　　Rolled seaward, shoreward, sands and wandering shells
And shifting weeds thy fellows, thou didst hide
　　　　Remote from all farewells,
Nor felt the sun, nor heard the fleeting rain,
230 Nor heeded Casa Magni's quenchless pain.

XXIV

Thou heedest not? Nay, for it was not thou,
　　That blind, mute clay relinquished by the waves
Reluctantly at last, and slumbering now
　　In one of kind earth's most compassionate graves!
Not thou, not thou, – for thou wert in the light
　　Of the Unspeakable, where time is not.
Thou sawest those tears; but in thy perfect sight
　　　　And thy eternal thought
Were they not even now all wiped away
240 In the reunion of the infinite day!

XXV

There face to face thou sawest the living God
    And worshippedst, beholding Him the same
Adored on earth as Love, the same whose rod
    Thou hadst endured as Life, whose secret name
Thou now didst learn, the healing name of Death.
    In that unroutable profound of peace,
Beyond experience of pulse and breath,
      Beyond the last release
Of longing, rose to greet thee all the lords
250 Of Thought, with consummation in their words:

XXVI

He of the seven cities claimed, whose eyes,
    Though blind, saw gods and heroes, and the fall
Of Ilium, and many alien skies,
    And Circe's Isle; and he whom mortals call
The Thunderous, who sang the Titan bound
    As thou the Titan victor; the benign
Spirit of Plato; Job; and Judah's crowned
      Singer and seer divine;
Omar; the Tuscan; Milton, vast and strong;
260 And Shakespeare, captain of the host of Song.

XXVII

Back from the underworld of whelming change
    To the wide-glittering beach thy body came;
And thou didst contemplate with wonder strange
    And curious regard thy kindred flame,
Fed sweet with frankincense and wine and salt,
    With fierce purgation search thee, soon resolving
Thee to the elements of the airy vault
      And the far spheres revolving,
The common waters, the familiar woods,
270 And the great hills' inviolate solitudes.

XXVIII

Thy close companions there officiated
   With solemn mourning and with mindful tears, –
The pained, imperious wanderer unmated
   Who voiced the wrath of those rebellious years;
Trelawney, lion-limbed and high of heart;
   And he, that gentlest sage and friend most true,
Whom Adonais loved. With these bore part
     One grieving ghost, that flew
Hither and thither through the smoke unstirred
280 In wailing semblance of a wild white bird.

XXIX

O heart of fire, that fire might not consume,
   Forever glad the world because of thee;
Because of thee forever eyes illume
   A more enchanted earth, a lovelier sea!
O poignant voice of the desire of life,
   Piercing our lethargy, because thy call
Aroused our spirits to a nobler strife
     Where base and sordid fall,
Forever past the conflict and the pain
290 More clearly beams the goal we shall attain!

XXX

And now once more, O marshes, back to you
   From whatsoever wanderings, near or far,
To you I turn with joy forever new,
   To you, O sovereign vasts of Tantramar!
Your tides are at the full. Your wizard flood,
   With every tribute stream and brimming creek,
Ponders, possessor of the utmost good,
     With no more left to seek, –
But the hour wanes and passes; and once more
300 Resounds the ebb with destiny in its roar.

XXXI

So might some lord of men, whom force and fate
   And his great heart's unvanquishable power
Have thrust with storm to his supreme estate,
   Ascend by night his solitary tower
High o'er the city's lights and cries uplift.
   Silent he ponders the scrolled heaven to read
And the keen stars' conflicting message sift,
      Till the slow signs recede,
And ominously scarlet dawns afar
310 The day he leads his legions forth to war.

                     (1892)

The Herring Weir

Back to the green deeps of the outer bay
   The red and amber currents glide and cringe,
   Diminishing behind a luminous fringe
Of cream-white surf and wandering wraiths of spray.
Stealthily, in the old reluctant way,
   The red flats are uncovered, mile on mile,
   To glitter in the sun a golden while.
Far down the flats, a phantom sharply grey,

The herring weir emerges, quick with spoil.
10   Slowly the tide forsakes it. Then draws near,
   Descending from the farm-house on the height,
A cart, with gaping tubs. The oxen toil
   Sombrely o'er the level to the weir,
   And drag a long black trail across the light.

                     (1893)

In an Old Barn

Tons upon tons the brown-green fragrant hay
    O'erbrims the mows beyond the time-warped eaves,
    Up to the rafters where the spider weaves,
Though few flies wander his secluded way.
Through a high chink one lonely golden ray,
    Wherein the dust is dancing, slants unstirred.
    In the dry hush some rustlings light are heard,
Of winter-hidden mice at furtive play.

Far down, the cattle in their shadowed stalls,
10   Nose-deep in clover fodder's meadowy scent,
    Forget the snows that whelm their pasture streams,
The frost that bites the world beyond their walls.
    Warm housed, they dream of summer, well content
    In day-long contemplation of their dreams.

(1893)

In a City Room

O city night of noises and alarms,
    Your lights may flare, your cables clang and rush,
But in the sanctuary of my love's arms
    Your blinding tumult dies into a hush.

My doors are surged about with your unrest;
    Your plangent cares assail my realm of peace;
But when I come unto her quiet breast
    How suddenly your jar and clamour cease!

Then even remembrance of your strifes and pains
10   Diminishes to a ghost of sorrows gone,
Remoter than a dream of last year's rains
    Gusty against my window in the dawn.

(1898)

The Fear of Love

Oh, take me into the still places of your heart,
And hide me under the night of your deep hair;
For the fear of love is upon me;
I am afraid lest God should discover the wonderfulness
                                    of our love.

Shall I find life but to lose it?
Shall I stretch out my hands at last to joy
And take but the irremediable anguish?
For the cost of heaven is the fear of hell;
The terrible cost of love
10 Is the fear to be cast out therefrom.

Oh, touch me! Oh, look upon me!
Look upon my spirit with your eyes
And touch me with the benediction of your hands!
Breathe upon me, breathe upon me,
And my soul shall live.
Kiss me with your mouth upon my mouth
And I shall be strong.

                                    (1900)

The Skater

My glad feet shod with the glittering steel
I was the god of the wingèd heel.

The hills in the far white sky were lost;
The world lay still in the wide white frost;

And the woods hung hushed in their long white dream
By the ghostly, glimmering, ice-blue stream.

Here was a pathway, smooth like glass,
Where I and the wandering wind might pass

To the far-off palaces, drifted deep,
10   Where Winter's retinue rests in sleep.

I followed the lure, I fled like a bird,
Till the startled hollows awoke and heard

A spinning whisper, a sibilant twang,
As the stroke of the steel on the tense ice rang;

And the wandering wind was left behind
As faster, faster I followed my mind;

Till the blood sang high in my eager brain,
And the joy of my flight was almost pain.

Then I stayed the rush of my eager speed
20   And silently went as a drifting seed, –

Slowly, furtively, till my eyes
Grew big with the awe of a dim surmise,

And the hair of my neck began to creep
At hearing the wilderness talk in sleep.

Shapes in the fir-gloom drifted near.
In the deep of my heart I heard my fear.

And I turned and fled, like a soul pursued,
From the white, inviolate solitude.

                                        (1901)

Heat in the City

Over the scorching roofs of iron
The red moon rises slow.
Uncomforted beneath its light
The pale crowds gasping go.

The heart-sick city, spent with day,
Cries out in vain for sleep.

The childless wife beside her dead
Is too outworn to weep.

The children in the upper rooms
10 Lie faint, with half-shut eyes.
In the thick-breathing, lighted ward
The stricken workman dies.

From breathless pit and sweltering loft
Dim shapes creep one by one
To throng the curb and crowd the stoops
And fear to-morrow's sun.

(1902)

Philander's Song

(From "The Sprightly Pilgrim")

I sat and read Anacreon.
  Moved by the gay, delicious measure
I mused that lips were made for love,
  And love to charm a poet's leisure.

And as I mused a maid came by
  With something in her look that caught me.
Forgotten was Anacreon's line,
  But not the lesson he had taught me.

[1904] (1927)

Going Over

[The Somme, 1917]

A girl's voice in the night troubled my heart
Across the roar of the guns, the crash of the shells,
Low and soft as a sigh, clearly I heard it.

Where was the broken parapet, crumbling about me?
Where my shadowy comrades, crouching expectant?
A girl's voice in the dark troubled my heart.

A dream was the ooze of the trench, the wet clay
                                    slipping.
A dream the sudden out-flare of the wide-flung Verys.
I saw but a garden of lilacs, a-flower in the dusk.

10 What was the sergeant saying? – I passed it along. –
Did *I* pass it along? I was breathing the breath of the lilacs.
For a girl's voice in the night troubled my heart.

Over! How the mud sucks! Vomits red the barrage.
But I am far off in the hush of a garden of lilacs.
For a girl's voice in the night troubled my heart.
Tender and soft as a sigh, clearly I heard it.

                                    [1918] (1919)

The Iceberg

        I was spawned from the glacier,
A thousand miles due north
Beyond Cape Chidley;
And the spawning,
When my vast, wallowing bulk went under,
Emerged and heaved aloft,
Shaking down cataracts from its rocking sides,
With mountainous surge and thunder
Outraged the silence of the Arctic sea.

10   Before I was thrust forth
A thousand years I crept,
Crawling, crawling, crawling irresistibly,
Hid in the blue womb of the eternal ice,
While under me the tortured rock
Groaned,
And over me the immeasurable desolation slept.

Under the pallid dawning
Of the lidless Arctic day
Forever no life stirred.
20 No wing of bird –
Of ghostly owl low winnowing
Or fleet-winged ptarmigan fleeing the pounce of
                                            death, –
No foot of backward-glancing fox
Half glimpsed, and vanishing like a breath, –
No lean and gauntly stalking bear,
Stalking his prey.
Only the white sun, circling the white sky.
Only the wind screaming perpetually.

And then the night –
30 The long night, naked, high over the roof of the world,
Where time seemed frozen in the cold of space, –
Now black, and torn with cry
Of unseen voices where the storm raged by,
Now radiant with spectral light
As the vault of heaven split wide
To let the flaming Polar cohorts through,
And close ranked spears of gold and blue,
Thin scarlet and thin green,
Hurtled and clashed across the sphere
40 And hissed in sibilant whisperings,
And died.
And then the stark moon, swinging low,
Silver, indifferent, serene,
Over the sheeted snow.

But now, an Alp afloat,
In seizure of the surreptitious tide,
Began my long drift south to a remote
And unimagined doom.
Scornful of storm,

50 Unjarred by thunderous buffeting of seas,
Shearing the giant floes aside,
Ploughing the wide-flung ice-fields in a spume
That smoked far up my ponderous flanks,
Onward I fared,
My ice-blue pinnacles rendering back the sun
In darts of sharp radiance;
My bases fathoms deep in the dark profound.

    And now around me
Life and the frigid waters all aswarm.
60 The smooth wave creamed
With tiny capelin and the small pale squid, –
So pale the light struck through them.
Gulls and gannets screamed
Over the feast, and gorged themselves, and rose,
A clamour of weaving wings, and hid
Momently my face.
The great bull whales
With cavernous jaws agape,
Scooped in the spoil, and slept,
70 Their humped forms just awash, and rocking softly, –
Or sounded down, down to the deeps, and nosed
Along my ribbed and sunken roots,
And in the green gloom scattered the pasturing cod.

    And so I voyaged on, down the dim parallels,
Convoyed by fields
Of countless calving seals
Mild-featured, innocent-eyed, and unforeknowing
The doom of the red flenching knives.
I passed the storm-racked gate
80 Of Hudson Strait,
And savage Chidley where the warring tides
In white wrath seethe forever.
Down along the sounding shore

Of iron-fanged, many-watered Labrador
Slow weeks I shaped my course, and saw
Dark Mokkowic and dark Napiskawa,
And came at last off lone Belle Isle, the bane
Of ships and snare of bergs.
Here, by the deep conflicting currents drawn,
90 I hung,
And swung,
The inland voices Gulfward calling me
To ground amid my peers on the alien strand
And roam no more.
But then an off-shore wind,
A great wind fraught with fate,
Caught me and pressed me back,
And I resumed my solitary way.
Slowly I bore
100 South-east by bastioned Bauld,
And passed the sentinel light far-beaming late
Along the liners' track,
And slanted out Atlanticwards, until
Above the treacherous swaths of fog
Faded from the view the loom of Newfoundland.

Beautiful, ethereal
In the blue sparkle of the gleaming day,
A soaring miracle
Of white immensity,
110 I was the cynosure of passing ships
That wondered and were gone,
Their wreathed smoke trailing them beyond the verge.
And when in the night they passed –
The night of stars and calm,
Forged up and passed, with churning surge
And throb of huge propellers, and long-drawn
Luminous wake behind,

And sharp, small lights in rows,
I lay a ghost of menace chill and still,
120 A shape pearl-pale and monstrous, off to leeward,
Blurring the dim horizon line.

        Day dragged on day,
And then came fog,
By noon, blind-white,
And in the night
Black-thick and smothering the sight.
Folded therein I waited,
Waited I knew not what
And heeded not,
130 Greatly incurious and unconcerned.
I heard the small waves lapping along my base,
Lipping and whispering, lisping with bated breath
A casual expectancy of death.
I heard remote
The deep, far carrying note
Blown from the hoarse and hollow throat
Of some lone tanker groping on her course.
Louder and louder rose the sound
In deepening diapason, then passed on,
140 Diminishing, and dying, –
And silence closed around.
And in the silence came again
Those stealthy voices,
That whispering of death.

        And then I heard
The thud of screws approaching.
Near and more near,
Louder and yet more loud,
Through the thick dark I heard it, –
150 The rush and hiss of waters as she ploughed
Head on, unseen, unseeing,

Toward where I stood across her path, invisible.
And then a startled blare
Of horror close re-echoing, – a glare
Of sudden, stabbing searchlights
That but obscurely pierced the gloom;
And there
I towered, a dim immensity of doom.

A roar
160 Of tortured waters as the giant screws,
Reversed, thundered full steam astern.
Yet forward still she drew, until,
Slow answering desperate helm,
She swerved, and all her broadside came in view,
Crawling beneath me;
And for a moment I saw faces, blanched,
Stiffly agape, turned upward, and wild eyes
Astare; and one long, quavering cry went up
As a submerged horn gored her through and through,
170 Ripping her beam wide open;
And sullenly she listed, till her funnels
Crashed on my steep,
And men sprang, stumbling, for the boats.
But now, my deep foundations
Mined by those warmer seas, the hour had come
When I must change.
Slowly I leaned above her,
Slowly at first, then faster,
And icy fragments rained upon her decks.
180 Then my enormous mass descended on her,
A falling mountain, all obliterating, –
And the confusion of thin, wailing cries,
The Babel of shouts and prayers
And shriek of steam escaping
Suddenly died.

And I rolled over,
Wallowing,
And once more came to rest,
My long hid bases heaved up high in air.

190   And now, from fogs emerging,
I traversed blander seas,
Forgot the fogs, the scourging
Of sleet-whipped gales, forgot
My austere origin, my tremendous birth,
My journeyings, and that last cataclysm
Of overwhelming ruin.
My squat, pale, alien bulk
Basked in the ambient sheen;
And all about me, league on league outspread,
200 A gulf of indigo and green.
I laughed in the light waves laced with white, –
Nor knew
How swiftly shrank my girth
Under their sly caresses, how the breath
Of that soft wind sucked up my strength, nor how
The sweet, insidious fingers of the sun
Their stealthy depredations wrought upon me.

      Slowly now
I drifted, dreaming.
210 I saw the flying-fish
With silver gleaming
Flash from the peacock-bosomed wave
And flicker through an arc of sunlit air
Back to their element, desperate to elude
The jaws of the pursuing albacore.

      Day after day
I swung in the unhasting tide.
Sometimes I saw the dolphin folk at play,

Their lithe sides iridescent-dyed,
220 Unheeding in their speed
That long grey wraith,
The shark that followed hungering beneath.
Sometimes I saw a school
Of porpoise rolling by
In ranked array,
Emerging and submerging rhythmically,
Their blunt black bodies heading all one way
Until they faded
In the horizon's dazzling line of light.
230 Night after night
I followed the low, large moon across the sky,
Or counted the large stars on the purple dark,
The while I wasted, wasted and took no thought,
In drowsed entrancement caught; –
Until one noon a wave washed over me,
Breathed low a sobbing sigh,
Foamed indolently, and passed on;
And then I knew my empery was gone;
As I, too, soon must go.
240 Nor was I ill content to have it so.

     Another night
Gloomed o'er my sight,
With cloud, and flurries of warm, wild rain.
Another day,
Dawning delectably
With amber and scarlet stain,
Swept on its way,
Glowing and shimmering with heavy heat.
A lazing tuna rose
250 And nosed me curiously,
And shouldered me aside in brusque disdain,
So had I fallen from my high estate.

A foraging gull
Stooped over me, touched me with webbed pink feet,
And wheeled and skreeled away,
Indignant at the chill.

    Last I became
A little glancing globe of cold
That slid and sparkled on the slow-pulsed swell.
260 And then my fragile, scintillating frame
Dissolved in ecstasy
Of many coloured light,
And I breathed up my soul into the air
And merged forever in the all-solvent sea.   (1931)

As Down the Woodland Ways

As down the woodland ways I went
   With every wind asleep
I felt the surge of endless life
   About my footsteps creep.

I felt the urge of quickening mould
   That had been once a flower
Mount with the sap to bloom again
   At its appointed hour.

I saw gray stumps go crumbling down
10   In sodden, grim decay,
To soar in pillared green again
   On some remoter day.

I saw crushed beetles, mangled grubs,
   All crawling, perished things,
Whirl up in air, an ecstasy
   Of many-coloured wings.

Through weed and world, through worm and star,
   The sequence ran the same: –
Death but the travail-pang of life,
20   Destruction but a name.   [1936] (1937)

BLISS CARMAN
1861–1929

Born in Fredericton, New Brunswick, Bliss Carman studied at the universities of New Brunswick, Oxford, Edinburgh, and Harvard before settling in the United States as a poet, literary editor, and essayist. A cousin and close friend of Charles G.D. Roberts, he collaborated with American poet Richard Hovey on a series of Vagabondia poems (1894-1900) celebrating the joys of the open road. His works include *Low Tide on Grand Pré* (1893), *Ballads of Lost Haven: A Book of the Sea* (1897), *Sappho, One Hundred Lyrics* (1903), and *Sanctuary: Sunshine House Sonnets* (1929). To show the evolution of "Low Tide on Grand Pré," one of Bliss Carman's best known poems, it is here reprinted following its first version, "Low Tide on Avon."

Low Tide on Avon

The sun goes down, and over all
    These barren reaches by the tide
Such unelusive glories fall,
    I almost dream they yet will bide
    Until the coming of the tide.

And yet I know that not for us,
    By any ecstacy of dream,
He lingers to keep luminous
    A little while the grievous stream,
10   That frets uncomforted of dream.

I know too well that not for thee,
    And not for any smile of thine,
He stays, but failing utterly,
    Some day across a waste of brine
    Shall draw to prayer those hands of thine!

A grievous stream that to and fro,
   Athrough the fields of Acadie,
Goes wandering, as if to know
   Why one beloved face should be
20   So long from home and Acadie!

And every year in June for him
   There comes a dream – Evangeline,
As on that day her loss made dim!
   Through all the years that intervene
   His deathless love Evangeline!

At evening fall in midsummer,
   Just when the radiant fleurs-de-lis
From trammel of winter and the stir
   Of breathing Death one hour are free,
30   She comes with radiant fleurs-de-lis!

Above the ageless hills there breaks,
   Over their purple bloom of pine
And blue ravines, in crimson flakes,
   Her light whose hands are come to twine
   Shadow of rose with shade of pine.

And all the land makes glad her coming,
   If only once in a year of time,
The Underking's strong hands o'ercoming,
   She move one night through a dream sublime,
40   In beauty still untouched of time.

Was it a year or lives ago
   We took the grasses in our hands,
And caught the summer flying low
   Over the waving meadow lands
   And held it there between our hands?

The while the river at our feet,
   A drowsy inland meadow stream,

At slip of son the afterheat
　　Made running gold, and in the gleam
50　　We freed our birch upon the stream.

And down along the elms at dusk
　　We lifted dripping blade to drift
Through twilight scented fine like musk,
　　Where night and gloam awhile uplift
　　Nor sunder soul and soul adrift.

And that we took into our hands,
　　Spirit of life or subtler thing,
Breathed on us there and loosed the bands
　　Of death, and taught us whispering
60　　The secret of some wonder thing.

And all your face grew light and seemed
　　To hold the shadow of the sun;
The evening wavered, and I deemed
　　That time was ripe and years had done
　　Their wheeling underneath the sun.

And all desire and all regret,
　　And fear and memory were nought;
One, to remember or forget
　　The keen delight our hands had caught;
70　　Morrow and yesterday were nought!

　　　*　　*　　*　　*　　*　　*

The night has fallen, and the tide –
　　Now and again comes drifting home,
Across these arching barrens wide,
　　A sigh like driven wind or foam:
　　In grief the flood is bursting home!
　　　　　　　　　　　(1886)

Low Tide on Grand Pré

The sun goes down, and over all
    These barren reaches by the tide
Such unelusive glories fall,
    I almost dream they yet will bide
    Until the coming of the tide.

And yet I know that not for us,
    By any ecstasy of dream,
He lingers to keep luminous
    A little while the grievous stream,
10   Which frets, uncomforted of dream –

A grievous stream, that to and fro
    Athrough the fields of Acadie
Goes wandering, as if to know
    Why one beloved face should be
    So long from home and Acadie.

Was it a year or lives ago
    We took the grasses in our hands,
And caught the summer flying low
    Over the waving meadow lands,
20   And held it there between our hands?

The while the river at our feet –
    A drowsy inland meadow stream –
At set of sun the after-heat
    Made running gold, and in the gleam
    We freed our birch upon the stream.

There down along the elms at dusk
    We lifted dripping blade to drift,
Through twilight scented fine like musk,
    Where night and gloom awhile uplift,
30   Nor sunder soul and soul adrift.

And that we took into our hands
    Spirit of life or subtler thing –
Breathed on us there, and loosed the bands
    Of death, and taught us, whispering,
    The secret of some wonder-thing.

Then all your face grew light, and seemed
    To hold the shadow of the sun;
The evening faltered, and I deemed
    That time was ripe, and years had done
40   Their wheeling underneath the sun.

So all desire and all regret,
    And fear and memory, were naught;
One to remember or forget
    The keen delight our hands had caught;
    Morrow and yesterday were naught.

The night has fallen, and the tide . . .
    Now and again comes drifting home,
Across these aching barrens wide,
    A sigh like driven wind or foam:
50   In grief the flood is bursting home.

                                (1887)

A Windflower

Between the roadside and the wood,
    Between the dawning and the dew,
A tiny flower before the sun,
    Ephemeral in time, I grew.

And there upon the trail of spring,
    Not death nor love nor any name
Known among men in all their lands
    Could blur the wild desire with shame.

But down my dayspan of the year
10   The feet of straying winds came by;
And all my trembling soul was thrilled
    To follow one lost mountain cry.

And then my heart beat once and broke
    To hear the sweeping rain forebode
Some ruin in the April world,
    Between the woodside and the road.

To-night can bring no healing now;
    The calm of yesternight is gone;
Surely the wind is but the wind,
20   And I a broken waif thereon.

                    (1889)

The Eavesdropper

In a still room at hush of dawn,
    My Love and I lay side by side
And heard the roaming forest wind
    Stir in the paling autumn-tide.

I watched her earth-brown eyes grow glad
    Because the round day was so fair;
While memories of reluctant night
    Lurked in the blue dusk of her hair.

Outside, a yellow maple tree,
10   Shifting upon the silvery blue
With tiny multitudinous sound,
    Rustled to let the sunlight through.

The livelong day the elvish leaves
    Danced with their shadows on the floor;
And the lost children of the wind
    Went straying homeward by our door.

And all the swarthy afternoon
    We watched the great deliberate sun
Walk through the crimsoned hazy world,
20   Counting his hilltops one by one.

Then as the purple twilight came
    And touched the vines along our eaves,
Another Shadow stood without
    And gloomed the dancing of the leaves.

The silence fell on my Love's lips;
    Her great brown eyes were veiled and sad
With pondering some maze of dream,
    Though all the splendid year was glad.

Restless and vague as a gray wind
30   Her heart had grown, she knew not why.
But hurrying to the open door,
    Against the verge of western sky

I saw retreating on the hills,
    Looming and sinister and black,
The stealthy figure swift and huge
    Of One who strode and looked not back.
                    (1893)

A Sea Child

The lover of child Marjory
    Had one white hour of life brim full;
Now the old nurse, the rocking sea,
    Hath him to lull.

The daughter of child Marjory
    Hath in her veins, to beat and run,
The glad indomitable sea,
    The strong white sun.
                    (1893)

The Ships of St. John

Smile, you inland hills and rivers!
Flush, you mountains in the dawn!
But my roving heart is seaward
With the ships of gray St. John.

Fair the land lies, full of August,
Meadow island, shingly bar,
Open barns and breezy twilight,
Peace and the mild evening star.

Gently now this gentlest country
10   The old habitude takes on,
But my wintry heart is outbound
With the great ships of St. John.

Once in your wide arms you held me,
Till the man-child was a man,
Canada, great nurse and mother
Of the young sea-roving clan.

Always your bright face above me
Through the dreams of boyhood shone;
Now far alien countries call me
20   With the ships of gray St. John.

Swing, you tides, up out of Fundy!
Blow, you white fogs, in from sea!
I was born to be your fellow;
You were bred to pilot me.

At the touch of your strong fingers,
Doubt, the derelict, is gone;
Sane and glad I clear the headland
With the white ships of St. John.

Loyalists, my fathers, builded
30 This gray port of the gray sea,
When the duty to ideals
Could not let well-being be.

When the breadth of scarlet bunting
Puts the wreath of maple on,
I must cheer too, – slip my moorings
With the ships of gray St. John.

Peerless-hearted port of heroes,
Be a word to lift the world,
Till the many see the signal
40 Of the few once more unfurled.

Past the lighthouse, past the nunbuoy,
Past the crimson rising sun,
There are dreams go down the harbor
With the tall ships of St. John.

In the morning I am with them
As they clear the island bar, –
Fade, till speck by speck the midday
Has forgotten where they are.

But I sight a vaster sea-line,
50 Wider lee-way, longer run,
Whose discoverers return not
With the ships of gray St. John.

                (1893)

Noons of Poppy

Noons of poppy, noons of poppy,
Scarlet leagues along the sea;
Flaxen hair afloat in sunlight,
Love, come down the world to me!

There's a Captain I must ship with,
(Heart, that day be far from now!)
Wears his dark command in silence
With the sea-frost on his brow.

Noons of poppy, noons of poppy,
10　Purple shadows by the sea;
How should love take thought to wonder
What the destined port may be?

Nay, if love have joy for shipmate
For a night-watch or a year,
Dawn will light o'er Lonely Haven,
Heart to happy heart, as here.

Noons of poppy, noons of poppy,
Scarlet acres by the sea
Burning to the blue above them;
20　Love, the world is full for me.　(1894)

A Vagabond Song

There is something in the autumn that is native to my
blood –
Touch of manner, hint of mood;
And my heart is like a rhyme,
With the yellow and the purple and the crimson keeping
time.

The scarlet of the maples can shake me like a cry
Of bugles going by.
And my lonely spirit thrills
To see the frosty asters like a smoke upon the hills.

There is something in October sets the gypsy blood astir;
10　We must rise and follow her,
When from every hill of flame
She calls and calls each vagabond by name.　(1895)

The Lanterns of St. Eulalie

In the October afternoon
Orange and purple and maroon,

Goes quiet Autumn, lamp in hand,
About the apple-coloured land,

To light in every apple-tree
The Lanterns of St. Eulalie.

They glimmer in the orchard shade
Like fiery opals set in jade, –

Crimson and russet and raw gold,
10 Yellow and green and scarlet old.

And O when I am far away
By foaming reel or azure bay,

In crowded street or hot lagoon,
Or under the strange austral moon, –

When the homesickness comes on me
For the great Marshes by the sea,

The running dikes, the brimming tide,
And the dark firs on Fundy side,

In dream once more I shall behold,
20 Like signal lights, those globes of gold

Hung out in every apple-tree –
The Lanterns of St. Eulalie.

(1900)

from Sappho: One Hundred Lyrics

XXII

Once you lay upon my bosom,
While the long blue-silver moonlight
Walked the plain, with that pure passion
All your own.

Now the moon is gone, the Pleiads
Gone, the dead of night is going,
Slips the hour, and on my bed
I lie alone.

XXIII

I loved thee, Atthis, in the long ago,
When the great oleanders were in flower
In the broad herded meadows full of sun.
And we would often at the fall of dusk
Wander together by the silver stream,
When the soft grass-heads were all wet with dew
And purple-misted in the fading light.
The joy I knew and sorrow at thy voice,
And the superb magnificence of love, –
10 The loneliness that saddens solitude,
And the sweet speech that makes it durable, –
The bitter longing and the keen desire,
The sweet companionship through quiet days
In the slow ample beauty of the world,
And the unutterable glad release
Within the temple of the holy night.
O Atthis, how I loved thee long ago
In that fair perished summer by the sea!

XXV

It was summer when I found you
In the meadow long ago,
And the golden vetch was growing
By the shore.

Did we falter when love took us
With a gust of great desire?
Does the barley bid the wind wait
In his course?

XXVIII

With your head thrown backward
In my arm's safe hollow,
And your face all rosy
With the mounting fervour;

While the grave eyes greaten
With the wise new wonder,
Swimming in a love-mist
Like the haze of Autumn;

From that throat, the throbbing
10 Nightingale's for pleading
Wayward soft and welling
Inarticulate love-notes,

Come the words that bubble
Up through broken laughter,
Sweeter than spring water,
"Gods, I am so happy!"

XLV

Softer than the hill fog to the forest
Are the loving hands of my dear lover,
When she sleeps beside me in the starlight
And her beauty drenches me with rest.

As the quiet mist enfolds the beech-trees,
Even as she dreams her arms enfold me,
Half awaking with a hundred kisses
On the scarlet lily of her mouth.

LIV

How soon will all my lovely days be over,
And I no more be found beneath the sun, –
Neither beside the many-murmuring sea,
Nor where the plain winds whisper to the reeds,
Nor in the tall beech-woods among the hills
Where roam the bright-lipped oreads, nor along
The pasture sides where berry-pickers stray
And harmless shepherds pipe their sheep to fold!

For I am eager, and the flame of life
10 Burns quickly in the fragile lamp of clay.
Passion and love and longing and hot tears
Consume this mortal Sappho, and too soon
A great wind from the dark will blow upon me,
And I be no more found in the fair world,
For all the search of the revolving moon
And patient shine of everlasting stars.

XCVIII

I am more tremulous than shaken reeds,
And love has made me like the river water.

Thy voice is as the hill wind over me,
And all my changing heart gives heed, my lover.

Before thy least lost murmur I must sigh,
Or gladden with thee as the sun-path glitters.

[1902] (1903)

Before the Snow

Now soon, ah, very soon, I know
The trumpets of the north will blow,
And the great winds will come to bring
The pale, wild riders of the snow.

Darkening the sun with level flight,
At arrowy speed, they will alight,
Unnumbered as the desert sands,
To bivouac on the edge of night.

Then I, within their somber ring,
10 Shall hear a voice that seems to sing,
Deep, deep within my tranquil heart,
The valiant prophecy of spring.

(1916)

The Ghost-yard of the Goldenrod

When the first silent frost has trod
The ghost-yard of the goldenrod,

And laid the blight of his cold hand
Upon the warm autumnal land,

And all things wait the subtle change
That men call death, is it not strange

That I – without a care or need,
Who only am an idle weed –

Should wait unmoved, so frail, so bold,
10 The coming of the final cold!

(1921)

Wild Geese

To-night with snow in the November air,
Over the roof I heard that startling cry
Passing along the highway of the dark –
The Wild Geese going South. Confused commands
As of a column on the march rang out
Clamorous and sharp against the frosty air.
And with an answering tumult in my heart
I too went hurrying out into the night
Was it from some deep immemorial past
10 I learned those summoning signals and alarms,
And still must answer to my brothers' call?
I knew the darkling hope that bade them rise
From Northern lakes, and with courageous hearts
Adventure forth on their uncharted quest.

(1929)

The Winter Scene

I

The rutted roads are all like iron; skies
Are keen and brilliant; only the oak-leaves cling
In the bare woods, or the hardy bitter-sweet;
Drivers have put their sheepskin jackets on;
And all the ponds are sealed with sheeted ice
That rings with stroke of skate and hockey-stick,
Or in the twilight cracks with running whoop.
Bring in the logs of oak and hickory,
And make an ample blaze on the wide hearth.
10 Now is the time, with winter o'er the world,
For books and friends and yellow candle-light,
And timeless lingering by the settling fire.
While all the shuddering stars are keen with cold.

II

Out from the silent portal of the hours,
When frosts are come and all the hosts put on
Their burnished gear to march across the night
And o'er a darkened earth in splendor shine,
Slowly above the world Orion wheels
His glittering square, while on the shadowy hill
20 And throbbing like a sea-light through the dusk,
Great Sirius rises in his flashing blue.
Lord of the winter night, august and pure,
Returning year on year untouched by time,
To hearten faith with thine unfaltering fire,
There are no hurts that beauty cannot ease,
No ills that love cannot at last repair,
In the victorious progress of the soul.

III

Russet and white and gray is the oak wood
In the great snow. Still from the North it comes,
30 Whispering, settling, sifting through the trees,
O'erloading branch and twig. The road is lost.
Clearing and meadow, stream and ice-bound pond
Are made once more a trackless wilderness
In the white hush where not a creature stirs;
And the pale sun is blotted from the sky.
In that strange twilight the lone traveller halts
To listen to the stealthy snowflakes fall.
And then far off toward the Stamford shore,
Where through the storm the coastwise liners go,
40 Faint and recurrent on the muffled air,
A foghorn booming through the smother – hark!

IV

When the day changed and the mad wind died down,
The powdery drifts that all day long had blown

Across the meadows and the open fields,
Or whirled like diamond dust in the bright sun,
Settled to rest, and for a tranquil hour
The lengthening bluish shadows on the snow
Stole down the orchard slope, and a rose light
Flooded the earth with beauty and with peace.
50 Then in the west behind the cedars black
The sinking sun stained red the winter dusk
With sullen flare upon the snowy ridge, –
As in a masterpiece by Hokusai,
Where on a background gray, with flaming breath
A scarlet dragon dies in dusky gold.

(1929)

May in the Selkirks

Up the Illecillewaet and down the yellow Beaver,
Over skyward passes where snow-peaks touch the blue.
Shining silver rivers dropping down from Heaven,
With the spring-call of the wilderness waking Spring anew.

Far gleaming glaciers like the Gates of Glory,
And the hosts in new green marching up the slopes,
Organ-voiced torrents singing through the gorges, –
Songs for the high trail and visions for our hopes.

Hints of light supernal on the rocky ledges,
10 Echoes of wild music from the valley floors,
And the tall evergreens watching at the Threshold, –
Keeping the silence of the Lord of out-of-doors.

Balm out of Paradise blown across the canyons
From the balsam-poplar buds and bronze leaves
                       uncurled. . . .
Soul in her wonder lifts the new *Magnificat.*
Alight with the rapture of the morning of the world.

(1929)

ARCHIBALD LAMPMAN

1862–1899

Son of an Anglican clergyman, Archibald Lampman was
born in Morpeth in southern Ontario, and published his
first poems while a student at Trinity College in the Uni-
versity of Toronto. After an unhappy attempt at teaching,
he obtained a junior position in the post office in Ottawa.
During his lifetime Lampman published two volumes of
poetry, *Among the Millet, and Other Poems* (1888) and
Lyrics of Earth (1895); at the time of his death, a third book,
Alcyone, was in press. The posthumous publication of *The
Poems of Archibald Lampman* (1900) was supervised by his
close friend, Duncan Campbell Scott.

Love Doubt

[The Growth of Love I]

Yearning upon the faint rose-curves that flit
    About her child-sweet mouth and innocent cheek,
    And in her eyes watching with eyes all meek
The light and shadow of laughter, I would sit
Mute, knowing our two souls might never knit;
    As if a pale proud lily-flower should seek
    The love of some red rose, but could not speak
One word of her blithe tongue to tell of it.

For oh, my Love was sunny-lipped and stirred
10   With all swift light and sound and gloom not long
Retained; I, with dreams weighed, that ever heard
    Sad burdens echoing through the loudest throng,
She, the wild song of some May-merry bird;
    I, but the listening maker of a song.

                              [1884] (1888)

For my Darling

[The Growth of Love II]

My lady is not learned in many books,
    Nor hath much love for grave discourses, strung
    With gaudy similes; for she is young,
And full of merry pranks and laughing looks;
But yet her heart hath many tender nooks
    Of fervour and sweet charity: her tongue,
    For all its laughter, yet is often wrung
With soft compassion for life's painful crooks.

I love my lady for her lovely face,
10   And for her mouth, and for her eyes, and hair;
More still I love her for her laughing grace,
    And for her wayward ways, and changeful air;
But most of all love gaineth ground apace,
    Because my lady's heart is pure and fair.

                      [1885] (1943)

Among the Timothy

Long hours ago, while yet the morn was blithe,
    Nor sharp athirst had drunk the beaded dew,
A reaper came, and swung his cradled scythe
    Around this stump, and, shearing slowly, drew
    Far round among the clover, ripe for hay,
        A circle clean and grey;
And here among the scented swathes that gleam,
    Mixed with dead daisies, it is sweet to lie
    And watch the grass and the few-clouded sky,
10   Nor think but only dream.

For when the noon was turning, and the heat
    Fell down most heavily on field and wood,
I too came hither, borne on restless feet,

Seeking some comfort for an aching mood.
  Ah, I was weary of the drifting hours,
    The echoing city towers,
The blind grey streets, the jingle of the throng,
  Weary of hope that like a shape of stone
  Sat near at hand without a smile or moan,
20   And weary most of song.

And those high moods of mine that sometime made
  My heart a heaven, opening like a flower,
A sweeter world where I in wonder strayed,
  Begirt with shapes of beauty and the power
  Of dreams that moved through that enchanted clime
    With changing breaths of rhyme,
Were all gone lifeless now like those white leaves
  That hang all winter, shivering dead and blind
  Among the sinewy beeches in the wind,
30   That vainly calls and grieves.

Ah! I will set no more mine overtaskèd brain
  To barren search and toil that beareth nought,
Forever following with sorefooted pain
  The crossing pathways of unbournèd thought;
  But let it go, as one that hath no skill,
    To take what shape it will,
An ant slow-burrowing in the earthy gloom,
  A spider bathing in the dew at morn,
  Or a brown bee in wayward fancy borne
40   From hidden bloom to bloom.

Hither and thither o'er the rocking grass
  The little breezes, blithe as they are blind,
Teasing the slender blossoms pass and pass,
  Soft-footed children of the gipsy wind,
  To taste of every purple-fringèd head
    Before the bloom is dead;

And scarcely heed the daisies that, endowed
   With stems so short they cannot see, up-bear
   Their innocent sweet eyes distressed, and stare
50   Like children in a crowd.

Not far to fieldward in the central heat,
   Shadowing the clover, a pale poplar stands
With glimmering leaves that, when the wind comes, beat
   Together like innumerable small hands,
     And with the calm, as in vague dreams astray,
       Hang wan and silver-grey;
Like sleepy maenads, who in pale surprise,
   Half-wakened by a prowling beast, have crept
   Out of the hidden covert, where they slept,
60   At noon with languid eyes.

The crickets creak, and through the noonday glow,
   That crazy fiddler of the hot mid-year,
The dry cicada plies his wiry bow
   In long-spun cadence, thin and dusty sere:
     From the green grass the small grasshoppers' din
      Spreads soft and silvery thin:
And ever and anon a murmur steals
   Into mine ears of toil that moves alway,
   The crackling rustle of the pitch-forked hay
70   And lazy jerk of wheels.

As so I lie and feel the soft hours wane,
   To wind and sun and peaceful sound laid bare,
That aching dim discomfort of the brain
   Fades off unseen, and shadowy-footed care
     Into some hidden corner creeps at last
      To slumber deep and fast;
And gliding on, quite fashioned to forget,
   From dream to dream I bid my spirit pass

Out into the pale green ever-swaying grass
80   To brood, but no more fret.

And hour by hour among all shapes that grow
    Of purple mints and daisies gemmed with gold
In sweet unrest my visions come and go;
    I feel and hear and with quiet eyes behold;
    And hour by hour, the ever-journeying sun,
     In gold and shadow spun,
Into mine eyes and blood, and through the dim
    Green glimmering forest of the grass shines down,
    Till flower and blade, and every cranny brown,
90   And I are soaked with him.

                    [1885] (1888)

Morning on the Lièvre

Far above us where a jay
Screams his matins to the day,
Capped with gold and amethyst,
Like a vapour from the forge
Of a giant somewhere hid,
Out of hearing of the clang
Of his hammer, skirts of mist
Slowly up the woody gorge
Lift and hang.

10 Softly as a cloud we go,
Sky above and sky below,
Down the river, and the dip
Of the paddles scarcely breaks,
With the little silvery drip
Of the water as it shakes
From the blades, the crystal deep
Of the silence of the morn,
Of the forest yet asleep,

And the river reaches borne
20 In a mirror, purple grey,
Sheer away
To the misty line of light,
Where the forest and the stream
In the shadow meet and plight,
Like a dream.

From amid a stretch of reeds,
Where the lazy river sucks
All the water as it bleeds
From a little curling creek,
30 And the muskrats peer and sneak
In around the sunken wrecks
Of a tree that swept the skies
Long ago,
On a sudden seven ducks
With a splashy rustle rise,
Stretching out their seven necks,
One before, and two behind,
And the others all arow,
And as steady as the wind
40 With a swivelling whistle go,
Through the purple shadow led,
Till we only hear their whir
In behind a rocky spur,
Just ahead.

[1886] (1888)

The Railway Station

The darkness brings no quiet here, the light
   No waking: ever on my blinded brain
    The flare of lights, the rush, and cry, and strain,
The engines' scream, the hiss and thunder smite:
I see the hurrying crowds, the clasp, the flight,

Faces that touch, eyes that are dim with pain:
   I see the hoarse wheels turn, and the great train
Move labouring out into the bourneless night.

So many souls within its dim recesses,
10   So many bright, so many mournful eyes:
   Mine eyes that watch grow fixed with dreams and
                                            guesses;
      What threads of life, what hidden histories,
   What sweet or passionate dreams and dark distresses,
      What unknown thoughts, what various agonies!
                                            (1887)

In November

The hills and leafless forests slowly yield
   To the thick-driving snow. A little while
   And night shall darken down. In shouting file
The woodmen's carts go by me homeward-wheeled,
Past the thin fading stubbles, half-concealed,
   Now golden-grey, sowed softly through with snow,
   Where the last ploughman follows still his row,
Turning black furrows through the whitening field.

Far off the village lamps begin to gleam,
10   Fast drives the snow, and no man comes this way;
      The hills grow wintery white, and bleak winds
                                            moan
         About the naked uplands. I alone
      Am neither sad, nor shelterless, nor grey,
Wrapped round with thought, content to watch and
                                            dream.
                                       [1887] (1888)

Heat

From plains that reel to southward, dim,
   The road runs by me white and bare;
Up the steep hill it seems to swim
   Beyond, and melt into the glare.
Upward half way, or it may be
   Nearer the summit, slowly steals
A hay-cart, moving dustily
   With idly clacking wheels.

By his cart's side the wagoner
10   Is slouching slowly at his ease,
Half-hidden in the windless blur
   Of white dust puffing to his knees.
This wagon on the height above,
   From sky to sky on either hand,
Is the sole thing that seems to move
   In all the heat-held land.

Beyond me in the fields the sun
   Soaks in the grass and hath his will;
I count the marguerites one by one;
20   Even the buttercups are still.
On the brook yonder not a breath
   Disturbs the spider or the midge.
The water-bugs draw close beneath
   The cool gloom of the bridge.

Where the far elm-tree shadows flood
   Dark patches in the burning grass,
The cows, each with her peaceful cud,
   Lie waiting for the heat to pass.
From somewhere on the slope near by
30   Into the pale depth of the noon
A wandering thrush slides leisurely
   His thin revolving tune.

In intervals of dreams I hear
    The cricket from the droughty ground;
The grass-hoppers spin into mine ear
    A small innumerable sound.
I lift mine eyes sometimes to gaze:
    The burning sky-line blinds my sight:
The woods far off are blue with haze:
40   The hills are drenched in light.

And yet to me not this or that
    Is always sharp or always sweet;
In the sloped shadow of my hat
    I lean at rest, and drain the heat;
Nay more, I think some blessèd power
    Hath brought me wandering idly here:
In the full furnace of this hour
    My thoughts grow keen and clear.

                        [1887] (1888)

A Night of Storm

Oh city, whom grey stormy hands have sown
    With restless drift, scarce broken now of any,
    Out of the dark thy windows dim and many
Gleam red across the storm. Sound is there none,
Save evermore the fierce wind's sweep and moan,
    From whose grey hands the keen white snow is shaken
    In desperate gusts, that fitfully lull and waken,
Dense as night's darkness round thy towers of stone.

Darkling and strange art thou thus vexed and chidden;
10   More dark and strange thy veilèd agony,
City of storm, in whose grey heart are hidden
    What stormier woes, what lives that groan and beat,

Stern and thin-cheeked, against time's heavier sleet,
Rude fates, hard hearts, and prisoning poverty.

[1887] (1888)

Solitude

How still it is here in the woods. The trees
    Stand motionless, as if they did not dare
    To stir, lest it should break the spell. The air
Hangs quiet as spaces in a marble frieze.
Even this little brook, that runs at ease,
    Whispering and gurgling in its knotted bed,
    Seems but to deepen with its curling thread
Of sound the shadowy sun-pierced silences.

Sometimes a hawk screams or a woodpecker
10   Startles the stillness from its fixèd mood
With his loud careless tap. Sometimes I hear
      The dreamy white-throat from some far off tree
    Pipe slowly on the listening solitude
      His five pure notes succeeding pensively.

(1888)

Winter Evening

To-night the very horses springing by
Toss gold from whitened nostrils. In a dream
The streets that narrow to the westward gleam
Like rows of golden palaces; and high
From all the crowded chimneys tower and die
A thousand aureoles. Down in the west
The brimming plains beneath the sunset rest,
One burning sea of gold. Soon, soon shall fly
The glorious vision, and the hours shall feel
10 A mightier master; soon from height to height,
With silence and the sharp unpitying stars,

Stern creeping frosts, and winds that touch like steel,
Out of the depth beyond the eastern bars,
Glittering and still shall come the awful night.

(1888)

A January Morning

The glittering roofs are still with frost; each worn
    Black chimney builds into the quiet sky
    Its curling pile, to crumble silently;
Far out to westward on the edge of morn
The slender, misty city towers upborne,
    Glimmer faint rose against the pallid blue;
    And yonder on those northern hills, the hue
Of amethyst, hang fleeces dull as horn;
But here behind me come the woodmen's sleighs
10   With shouts and clamorous squeakings; might and
                        main
    Up the steep slope the horses stamp and strain,
Urged on by hoarse-tongued drivers – cheeks ablaze,
    Iced beards and frozen eyelids – team by team,
    With frost-fringed flanks and nostrils jetting steam.

(1889)

Evening

From upland slopes I see the cows file by,
Lowing, great-chested, down the homeward trail,
By dusking fields and meadows shining pale
With moon-tipped dandelions. Flickering high,
A peevish night-hawk in the western sky
Beats up into the lucent solitudes,
Or drops with griding wing. The stilly woods
Grow dark and deep and gloom mysteriously.
Cool night-winds creep, and whisper in mine ear.
10 The homely cricket gossips at my feet.

From far-off pools and wastes of reeds I hear,
Clear and soft-piped, the chanting frogs break sweet
In full Pandean chorus. One by one
Shine out the stars, and the great night comes on.

[c. 1889] (1899)

In November

With loitering step and quiet eye,
Beneath the low November sky,
I wandered in the woods, and found
A clearing, where the broken ground
Was scattered with black stumps and briers,
And the old wreck of forest fires.
It was a bleak and sandy spot,
And, all about, the vacant plot
Was peopled and inhabited
10 By scores of mulleins long since dead.
A silent and forsaken brood
In that mute opening of the wood,
So shrivelled and so thin they were,
So grey, so haggard, and austere,
Not plants at all they seemed to me,
But rather some spare company
Of hermit folk, who long ago,
Wandering in bodies to and fro,
Had chanced upon this lonely way,
20 And rested thus, till death one day
Surprised them at their compline prayer,
And left them standing lifeless there.

There was no sound about the wood
Save the wind's secret stir. I stood
Among the mullein-stalks as still
As if myself had grown to be
One of their sombre company,

A body without wish or will.
And as I stood, quite suddenly,
30 Down from a furrow in the sky
The sun shone out a little space
Across that silent sober place,
Over the sand heaps and brown sod,
The mulleins and dead goldenrod,
And passed beyond the thickets grey,
And lit the fallen leaves that lay,
Level and deep within the wood,
A rustling yellow multitude.

And all around me the thin light,
40 So sere, so melancholy bright,
Fell like the half-reflected gleam
Or shadow of some former dream;
A moment's golden reverie
Poured out on every plant and tree
A semblance of weird joy, or less,
A sort of spectral happiness;
And I, too, standing idly there,
With muffled hands in the chill air,
Felt the warm glow about my feet,
50 And shuddering betwixt cold and heat,
Drew my thoughts closer, like a cloak,
While something in my blood awoke,
A nameless and unnatural cheer,
A pleasure secret and austere.

[1889] (1890)

Across the Pea-Fields

Field upon field to westward hum and shine
    The gray-green sun-drenched mists of blossoming peas;
    Beyond them are great elms and poplar trees
That guard the noon-stilled farm-yards, groves of pine,
And long dark fences muffled thick with vine;
    Then the high city, murmurous with mills;
    And last upon the sultry west blue hills,
Misty, far-lifted, a mere filmy line.

Across these blackening rails into the light
10   I lean and listen, lolling drowsily;
On the fence corner, yonder to the right,
    A red squirrel whisks and chatters; nearer by
        A little old brown woman on her knees
        Searches the deep hot grass for strawberries.

                        [1889] (1900)

A Sunset on the Lower St. Lawrence

[A Sunset at Les Eboulements]

Broad shadows fall. On all the mountain side
The scythe-swept fields are silent. Slowly home
By the long beach the high-piled hay-carts come,
Splashing the pale salt shallows. Over wide
Fawn-coloured wastes of mud the slipping tide,
Round the dun rocks and wattled fisheries,
Creeps murmuring in. And now by twos and threes,
O'er the slow spreading pools with clamorous chide,
Belated crows from strip to strip take flight.
10 Soon will the first star shine; yet ere the night
Reach onward to the pale-green distances,
The sun's last shaft beyond the gray sea-floor
Still dreams upon the Kamouraska shore,
And the long line of golden villages.

                        [1890] (1891)

To a Millionaire

The world in all its gloom and splendour passes by,
And thou in the midst of it with brows that gleam,
A creature of that old distorted dream,
That makes the sound of life an evil cry.
Good men perform just deeds, and brave men die,
And win not honour such as gold can give,
While the vain multitudes plod on, and live,
And serve the curse that pins them down, but I –
I think only of the unnumbered broken hearts,
10 The hunger and the mortal strife for bread,
Old age and youth alike mistaught, misfed,
By want and rags and homelessness made vile,
The griefs and hates, and all the meaner parts
That balance thy one grim misgotten pile.

[1891] (1894)

The City of the End of Things

Beside the pounding cataracts
Of midnight streams unknown to us
'Tis builded in the leafless tracts
And valleys huge of Tartarus.
Lurid and lofty and vast it seems;
It hath no rounded name that rings,
But I have heard it called in dreams
The City of the End of Things.

Its roofs and iron towers have grown
10 None knoweth how high within the night,
But in its murky streets far down
A flaming terrible and bright
Shakes all the stalking shadows there,
Across the walls, across the floors,
And shifts upon the upper air

From out a thousand furnace doors;
And all the while an awful sound
Keeps roaring on continually,
And crashes in the ceaseless round
20 Of a gigantic harmony.
Through its grim depths re-echoing
And all its weary height of walls,
With measured roar and iron ring,
The inhuman music lifts and falls.
Where no thing rests and no man is,
And only fire and night hold sway;
The beat, the thunder and the hiss
Cease not, and change not, night nor day.
And moving at unheard commands,
30 The abysses and vast fires between,
Flit figures that with clanking hands
Obey a hideous routine;
They are not flesh, they are not bone,
They see not with the human eye,
And from their iron lips is blown
A dreadful and monotonous cry;
And whoso of our mortal race
Should find that city unaware,
Lean Death would smite him face to face,
40 And blanch him with its venomed air:
Or caught by the terrific spell,
Each thread of memory snapt and cut,
His soul would shrivel and its shell
Go rattling like an empty nut.

It was not always so, but once,
In days that no man thinks upon,
Fair voices echoed from its stones,
The light above it leaped and shone:
Once there were multitudes of men,

50 That built that city in their pride,
     Until its might was made, and then
     They withered age by age and died.
     But now of that prodigious race,
     Three only in an iron tower,
     Set like carved idols face to face,
     Remain the masters of its power;
     And at the city gate a fourth,
     Gigantic and with dreadful eyes,
     Sits looking toward the lightless north,
60 Beyond the reach of memories;
     Fast rooted to the lurid floor,
     A bulk that never moves a jot,
     In his pale body dwells no more,
     Or mind, or soul, – an idiot!

     But sometime in the end those three
     Shall perish and their hands be still,
     And with the master's touch shall flee
     Their incommunicable skill.
     A stillness absolute as death
70 Along the slacking wheels shall lie,
     And, flagging at a single breath,
     The fires shall moulder out and die.
     The roar shall vanish at its height,
     And over that tremendous town
     The silence of eternal night
     Shall gather close and settle down.
     All its grim grandeur, tower and hall,
     Shall be abandoned utterly,
     And into rust and dust shall fall
80 From century to century;
     Nor ever living thing shall grow,
     Or trunk of tree, or blade of grass;
     No drop shall fall, no wind shall blow,

Nor sound of any foot shall pass:
Alone of its accursèd state,
One thing the hand of Time shall spare,
For the grim Idiot at the gate
Is deathless and eternal there.

[1892] (1894)

White Pansies

Day and night pass over, rounding,
　　Star and cloud and sun,
Things of drift and shadow, empty
　　Of my dearest one.

Soft as slumber was my baby,
　　Beaming bright and sweet;
Daintier than bloom or jewel
　　Were his hands and feet.

He was mine, mine all, mine only,
10　　Mine and his the debt;
Earth and Life and Time are changers;
　　I shall not forget.

Pansies for my dear one – heartsease –
　　Set them gently so;
For his stainless lips and forehead,
　　Pansies white as snow.

Would that in the flower-grown little
　　Grave they dug so deep,
I might rest beside him, dreamless,
20　　Smile no more, nor weep.

[1894] (1899)

On Lake Temiscamingue

A single dreamy elm that stands between
The sombre forest and the wan-lit lake
Halves with its slim grey stem and pendent green
The shadowed point. Beyond it, without break,
Bold brows of pine-topped granite bend away
Far to the southward fading off in grand
Soft folds of looming purple. Cold and grey,
The point runs out, a blade of thinnest sand.
Two rivers meet beyond it, wild and clear,
10 Their deepening thunder breaks upon the ear –
The one descending from its forest home
By many an eddied pool and murmuring fall,
The other cloven through the mountain wall,
A race of tumbled rocks, a roar of foam.

                              [1896] (1900)

from *A Portrait in Six Sonnets*

I

Tall is my friend, for Nature would have marred
Her breadth of vision with a meaner height:
Full-browed, for at her bidding are unbarred
The gates of Beauty and the inward sight:
And slender, for her eager soul denies
A needless burden to the delicate frame:
Grey-eyed, for grey is wisdom – yet with eyes,
Mobile and deep, and quick for thought or flame
A voice of many notes that breaks and changes
10 And fits each meaning with its vital chord,
A speech, true to the heart, that lightly ranges
From jocund laughter to the serious word,
And over all a bearing proud and free,
A noble grace, a conscious dignity.

VI

To hold for a possession in the mind,
In every hour of life, in every place,
A noble spirit's influence, pure and kind,
The image of an honoured form and face, –
Better than any soundest article
Of any creed is this; and this to me,
This image and this faith unchangeable,
This pattern of the fairest dignity,
Is present ever in my friend, – my friend, –
10 Whom only shall high thoughts and deeds attend,
The gentlest and the wisest. Touched by her,
A world of finer vision I have found;
Less heedful of the common fret and stir,
I tread, grave-hearted, upon loftier ground.

[c. 1896] (1943)

In the Wilds

We run with rushing streams that toss and spume;
We speed or dream upon the open meres;
The pine-woods fold us in their ancient gloom;
The thunder of wild water fills our ears;
The rain we take, we take the beating sun;
The stars are cold above our heads at night;
On the rough earth we lie when day is done,
And slumber even in the storm's despite.
The savage vigor of the forest creeps
10 Into our veins, and laughs upon our lips;
The warm blood kindles from forgotten deeps,
And surges tingling to the finger-tips.
The deep-pent life awakes, and bursts its bands;
We feel the strength and goodness of our hands.

(1897)

Winter Uplands

The frost that stings like fire upon my cheek,
The loneliness of this forsaken ground,
The long white drift upon whose powdered peak
I sit in the great silence as one bound;
The rippled sheet of snow where the wind blew
Across the open fields for miles ahead;
The far-off city towered and roofed in blue
A tender line upon the western red;
The stars that singly, then in flocks appear,
10 Like jets of silver from the violet dome,
So wonderful, so many and so near,
And then the golden moon to light me home –
The crunching snowshoes and the stinging air,
And silence, frost and beauty everywhere.

[1899] (1900)

DUNCAN CAMPBELL SCOTT

1862–1947

The son of a Methodist minister, Duncan Campbell Scott was born in Ottawa, his home for most of his life. At the age of seventeen he became a clerk with the Department of Indian Affairs, where he rose to deputy superintendent-general, a position he held from 1913 until his retirement in 1932. An accomplished author of short stories as well as poetry, he enjoyed a long literary career, from the publication of *The Magic House, and Other Poems* (1893) to *The Circle of Affection, and Other Pieces in Prose and Verse* (1947).

Ottawa

Before Dawn

The stars are stars of morn; a keen wind wakes
The birches on the slope; the distant hills
Rise in the vacant North; the Chaudière fills
The calm with its hushed roar; the river takes
An unquiet rest, and a bird stirs, and shakes
The morn with music; a snatch of singing thrills
From the river; and the air clings and chills.
Fair, in the South, fair as a shrine that makes
The wonder of a dream, imperious towers
10 Pierce and possess the sky, guarding the halls
Where our young strength is welded strenuously;
While in the East, the star of morning dowers
The land with a large tremulous light, that falls
A pledge and presage of our destiny.

(1889)

At the Cedars
(To W.W.C.)

You had two girls – Baptiste –
One is Virginie –
Hold hard – Baptiste!
Listen to me.

The whole drive was jammed
In that bend at the Cedars,
The rapids were dammed
With the logs tight rammed
And crammed; you might know
10 The Devil had clinched them below.

We worked three days – not a budge,
"She's as tight as a wedge, on the ledge,"
Says our foreman;
"Mon Dieu! boys, look here,
We must get this thing clear."
He cursed at the men
And we went for it then;
With our cant-dogs arow,
We just gave he-yo-ho;
20 When she gave a big shove
From above.

The gang yelled and tore
For the shore,
The logs gave a grind
Like a wolf's jaws behind,
And as quick as a flash,
With a shove and a crash,
They were down in a mash,
But I and ten more,

30 All but Isaàc Dufour,
    Were ashore.

    He leaped on a log in the front of the rush,
    And shot out from the bind
    While the jam roared behind;
    As he floated along
    He balanced his pole
    And tossed us a song.
    But just as we cheered,
    Up darted a log from the bottom,
40 Leaped thirty feet square and fair,
    And came down on his own.

    He went up like a block
    With the shock,
    And when he was there
    In the air,
    Kissed his hand
    To the land;
    When he dropped
    My heart stopped,
50 For the first logs had caught him
    And crushed him;
    When he rose in his place
    There was blood on his face.

    There were some girls, Baptiste,
    Picking berries on the hillside,
    Where the river curls, Baptiste,
    You know – on the still side
    One was down by the water,
    She saw Isaàc
60 Fall back.

    She did not scream, Baptiste,
    She launched her canoe;

It did seem, Baptiste,
That she wanted to die too,
For before you could think
The birch cracked like a shell
In that rush of hell,
And I saw them both sink –

Baptiste! –
70 He had two girls,
One is Virginie,
What God calls the other
Is not known to me.

(1889)

The Onondaga Madonna

She stands full-throated and with careless pose,
This woman of a weird and waning race,
The tragic savage lurking in her face,
Where all her pagan passion burns and glows;
Her blood is mingled with her ancient foes,
And thrills with war and wildness in her veins;
Her rebel lips are dabbled with the stains
Of feuds and forays and her father's woes.

And closer in the shawl about her breast,
10 The latest promise of her nation's doom,
Paler than she her baby clings and lies,
The primal warrior gleaming from his eyes;
He sulks, and burdened with his infant gloom,
He draws his heavy brows and will not rest.

(1894)

Watkwenies*

Vengeance was once her nation's lore and law:
When the tired sentry stooped above the rill,
Her long knife flashed, and hissed, and drank its fill;
Dimly below her dripping wrist she saw,
One wild hand, pale as death and weak as straw,
Clutch at the ripple in the pool; while shrill
Sprang through the dreaming hamlet on the hill,
The war-cry of the triumphant Iroquois.

Now clothed with many an ancient flap and fold,
10 And wrinkled like an apple kept till May,
She weighs the interest-money in her palm,
And, when the Agent calls her valiant name,
Hears, like the war-whoops of her perished day,
The lads playing snow-snake in the stinging cold.

———

*The Woman who Conquers

(1898)

Night Hymns on Lake Nipigon

Here in the midnight, where the dark mainland and
island
Shadows mingle in shadow deeper, profounder,
Sing we the hymns of the churches, while the dead water
Whispers before us.

Thunder is travelling slow on the path of the lightning;
One after one the stars and the beaming planets
Look serene in the lake from the edge of the storm-cloud,
Then have they vanished.

While our canoe, that floats dumb in the bursting thunder,

10 Gathers her voice in the quiet and thrills and whispers,
     Presses her prow in the star-gleam, and all her ripple
          Lapses in blackness.

Sing we the sacred ancient hymns of the churches,
Chanted first in old-world nooks of the desert,
While in the wild, pellucid Nipigon reaches
     Hunted the savage.

Now have the ages met in the Northern midnight,
And on the lonely, loon-haunted Nipigon reaches
Rises the hymn of triumph and courage and comfort,
20   Adeste Fideles.

Tones that were fashioned when the faith brooded in
                                        darkness,
Joined with sonorous vowels in the noble Latin,
Now are married with the long-drawn Ojibwa,
     Uncouth and mournful.

Soft with the silver drip of the regular paddles
Falling in rhythm, timed with the liquid, plangent
Sounds from the blades where the whirlpools break and
                                        are carried
     Down into darkness;

Each long cadence, flying like a dove from her shelter
30 Deep in the shadow, wheels for a throbbing moment,
Poises in utterance, returning in circles of silver
     To nest in the silence.

All wild nature stirs with the infinite, tender
Plaint of a bygone age whose soul is eternal,
Bound in the lonely phrases that thrill and falter
     Back into quiet.

Back they falter as the deep storm overtakes them,
Whelms them in splendid hollows of booming thunder,
Wraps them in rain, that, sweeping, breaks and
                                            onrushes
40   Ringing like cymbals.

                                            (1900)

The Forsaken*

I

Once in the winter
Out on a lake
In the heart of the north-land,
Far from the Fort
And far from the hunters,
A Chippewa woman
With her sick baby,
Crouched in the last hours
Of a great storm.
10 Frozen and hungry,
She fished through the ice
With a line of the twisted
Bark of the cedar,
And a rabbit-bone hook
Polished and barbed;
Fished with the bare hook

---

* This story is true. The fact may be of interest and value,
perhaps, as proof of a well-known Indian characteristic,
although the incident, as material for poetry, gains nothing
in value from its truth. It was told me by the Hudson's Bay
Company's factor at Nepigon House. "Tikanagan" is the
Ojibeway word for the Indian cradle, about the construction
and uses of which a little chapter might be written. Huskies
are sledge dogs, a corruption of Eskimo.

All through the wild day,
Fished and caught nothing;
While the young chieftain
20 Tugged at her breasts,
Or slept in the lacings
Of the warm *tikanagan*.
All the lake-surface
Streamed with the hissing
Of millions of iceflakes
Hurled by the wind;
Behind her the round
Of a lonely island
Roared like a fire
30 With the voice of the storm
In the deeps of the cedars.
Valiant, unshaken,
She took of her own flesh,
Baited the fish-hook,
Drew in a gray-trout,
Drew in his fellows,
Heaped them beside her,
Dead in the snow.
Valiant, unshaken,
40 She faced the long distance,
Wolf-haunted and lonely,
Sure of her goal
And the life of her dear one:
Tramped for two days,
On the third in the morning,
Saw the strong bulk
Of the Fort by the river,
Saw the wood-smoke
Hang soft in the spruces,
50 Heard the keen yelp
Of the ravenous huskies

Fighting for whitefish:
Then she had rest.

II

Years and years after,
When she was old and withered,
When her son was an old man
And his children filled with vigour,
They came in their northern tour on the verge of winter,
To an island in a lonely lake.
60 There one night they camped, and on the morrow
Gathered their kettles and birch-bark
Their rabbit-skin robes and their mink-traps,
Launched their canoes and slunk away through the
                                                islands,
Left her alone forever,
Without a word of farewell,
Because she was old and useless,
Like a paddle broken and warped,
Or a pole that was splintered.
Then, without a sigh,
70 Valiant, unshaken,
She smoothed her dark locks under her kerchief,
Composed her shawl in state,
Then folded her hands ridged with sinews and corded
                                                with veins,
Folded them across her breasts spent with the
                                        nourishing of children,
Gazed at the sky past the tops of the cedars,
Saw two spangled nights arise out of the twilight,
Saw two days go by filled with the tranquil sunshine,
Saw, without pain, or dread, or even a moment of
                                                longing:
Then on the third great night there came thronging and
                                                thronging

80 Millions of snowflakes out of a windless cloud;
  They covered her close with a beautiful crystal shroud,
  Covered her deep and silent.
  But in the frost of the dawn,
  Up from the life below,
  Rose a column of breath
  Through a tiny cleft in the snow,
  Fragile, delicately drawn,
  Wavering with its own weakness,
  In the wilderness a sign of the spirit,
90 Persisting still in the sight of the sun
  Till day was done.
  Then all light was gathered up by the hand of God and
                                   hid in His breast,
  Then there was born a silence deeper than silence,
  Then she had rest.

                                                    (1903)

Dulse Gathering

We watched the tide with the current fight,
    And the shingle clash before
And the wild floods of fugitive light
    Play on the pale south-shore.

We gathered dulse that the sea had cast,
    In many a glistering heap;
We bore it back to the farm on the hill
    Where the corn and the flax-fields sleep.

There in the loft of an upland barn,
10   A league from its tossing bed,
It gathered salt and shrivelled with age
    To a parchment purple and red.

But still it holds the soul of the tide –
    This rag of wizened dulse;

The keen free scent and the tang of the salt
　　Brings the sea into the pulse.

And memories lone on the heart are hurled,
　　Like the waves on the shingle flung,
When the sun was young, and young was the world,
20　　When we were young.

(1905)

The Wood Peewee

He comes in Springtime with the breeze
　　That shakes the flowering maples,
He builds his nest in greening trees
　　Where shower and sunshine dapples;
When all the woods are tranced and still,
　　Amid the virgin leaves
His pensive note he sounds at will,
　　He grieves.

At dawning when the cool air floats,
10　　When dove-wing tints are streaming,
He, earliest of the early throats,
　　Begins his song adreaming;
While round his nest still clings the night,
　　He pipes in wistful flushes,
But when the wind lets in the light,
　　He hushes.

Yet is his heart with joyance filled
　　And not with brooding sadness;
If he might utter as he willed
20　　His strain would mount in gladness;
It meaneth joy in simple trust,
　　Though pensively it rings;
Not as he would but as he must
　　He sings.

(1905)

The Height of Land

Here is the height of land:
The watershed on either hand
Goes down to Hudson Bay
Or Lake Superior;
The stars are up, and far away
The wind sounds in the wood, wearier
Than the long Ojibwa cadence
In which Potàn the Wise
Declares the ills of life
10 And Chees-que-ne-ne makes a mournful sound
Of acquiescence. The fires burn low
With just sufficient glow
To light the flakes of ash that play
At being moths, and flutter away
To fall in the dark and die as ashes:
Here there is peace in the lofty air,
And Something comes by flashes
Deeper than peace; –
The spruces have retired a little space
20 And left a field of sky in violet shadow
With stars like marigolds in a water-meadow.

Now the Indian guides are dead asleep;
There is no sound unless the soul can hear
The gathering of the waters in their sources.

We have come up through the spreading lakes
From level to level, –
Pitching our tents sometimes over a revel
Of roses that nodded all night,
Dreaming within our dreams,
30 To wake at dawn and find that they were captured
With no dew on their leaves;
Sometimes mid sheaves

Of bracken and dwarf-cornel, and again
On a wide blueberry plain
Brushed with the shimmer of a bluebird' s wing;
A rocky islet followed
With one lone poplar and a single nest
Of white-throat-sparrows that took no rest
But sang in dreams or woke to sing, –
40 To the last portage and the height of land –:
Upon one hand
The lonely north enlaced with lakes and streams,
And the enormous targe of Hudson Bay,
Glimmering all night
In the cold arctic light;
On the other hand
The crowded southern land
With all the welter of the lives of men.
But here is peace, and again
50 That Something comes by flashes
Deeper than peace, – a spell
Golden and inappellable
That gives the inarticulate part
Of our strange being one moment of release
That seems more native than the touch of time,
And we must answer in chime;
Though yet no man may tell
The secret of that spell
Golden and inappellable.

60 Now are there sounds walking in the wood,
And all the spruces shiver and tremble,
And the stars move a little in their courses.
The ancient disturber of solitude
Breathes a pervasive sigh,
And the soul seems to hear
The gathering of the waters at their sources;

Then quiet ensues and pure starlight and dark;
The region-spirit murmurs in meditation,
The heart replies in exaltation
70 And echoes faintly like an inland shell
Ghost tremors of the spell;
Thought reawakens and is linked again
With all the welter of the lives of men.
Here on the uplands where the air is clear
We think of life as of a stormy scene, –
Of tempest, of revolt and desperate shock;
And here, where we can think, on the bright uplands
Where the air is clear, we deeply brood on life
Until the tempest parts, and it appears
80 As simple as to the shepherd seems his flock:
A Something to be guided by ideals –
That in themselves are simple and serene –
Of noble deed to foster noble thought,
And noble thought to image noble deed,
Till deed and thought shall interpenetrate,
Making life lovelier, till we come to doubt
Whether the perfect beauty that escapes
Is beauty of deed or thought or some high thing
Mingled of both, a greater boon than either:
90 Thus we have seen in the retreating tempest
The victor-sunlight merge with the ruined rain,
And from the rain and sunlight spring the rainbow.

The ancient disturber of solitude
Stirs his ancestral potion in the gloom,
And the dark wood
Is stifled with the pungent fume
Of charred earth burnt to the bone
That takes the place of air.
Then sudden I remember when and where, –
100 The last weird lakelet foul with weedy growths

And slimy viscid things the spirit loathes,
Skin of vile water over viler mud
Where the paddle stirred unutterable stenches,
And the canoes seemed heavy with fear,
Not to be urged toward the fatal shore
Where a bush fire, smouldering, with sudden roar
Leaped on a cedar and smothered it with light
And terror. It had left the portage-height
A tangle of slanted spruces burned to the roots,
110 Covered still with patches of bright fire
Smoking with incense of the fragrant resin
That even then began to thin and lessen
Into the gloom and glimmer of ruin.
'Tis overpast. How strange the stars have grown;
The presage of extinction glows on their crests
And they are beautied with impermanence;
They shall be after the race of men
And mourn for them who snared their fiery pinions,
Entangled in the meshes of bright words.

120 A lemming stirs the fern and in the mosses
Eft-minded things feel the air change, and dawn
Tolls out from the dark belfries of the spruces.
How often in the autumn of the world
Shall the crystal shrine of dawning be rebuilt
With deeper meaning! Shall the poet then,
Wrapped in his mantle on the height of land,
Brood on the welter of the lives of men
And dream of his ideal hope and promise
In the blush sunrise? Shall he base his flight
130 Upon a more compelling law than Love
As Life's atonement; shall the vision
Of noble deed and noble thought immingled
Seem as uncouth to him as the pictograph
Scratched on the cave side by the cave-dweller

To us of the Christ-time? Shall he stand
With deeper joy, with more complex emotion,
In closer commune with divinity,
With the deep fathomed, with the firmament charted,
With life as simple as a sheep-boy's song,
140 What lies beyond a romaunt that was read
Once on a morn of storm and laid aside
Memorious with strange immortal memories?
Or shall he see the sunrise as I see it
In shoals of misty fire the deluge-light
Dashes upon and whelms with purer radiance,
And feel the lulled earth, older in pulse and motion,
Turn the rich lands and the inundant oceans
To the flushed color, and hear as now I hear
The thrill of life beat up the planet's margin
150 And break in the clear susurrus of deep joy
That echoes and reëchoes in my being?
O Life is intuition the measure of knowledge
And do I stand with heart entranced and burning
At the zenith of our wisdom when I feel
The long light flow, the long wind pause, the deep
Influx of spirit, of which no man may tell
The Secret, golden and inappellable?

(1916)

The Closed Door

The dew falls and the stars fall,
The sun falls in the west,
But never more
Through the closed door,
Shall the one that I loved best
Return to me:
A salt tear is the sea,
All earth's air is a sigh,
But they never can mourn for me

10 With my heart's cry,
    For the one that I loved best
    Who caressed me with her eyes,
    And every morning came to me,
    With the beauty of sunrise,
    Who was health and wealth and all,
    Who never shall answer my call,
    While the sun falls in the west,
    The dew falls and the stars fall.

                            (1916)

To a Canadian Aviator Who Died
for His Country in France

Tossed like a falcon from the hunter's wrist,
A sweeping plunge, a sudden shattering noise,
And thou has dared, with a long spiral twist,
The elastic stairway to the rising sun.
Peril below thee and above, peril
Within thy car; but peril cannot daunt
Thy peerless heart: gathering wing and poise,
Thy plane transfigured, and thy motor-chant
Subduèd to a whisper – then a silence, –
10 And thou art but a disembodied venture
In the void.

But Death, who has learned to fly,
Still matchless when his work is to be done,
Met thee between the armies and the sun;
Thy speck of shadow faltered in the sky;
Then thy dead engine and thy broken wings
Drooped through the arc and passed in fire,
A wreath of smoke – a breathless exhalation.
But ere that came a vision sealed thine eyes,
20 Lulling thy senses with oblivion;

And from its sliding station in the skies
Thy dauntless soul upward in circles soared
To the sublime and purest radiance whence it sprang.

In all their eyries, eagles shall mourn thy fate,
And leaving on the lonely crags and scaurs
Their unprotected young, shall congregate
High in the tenuous heaven and anger the sun
With screams, and with a wild audacity
Dare all the battle danger of thy flight;
30 Till weary with combat one shall desert the light,
Fall like a bolt of thunder and check his fall
On the high ledge, smoky with mist and cloud,
Where his neglected eaglets shriek aloud,
And drawing the film across his sovereign sight
Shall dream of thy swift soul immortal
Mounting in circles, faithful beyond death.

(1917)

En Route

The train has stopped for no apparent reason
In the wilds;
A frozen lake is level and fretted over
With rippled wind lines;
The sun is burning in the South; the season
Is winter trembling at a touch of spring.
A little hill with birches and a ring
Of cedars – all so still, so pure with snow –
It seems a tiny landscape in the moon.
10 Long wisps of shadow from the naked birches
Lie on the white in lines of cobweb-grey;
From the cedar roots the snow has shrunk away,
One almost hears it tinkle as it thaws.
Traces there are of wild things in the snow –
Partridge at play, tracks of the foxes' paws

That broke a path to sun them in the trees.
They're going fast where all impressions go
On a frail substance – images like these,
Vagaries the unconscious mind receives
From nowhere, and lets go to nothingness
With the lost flush of last year's autumn leaves.

[1930-31] (1935)

At Gull Lake: August, 1810

Gull Lake set in the rolling prairie –
Still there are reeds on the shore,
As of old the poplars shimmer
As summer passes;
Winter freezes the shallow lake to the core;
Storm passes,
Heat parches the sedges and grasses,
Night comes with moon-glimmer,
Dawn with the morning-star;
10 All proceeds in the flow of Time
As a hundred years ago.

Then two camps were pitched on the shore,
The clustered teepees
Of Tabashaw Chief of the Saulteaux.
And on a knoll tufted with poplars
Two gray tents of a trader –
Nairne of the Orkneys.
Before his tents under the shade of the poplars
Sat Keejigo, third of the wives
20 Of Tabashaw Chief of the Saulteaux;
Clad in the skins of antelopes
Broidered with porcupine quills
Coloured with vivid dyes,

Vermilion here and there
In the roots of her hair,
A half-moon of powder-blue
On her brow, her cheeks
Scored with light ochre streaks.
Keejigo daughter of Launay
30 The Normandy hunter
And Oshawan of the Saulteaux,
Troubled by fugitive visions
In the smoke of the camp-fires,
In the close dark of the teepee,
Flutterings of colour
Along the flow of the prairies,
Spangles of flower tints
Caught in the wonder of dawn,
Dreams of sounds unheard –
40 The echoes of echo,
Star she was named for
Keejigo, star of the morning,
Voices of storm –
Wind-rush and lightning, –
The beauty of terror;
The twilight moon
Coloured like a prairie lily,
The round moon of pure snow,
The beauty of peace;
50 Premonitions of love and of beauty
Vague as shadows cast by a shadow.
Now she had found her hero,
And offered her body and spirit
With abject unreasoning passion,
As Earth abandons herself
To the sun and the thrust of the lightning.
Quiet were all the leaves of the poplars,
Breathless the air under their shadow,

As Keejigo spoke of these things to her heart
60 In the beautiful speech of the Saulteaux.

> *The flower lives on the prairie,*
> *The wind in the sky,*
> *I am here my beloved;*
> *The wind and the flower.*
>
> *The crane hides in the sand-hills,*
> *Where does the wolverine hide?*
> *I am here my beloved,*
> *Heart's-blood on the feathers*
> *The foot caught in the trap.*
>
> 70 *Take the flower in your hand,*
> *The wind in your nostrils;*
> *I am here my beloved;*
> *Release the captive*
> *Heal the wound under the feathers.*

A storm-cloud was marching
Vast on the prairie,
Scored with livid ropes of hail,
Quick with nervous vines of lightning –
Twice had Nairne turned her away
80 Afraid of the venom of Tabashaw,
Twice had the Chief fired at his tents
And now when two bullets
Whistled above the encampment
He yelled "Drive this bitch to her master."

Keejigo went down a path by the lake;
Thick at the tangled edges,
The reeds and the sedges
Were gray as ashes
Against the death-black water;
90 The lightning scored with double flashes

The dark lake-mirror and loud
Came the instant thunder.
Her lips still moved to the words of her music,
"Release the captive,
Heal the wound under the feathers."

At the top of the bank
The old wives caught her and cast her down
Where Tabashaw crouched by his camp-fire.
He snatched a live brand from the embers,
100 Seared her cheeks,
Blinded her eyes,
Destroyed her beauty with fire,
Screaming, "Take that face to your lover."
Keejigo held her face to the fury
And made no sound.
The old wives dragged her away
And threw her over the bank
Like a dead dog.

Then burst the storm –
110 The Indians' screams and the howls of the dogs
Lost in the crash of hail
That smashed the sedges and reeds,
Stripped the poplars of leaves,
Tore and blazed onwards,
Wasting itself with riot and tumult –
Supreme in the beauty of terror.
The setting sun struck the retreating cloud
With a rainbow, not an arc but a column
Built with the glory of seven metals;
120 Beyond in the purple deeps of the vortex
Fell the quivering vines of the lightning.
The wind withdrew the veil from the shrine of the moon,
She rose changing her dusky shade for the glow
Of the prairie lily, till free of all blemish of colour

She came to her zenith without a cloud or a star,
A lovely perfection, snow-pure in the heaven of
                                        midnight.
After the beauty of terror the beauty of peace.

But Keejigo came no more to the camps of her people;
Only the midnight moon knew where she felt her way,
130 Only the leaves of autumn, the snows of winter
Knew where she lay.

                                                (1935)

Chiostro Verde

Here in the old Green Cloister
At Santa Maria Novella
The grey well in the centre
Is dry to the granite curb;
No splashing will ever disturb
The cool depth of the shaft.
In the stone-bordered quadrangle
Daisies, in galaxy, spangle
The vivid cloud of grass.
10 Four young cypresses fold
Themselves in their mantles of shadow
Away from the sun's hot gold;
And roses revel in the light,
Hundreds of roses; if one could gather
The flush that fades over the Arno
Under Venus at sundown
And dye a snow-rose with the colour,
The ghost of the flame on the snow
Might give to a painter the glow
20 Of these roses.
Above the roof of the cloister
Rises the rough church wall

Worn with the tides of Time.
The burnished pigeons climb
And slide in the shadowed air,
Wing-whispering everywhere,
Coo and murmur and call
From their nooks in the crannied wall.
Then on the rustling space,
30 Falling with delicate grace,
Boys' voices from the far off choir,
The full close of a phrase,
A cadence of Palestrina
Or something of even older days,
No words – only the tune.
It dies now – too soon.
Will music forever die,
The soul bereft of its cry,
And no young throats
40 Vibrate to clear new notes?
While the cadence was hovering in air
The pigeons were flying
In front of the seasoned stone,
Visiting here and there,
Cooing from the cool shade
Of their nooks in the wall;
Who taught the pigeons their call
Their murmurous music?

Under the roof of the cloister
50 A few frescoes are clinging
Made by Paolo Uccello,
Once they were clear and mellow
Now they have fallen away
To a dull green-gray,
What has not fallen will fall;
Of all colour bereft

Will nothing at last be left
But a waste wall?
Will painting forever perish,
60 Will no one be left to cherish
The beauty of life and the world,
Will the soul go blind of the vision?
Who painted those silver lights in the daisies
That sheen in the grass-cloud
That hides their stars or discloses,
Who stained the bronze-green shroud
Wrapping the cypress
Who painted the roses?

(1935)

SOPHIA ALMON HENSLEY

1866–1946

Born in Bridgetown, Nova Scotia, Sophia Almon Hensley
was educated in England and in Paris before becoming a
literary protégée of Charles G.D. Roberts while she was
living in Windsor, Nova Scotia, in the late 1880s. After her
marriage in 1889, she lived in New York, London, and the
Channel Islands, returning regularly to Nova Scotia in the
summers, and eventually retiring to Windsor. In addition
to three volumes of poetry – *Poems* (1889), *A Woman's Love
Letters* (1895), and *The Heart of a Woman* (1906) – she
wrote a prose work, *Love and the Woman of Tomorrow*
(1913), which explicitly expresses her feminist ideas.

Rondeau – When Summer Comes

When summer comes, and when o'er hill and lea
The sun's strong wooing glow hath patiently
    Shed o'er the earth long days his golden dower,
    And then, by force of his own loving power,
Drawn the hard frost, and left it passive, free
To give forth all its sweets untiringly,
Shall not the day rise fair for thee and me,
    And all life seem but as an opening flower
        When summer comes?

10 The days move slowly, young hearts yearn to be
Together always, cannot brook to see
    Their love-days pass, and void each sunny hour,
    Yet may we smile, e'en when fate's storm-clouds lower,
Waiting fulfilment of our hearts' decree
        When summer comes.

                           (1889)

Slack Tide

My boat is still in the reedy cove
Where the rushes hinder its onward course,
For I care not now if we rest or move
O'er the slumberous tide to the river's source.

My boat is fast in the tall dank weeds
And I lay my oars in silence by,
And lean, and draw the slippery reeds
Through my listless fingers carelessly.

The bubbling froth of the surface foam
10 Clings close to the side of my moveless boat,
Like endless meshes of honeycomb, –
And I break it off, and send it afloat.

A faint wind stirs, and I drift along
Far down the stream to its utmost bound,
And the thick white foam-flakes gathering strong
Still cling, and follow, and fold around.

Oh! the weary green of the weedy waste,
The thickening scum of the frothy foam,
And the torpid heart by the reeds embraced
20 And shrouded and held in its cheerless home.

The fearful stillness of wearied calm,
The tired quiet of ended strife,
The echoed note of a heart's sad psalm,
The sighing end of a wasted life. –

The reeds cling close, and my cradle sways,
And the white gull dips in the waters' barm,
And the heart asleep in the twilight haze
Feels not its earth-bonds, knows not alarm.

(1889)

Triumph

The sky, grown dull through many waiting days,
    Flashed into crimson with the sunrise charm,
    So all my love, aroused to vague alarm,
Flushed into fire and burned with eager blaze.
I saw thee not as suppliant, with still gaze
    Of pleading, but as victor, – and thine arm
    Gathered me fast into embraces warm,
And I was taught the light of Love's dear ways.

This day of triumph is no longer thine,
10   Oh conqueror, in calm exclusive power. –
As evermore, through storm, and shade, and shine,
      Your woe my pain, your joy my ecstasy,
We breathe together, – so this blessed hour
      Of self-surrender makes my jubilee!

                    (1889)

Guiltless

She felt a touch of genuine pity rise,
And for an instant dim those wondrous eyes!

For, as he lay there, happy, at her feet,
Thinking the world so fair, and love so sweet,

She knew, more wise than he, the coming gloom
That soon must end his bliss and shroud his doom.

She, leaning, said, "Why waste the precious hours
"In fancies vain o'er quickly fading flowers.

"Soon will the vision melt and die away
10 "In the dim shadows of the waning day.

"As you love liberty, and life, and good,
"So trust not to a woman's changeful mood.

"Know you to souls like yours I can but bring
"Evil, and pain, and blind heart-sorrowing."

She laid her hand soft on his golden head.
"Go, while there is yet time," she gently said.

———

With upturned face he answered. Slow and clear
The words fell on the tranquil evening air:

20 "If I could know that, vampire-like, you drew
"My life-blood daily from me, – if I knew

"That just one drop of vital force remained,
"And I might leave you, life and freedom gained,

"I should not move, – but, striving to compress
"In that brief hour a life time happiness,

"Would give, with one dear thrill of ecstasy
"Even that drop, as you required, – and die."

———

The sunset tint halowed her queenly head.
30 "Ah well! so be it then," she lightly said.

(1895)

Somewhere in France

1918

Leave me alone here, proudly, with my dead,
    Ye mothers of brave sons adventurous;
He who once prayed: "If it be possible
    Let this cup pass" will arbitrate for us.
Your boy with iron nerves and careless smile
    Marched gaily by and dreamed of glory's goal;
Mine had blanched cheek, straight mouth and close-
                                gripped hands
    And prayed that somehow he might save his soul.

I do not grudge your ribbon or your cross,
10   The price of these my soldier, too, has paid;
I hug a prouder knowledge to my heart,
    The mother of the boy who was afraid!

He was a tender child with nerves so keen
    They doubled pain and magnified the sad;
He hated cruelty and things obscene
    And in all high and holy things was glad.
And so he gave what others could not give,
    The one supremest sacrifice he made,
A thing your brave boy could not understand;
20   He gave his all because he was afraid!

                   (1918)

SUSAN FRANCES HARRISON
("SERANUS")

1859–1935

Born in Toronto, her home for most of her life, Susan Frances Harrison developed a diversified career as a poet, novelist, journalist, musician, composer, and lecturer on the culture of French Canada. Under the pen name "Seranus" (derived from a misreading of her signature, S. Frances), she published a collection of stories, two novels, and six books and chapbooks of poetry. Her first volume of poems, *Pine, Rose, and Fleur de Lis* (1891), expresses the fascination with French Canada that informs much of her work.

March

With outstretched whirring wings of vandyked jet,
Two crows one day o'er house and pavement pass'd.
Swift silhouettes limned against the blue, they glass'd
Smooth beak and ebon feather in the wet
Of gaping pool and gutter, while, beset
By nestward longing, high their hoarse cry cast
In the face of fickle sun and treacherous blast,
Till all the City smelt the violet.

Then through that City quick the news did run.
10 Great wheels were slacken'd; belts were stopped in mill,
And fires in forges. Long ere set of sun
Dazed men, pale women sought the open hill –
They throng'd the streets. They caught the clarion cry –
"Spring has come back – trust Spring to never die!"

(1891)

Interim

We must have lain here for an hour or more,
    With a birch above for a ceiling –
We were both so glad to get ashore!

We sang as the skiff we rockward bore,
    With the eagle aloft and wheeling!
We must have lain here for an hour or more,

Learning again the sweet land lore,
    With the air so warm and healing!
We were both so glad to get ashore.

10 Watching the cumuli slowly soar,
    All the blue beneath revealing,
We must have lain here for an hour or more.

Brown pine tassels bestrew the floor,
    With the red birch fit for peeling!
We were both so glad to get ashore.

The summer's heart is ripe to the core,
    With our own hearts madly reeling!
We must have lain here for an hour or more,
We were both so glad to get ashore!

                (1891)

Les Chantiers

For know, my girl, there is always the axe
    Ready at hand in this latitude,
And how it stings and bites and hacks

When Alphonse the sturdy trees attacks!
    So fear, child, to cross him, or play the prude,
For know, my girl, there is always the axe.

See! it shines even now as his hands relax
  Their grip with a dread desire imbu'd,
And how it stings and bites and hacks,

10 And how it rips and cuts and cracks
  – Perhaps – in his brain as the foe is pursu'd,
For know, my girl, there is always the axe.

The giant boles in the forest tracks
  Stagger, soul-smitten, when afar it is view'd,
And how it stings and bites and hacks!

Then how, Madelon, should its fearful thwacks
  A slender lad like your own elude?
For know, my girl, there is always the axe,
And how it stings! and bites! and hacks!

         (1891)

September

I

Birds that were gray in the green are black in the yellow.
Here where the green remains rocks one little fellow.

Quaker in gray, do you know that the green is going?
More than that – do you know that the yellow is
         showing?

II

Singer of songs, do you know that your Youth is flying?
That Age will soon at the lock of your life be prying?

Lover of life, do you know that the brown is going?
More than that – do you know that the gray is showing?

         (1891)

Niagara in Winter

Nor similes nor metaphors avail!
All imagery vanishes, device
Dies in thy presence, wondrous dream of ice!
Ice-bound I stand, my face is pinched and pale,
Before such awful majesty I fail,
Sink low on this snow-lichened slab of gneiss,
Shut out the gleaming mass that can entice,
Enchain, enchant, but in whose light I quail.

While I from under frozen lashes peer,
10 My thoughts fly back and take a homeward course.
How dear to dwell in sweet placidity,
Instead of these colossal crystals, see
The slender icicles of some fairy "force,"
And break the film upon an English mere!

(1891)

PAULINE JOHNSON

1861–1913

Born on the Six Nations Reserve near Brantford, Ontario, to an English mother and a Mohawk father, Pauline Johnson chose to identify strongly with her Native heritage, publishing her poems and stories in newspapers and magazines. After she discovered her gift for oral performance in 1892, she toured Europe and North America for nearly two decades, presenting her poems in venues ranging from upper-class drawing rooms to frontier stages. Her first book of poetry, *The White Wampum* (1895), was followed by two more volumes of poetry and three of prose.

Re-Voyage

What of the days when we two dreamed together?
    Days marvellously fair,
As lightsome as a skyward floating feather
    Sailing on summer air –
Summer, summer, that came drifting through
Fate's hand to me, to you.

What of the days, my dear? I sometimes wonder
    If you too wish this sky
Could be the blue we sailed so softly under,
10   In that sun-kissed July;
Sailed in the warm and yellow afternoon,
With hearts in touch and tune.

Have you no longing to re-live the dreaming,
    Adrift in my canoe?
To watch my paddle blade all wet and gleaming
    Cleaving the waters through?
To lie wind-blown and wave-caressed, until
Your restless pulse grows still?

Do you not long to listen to the purling
20   Of foam athwart the keel?
To hear the nearing rapids softly swirling
    Among their stones, to feel
The boat's unsteady tremor as it braves
The wild and snarling waves?

What need of question, what of your replying?
    Oh! well I know that you
Would toss the world away to be but lying
    Again in my canoe,
In listless indolence entranced and lost,
30 Wave-rocked, and passion tossed.

Ah me! my paddle failed me in the steering
    Across love's shoreless seas;
All reckless, I had ne'er a thought of fearing
    Such dreary days as these,
When through the self-same rapids we dash by,
My lone canoe and I.

                      (1891)

The Song My Paddle Sings

West wind blow from your prairie nest?
Blow from the mountains, blow from the west.
The sail is idle, the sailor too;
O! wind of the west, we wait for you.
Blow, blow!
I have wooed you so,
But never a favour you bestow.
You rock your cradle the hills between,
But scorn to notice my white lateen.

10 I stow the sail, unship the mast:
I wooed you long but my wooing's past;
My paddle will lull you into rest.

O! drowsy wind of the drowsy west,
Sleep, sleep,
By your mountain steep,
Or down where the prairie grasses sweep!
Now fold in slumber your laggard wings,
For soft is the song my paddle sings.

August is laughing across the sky,
20 Laughing while paddle, canoe and I,
Drift, drift,
Where the hills uplift
On either side of the current swift.

The river rolls in its rocky bed;
My paddle is plying its way ahead;
Dip, dip,
While the waters flip
In foam as over their breast we slip.

And oh, the river runs swifter now;
30 The eddies circle about my bow.
Swirl, swirl!
How the ripples curl
In many a dangerous pool awhirl!

And forward far the rapids roar,
Fretting their margin for evermore.
Dash, dash,
With a mighty crash,
They seethe, and boil, and bound, and splash.

Be strong, O paddle! be brave, canoe!
40 The reckless waves you must plunge into.
Reel, reel,
On your trembling keel,
But never a fear my craft will feel.

We've raced the rapid, we're far ahead!
The river slips through its silent bed.
Sway, sway,
As the bubbles spray
And fall in tinkling tunes away.

And up on the hills against the sky,
50 A fir tree rocking its lullaby,
Swings, swings,
Its emerald wings,
Swelling the song that my paddle sings.
                                        (1892)

Ojistoh

I am Ojistoh, I am she, the wife
Of him whose name breathes bravery and life
And courage to the tribe that calls him chief.
I am Ojistoh, his white star, and he
Is land, and lake, and sky – and soul to me.

Ah! but they hated him, those Huron braves,
Him who had flung their warriors into graves,
Him who had crushed them underneath his heel,
Whose arm was iron, and whose heart was steel
10 To all – save me, Ojistoh, chosen wife
Of my great Mohawk, white star of his life.

Ah! but they hated him, and councilled long
With subtle witchcraft how to work him wrong;
How to avenge their dead, and strike him where
His pride was highest, and his fame most fair.
Their hearts grew weak as women at his name:
They dared no war-path since my Mohawk came
With ashen bow, and flinten arrow-head
To pierce their craven bodies; but their dead

20 Must be avenged. Avenged? They dared not walk
   In day and meet his deadly tomahawk;
   They dared not face his fearless scalping knife;
   So – Niyoh! * – then they thought of me, his wife.

   O! evil, evil face of them they sent
   With evil Huron speech: "Would I consent
   To take of wealth? be queen of all their tribe?
   Have wampum ermine?" Back I flung the bribe
   Into their teeth, and said, "While I have life
   Know this – Ojistoh is the Mohawk's wife."

30 Wah! how we struggled! But their arms were strong.
   They flung me on their pony's back, with thong
   Round ankle, wrist, and shoulder. Then upleapt
   The one I hated most: his eye he swept
   Over my misery, and sneering said,
   "Thus, fair Ojistoh, we avenge our dead."

   And we two rode, rode as a sea wind-chased,
   I, bound with buckskin to his hated waist,
   He, sneering, laughing, jeering, while he lashed
   The horse to foam, as on and on we dashed.
40 Plunging through creek and river, bush and trail,
   On, on we galloped like a northern gale.
   At last, his distant Huron fires aflame
   We saw, and nearer, nearer still we came.

   I, bound behind him in the captive's place,
   Scarcely could see the outline of his face.
   I smiled, and laid my cheek against his back:
   "Loose thou my hands," I said. "This pace let slack.
   Forget we now that thou and I are foes.
   I like thee well, and wish to clasp thee close;

----

* God, in the Mohawk language.

50 I like the courage of thine eye and brow;
    I like thee better than my Mohawk now."

He cut the cords; we ceased our maddened haste
I wound my arms about his tawny waist;
My hand crept up the buckskin of his belt;
His knife hilt in my burning palm I felt;
One hand caressed his cheek, the other drew
The weapon softly – "I love you, love you,"
I whispered, "love you as my life."
And – buried in his back his scalping knife.

60 Ha! how I rode, rode as a sea wind-chased,
    Mad with sudden freedom, mad with haste,
    Back to my Mohawk and my home. I lashed
    That horse to foam, as on and on I dashed.
    Plunging thro' creek and river, bush and trail,
    On, on I galloped like a northern gale.
    And then my distant Mohawk's fires aflame
    I saw, as nearer, nearer still I came,
    My hands all wet, stained with a life's red dye,
    But pure my soul, pure as those stars on high –
70 "My Mohawk's pure white star, Ojistoh, still am I."
                                            [1893] (1895)

Marshlands

A thin wet sky, that yellows at the rim,
And meets with sun-lost lip the marsh's brim.

The pools low lying, dank with moss and mould,
Glint through their mildews like large cups of gold.

Among the wild rice in the still lagoon,
In monotone the lizard shrills his tune.

The wild goose, homing, seeks a sheltering,
Where rushes grow, and oozing lichens cling.

Late cranes with heavy wing, and lazy flight,
10 Sail up the silence with the nearing night.

And like a spirit, swathed in some soft veil,
Steals twilight and its shadows o'er the swale.

Hushed lie the sedges, and the vapours creep,
Thick, grey and humid, while the marshes sleep.

(1895)

The Idlers

The sun's red pulses beat,
Full prodigal of heat,
Full lavish of its lustre unrepressed;
But we have drifted far
From where his kisses are,
And in this landward-lying shade we let our paddles
rest.

The river, deep and still,
The maple-mantled hill,
The little yellow beach whereon we lie,
10 The puffs of heated breeze,
All sweetly whisper – These
Are days that only come in a Canadian July.

So, silently we two
Lounge in our still canoe,
Nor fate, nor fortune matters to us now:
So long as we alone
May call this dream our own,
The breeze may die, the sail may droop, we care not
when or how.

Against the thwart, near by,
20 Inactively you lie,
And all too near my arm your temple bends.

Your indolently crude,
Abandoned attitude,
Is one of ease and art, in which a perfect languor blends.

Your costume, loose and light,
Leaves unconcealed your might
Of muscle, half suspected, half defined;
And falling well aside,
Your vesture opens wide,
30 Above your splendid sunburnt throat that pulses
                                        unconfined.

With easy unreserve,
Across the gunwale's curve,
Your arm superb is lying, brown and bare;
Your hand just touches mine
With import firm and fine,
(I kiss the very wind that blows about your tumbled
                                        hair).

Ah! Dear, I am unwise
In echoing your eyes
Whene'er they leave their far-off gaze, and turn
40 To melt and blur my sight;
For every other light
Is servile to your cloud-grey eyes, wherein cloud
                                        shadows burn.

But once the silence breaks,
But once your ardour wakes
To words that humanize this lotus-land;
So perfect and complete
Those burning words and sweet,
So perfect is the single kiss your lips lay on my hand.

The paddles lie disused,
50 The fitful breeze abused,

Has dropped to slumber, with no after-blow;
And hearts will pay the cost,
For you and I have lost
More than the homeward blowing wind that died an
                              hour ago.

                                    (1895)

The Corn Husker

Hard by the Indian lodges, where the bush
    Breaks in a clearing, through ill-fashioned fields,
She comes to labour, when the first still hush
    Of autumn follows large and recent yields.

Age in her fingers, hunger in her face,
    Her shoulders stooped with weight of work and years,
But rich in tawny colouring of her race,
    She comes a-field to strip the purple ears.

And all her thoughts are with the days gone by,
10   Ere might's injustice banished from their lands
Her people, that to-day unheeded lie,
    Like the dead husks that rustle through her hands.

                                    (1903)

Low Tide at St. Andrews

(New Brunswick)

The long red flats stretch open to the sky,
Breathing their moisture on the August air.
The seaweeds cling with flesh-like fingers where
The rocks give shelter that the sands deny;
And wrapped in all her summer harmonies
St. Andrews sleeps beside her sleeping seas.

The far-off shores swim blue and indistinct,
Like half-lost memories of some old dream.

The listless waves that catch each sunny gleam
10 Are idling up the waterways land-linked,
And, yellowing along the harbour's breast,
The light is leaping shoreward from the west.

And naked-footed children, tripping down,
Light with young laughter, daily come at eve
To gather dulse and sea clams and then heave
Their loads, returning laden to the town,
Leaving a strange grey silence when they go, –
The silence of the sands when tides are low.

(1903)

Lullaby of the Iroquois

Little brown baby-bird, lapped in your nest,
Wrapped in your nest,
Strapped in your nest,
Your straight little cradle-board rocks you to rest;
Its hands are your nest;
Its bands are your nest;
It swings from the down-bending branch of the oak;
You watch the camp flame, and the curling grey smoke;
But, oh, for your pretty black eyes sleep is best, –
10 Little brown baby of mine, go to rest.

Little brown baby-bird swinging to sleep,
Winging to sleep,
Singing to sleep,
Your wonder-black eyes that so wide open keep,
Shielding their sleep,
Unyielding to sleep,
The heron is homing, the plover is still,
The night-owl calls from his haunt on the hill,
Afar the fox barks, afar the stars peep, –
20 Little brown baby of mine, go to sleep.

(1903)

Silhouette

The sky-line melts from the russet into blue,
Unbroken the horizon, saving where
A wreath of smoke curls up the far, thin air,
And points the distant lodges of the Sioux.

Etched where the lands and cloudlands touch and die
A solitary Indian tepee stands,
The only habitation of these lands,
That roll their magnitude from sky to sky.

The tent poles lift and loom in thin relief,
10 The upward floating smoke ascends between,
And near the open doorway, gaunt and lean,
And shadow-like, there stands an Indian Chief.

With eyes that lost their lustre long ago,
With visage fixed and stern as fate's decree,
He looks towards the empty west, to see
The never-coming herd of buffalo.

Only the bones that bleach upon the plains,
Only the fleshless skeletons that lie
In ghastly nakedness and silence, cry
20 Out mutely that naught else to him remains.

(1903)

The Train Dogs

Out of the night and the north;
    Savage of breed and of bone,
Shaggy and swift comes the yelping band,
Freighters of fur from the voiceless land
    That sleeps in the Arctic zone.

Laden with skins from the north,
    Beaver and bear and raccoon,

Marten and mink from the polar belts,
Otter and ermine and sable pelts –
10   The spoils of the hunter's moon.

Out of the night and the north,
    Sinewy, fearless and fleet,
Urging the pack through the pathless snow,
The Indian driver, calling low,
    Follows with moccasined feet.

Ships of the night and the north,
    Freighters on prairies and plains,
Carrying cargoes from field and flood
They scent the trail through their wild red blood,
20   The wolfish blood in their veins.

(1904)

KATE SIMPSON HAYES

1852–1943

Born in New Brunswick, Kate Simpson Hayes was the first woman journalist in Western Canada, where she enjoyed a colourful and varied career. As "Mary Markwell" she enlivened the pages of the Regina *Leader* and later the Manitoba *Free Press* with her versatility and wit. Her first book, *Prairie Pot-Pourri*, published in Winnipeg in 1895, was followed by a novel and a volume of verse, *Derby Day in the Yukon* (1910), the latter issued under the pseudonym "Yukon Bill."

Riel

A wandering Wild-bird from its prairie nest
    Roamed amid clouds beneath an alien sky;
The poise of eagle in that haughty crest,
    And one wild dream: Higher and still more high
And o'er this lovely prairie land there fell
The blight of a proud heart's unrest: Riel!

Slumbered the camp. The fields were fair to see;
    Wigwam and shack grouped 'neath a peaceful sky,
And over this young land the bonds of harmony
10   Were rudely broken by a fierce war-cry –
And on swift wings of Hate from Passion's hell
Rose hand 'gainst brother's hand: Riel!

Above the din of battle, hollow sounds
    Of drum, sad dying moans we hear.
Empty saddles, broken ranks, new-made mounds
    Upon the prairie's bleeding breast. Then a British cheer
That ends in a wild wail! from wigwam hear the swell
In that deep cry of anguish and reproach: Riel!

Oh, Wild-bird! had'st thou raised thy voice –
20   Not in a note of discord – but in song

That would have made this prairie land rejoice
    To call thee son! But thou did'st quicken wrong,
And left to Time saddest of words to tell: –
Writ in his brother's blood the rebel name: Riel!

                                      (1895)

Prairie Verses

The smile of summer fainter grows and colder;
    The wild flower cowers close to drooping stem;
The wind grown keen and wild, now waxes bolder,
    Chills the soft dew, and makes each drop a gem.
From latticed clouds a burst of sunlit glory
    Wakes the dull fields mounded with yellow grain,
Rivalling the wild-bird comes the herd-boy's story,
    In joyous notes re-echoing across the rolling plain.
This storied land with all its dawning splendour
10   Touches the heart with a joy that breaks in pain,
Awakening regret for days that are no more, and tender
    Memories of happiness that long hath silent lain.

The prairie grasses twine green fingers close,
    The wild flowers bud and bloom, then with a sigh
Join in the west wind's frolic, first a dance
    Then a wild rush onward, and the sky
Frowns darkling down; Summer eyes askance
    Then timidly glides by.

Swift with blinding gloss
20   The snow comes like some fairy,
Mounting the stacks and covering the way;
    Sheltering the weakly roots that sway and curve and toss
Before the north wind coming down with sleet in battle
                                    fray,

    And in a sheen of brightest light
'Tis winter on the prairie.

                                        (1895)

AGNES ETHELWYN WETHERALD

1857–1940

Born into a large Quaker family in Rockwood, Ontario, Agnes Ethelwyn Wetherald spent several decades around the turn of the century working as a journalist, editorial assistant, and proof-reader in Toronto and the north-eastern United States. She returned to assist with the family farm near Fenwick, on the Niagara peninsula, where she spent the rest of her life. Her first book of poems, *The House of the Trees* (1895), was followed by five more books of poetry, the last of which, *Lyrics and Sonnets* (1931), includes an autobiographical memoir.

October

Against the winter's heav'n of white the blood
   Of earth runs very quick and hot to-day;
   A storm of fiery leaves are out at play
Around the lingering sunset of the wood.
Where rows of blackberries unnoticed stood,
   Run streams of ruddy color wildly gay;
   The golden lane half dreaming picks its way
Through whelming vines, as through a gleaming flood.

O warm outspoken earth, a little space
10   Against thy beating heart my heart shall beat,
    A little while they twain shall bleed and burn,
And then the cold touch and the gray, gray face,
   The frozen pulse, the drifted winding-sheet,
    And speechlessness, and the chill burial urn.

               (1895)

The Humming-bird

Against my window-pane
    He plunges at a mass
Of buds – and strikes in vain
    The intervening glass.

O sprite of wings and fire
    Outstretching eagerly,
My soul, with like desire
    To probe thy mystery,

Comes close as breast to bloom,
10   As bud to hot heart-beat,
And gains no inner room,
    And drains no hidden sweet.

                    (1895)

June Apples

Green apple branches full of green apples
    All around me unfurled,
Here where the shade and the sunlight dapples
    A grass-green, apple-green world.

Little green children stirred with the heaving
    Of the warm breast of the air,
When your old nurse, the wind, is grieving
    Comfortlessly you fare.

But now an old-time song she is crooning,
10   Nestle your heads again,
While I dream on through the golden nooning,
    Or look for the first red stain

On some round cheek that the sunshine dapples,
    Near me where I lie curled
Under green trees athrong with green apples,
    In a grass-green, apple-green world.

                    (1895)

The World Well Lost

My one dark love shall fix the day,
   The solemn day when we shall wed;
Nor know I if on green or gray,
   On winter white or autumn red,

My happy bridal moon shall rise,
   Nor which of all the blossoming Mays
Shall wreathe the gates of Paradise
   Upon my dark love's day of days.

But this I know: her steps will be
10   Like rose-leaves falling from the rose,
Her eyes a fathomless strange sea
   To which my stream of being flows.

And this I know: her lips will rest
   As lightly on the drowsing lid
As leafy shadows on the breast
   Of some sweet grave all flower-hid.

In some sweet grave all flower-hid
   A thousand times the blooms of May
Shall visit us the leaves amid,
20   When my love, Death, has named the day.

                     (1907)

A Winter Picture

An air as sharp as steel, a sky
   Pierced with a million points of fire;
The level fields, hard, white and dry,
   A road as straight and tense as wire.

No hint of human voice or face
   In frost below or fire above,
Save where the smoke's blue billowing grace
   Flies flag-like from the roofs of love.

                     (1907)

Each to Her Own

One took me to a skyward-climbing vine,
    Behind whose pointed leaves a poet sang
    Soul-stealingly, so that the stones outrang
In praise of her, and hearts that ache and pine
Felt through their tears a radiance divine
    From farthest stars, until within them sprang
    Responsive holiness that dulled the pang –
And said, "Her matchless power might be thine."

Then sharp I called to my light-thoughted muse,
10   Running with brook-like rapture through the marsh,
        Her berry-scented garments stained and torn,
And clothed her in white robe and careful shoes,
    And told her heaven was fair and earth was harsh,
        While she with hanging head looked all forlorn.
                                                    (1907)

Hester Prynne Speaks

Two fires are mine: one strong within, love-born;
One fierce without, of human hate and scorn,
And on my breast, my Pearl, my flower of fire.

Two woes are mine: the sharp pang of desire,
And that sick moan of her who anguished much
Until she found the Garment's hem to touch.

Two loves: my Pearl, and him who on my breast
Gave me my shame, my child, life's worst and best,
Of lowest hell, of highest heaven are such.

10 Two souls have I: one in these baby eyes,
    One answering human scorn with scornful cries.
    Lord, would I had Thy Garment's hem to touch!
                                                    (1931)

MARIE JOUSSAYE

1864?–1949

Born in Belleville, Ontario, into a working-class family, Marie Joussaye left school at the age of twelve to become a domestic servant. In the early 1890s she worked as a labour activist organizing servant girls in Toronto, then moved to British Columbia and the Yukon, where she married David Fotheringham in 1903. Her poetry appeared in several pamphlets and two books: *The Songs That Quinté Sang* (1895) and *Selections from Anglo-Saxon Songs* (1918).

Only a Working Girl

I know I am only a working girl,
  And I am not ashamed to say
I belong to the ranks of those who toil
  For a living, day by day.
With willing feet I press along
  In the paths that I must tread,
Proud that I have the strength and skill
  To earn my daily bread.

I belong to the "lower classes;"
10   That's a phrase we often meet.
There are some who sneer at working girls;
  As they pass us on the street,
They stare at us in proud disdain
  And their lips in scorn will curl,
And oftentimes we hear them say:
  "She's only a working girl."

"Only a working girl!" Thank God,
  With willing hands and heart,
Able to earn my daily bread,
20   And in Life's battle take my part.
You could offer me no title

318

I would be more proud to own,
And I stand as high in the sight of God
    As the Queen upon her throne.

Those gentle folk who pride themselves
    Upon their wealth and birth,
And look with scorn on those who have
    Naught else but honest worth,
Your gentle birth we laugh to scorn,
30   For we hold it as our creed
That none are gentle, save the one
    Who does a gentle deed.

We are only the "lower classes,"
    But the Holy Scriptures tell
How, when the King of Glory
    Came down on earth to dwell,
Not with the rich and mighty
    'Neath costly palace dome,
But with the poor and lowly
40   He chose to make His home.

He was one of the "lower classes,"
    And had to toil for bread,
So poor that oftentimes He had
    No place to lay His head.
He knows what it is to labor
    And toil the long day thro',
He knows when we are weary
    For He's been weary too.

O working girls! Remember,
50   It is neither crime or shame
To work for honest wages,
    Since Christ has done the same,
And wealth and high position
    Seem but of little worth

To us, whose fellow laborer
 Is King of Heaven and Earth.

So when you meet with scornful sneers,
 Just lift your heads in pride;
The shield of honest womanhood
60 Can turn such sneers aside,
And some day they will realize
 That the purest, fairest pearls
'Mid the gems of noble womankind
 Are "only working girls."

      (1895)

Two Poets

There lived a poet once, a famous bard,
 Whose muse, arrayed in robes of misty light,
Soared high above the common herd of men.
 So high she soared, she almost passed from sight,
Even as the cold and brilliant stars of Heaven
 That shine in chilly splendour from the skies
Withhold the radiance of their fairest beams
 Beyond the naked sight of human eyes.
Still there are some pretentious ones who read
10 The mystic dreams and fancies of his brain,
Pedantic minds, who, understanding naught,
 Would still have others think they grasp the strain,
Till, at some passage with strange meaning fraught,
 Too subtle far for them to understand,
They pause perplexed, then as with one accord
 Cry out in chorus: "How sublime and grand!"
O gifted bard! I would not try to pluck
 One leaf from out thy laurel wreath of fame
Because I fail to grasp thy subtle thought;
20 'Tis not in thee, but me, where lies the blame.

Around his tomb the world has bowed in grief,
    And strewed his grave with bay and laurel leaf.

There lived and died a poet, years ago –
    A hardy, humble ploughman of the soil
Who sang his heartfelt songs in simplest words
    And earned his daily bread by humble toil.
His songs brought gladness unto many hearts
    And soothed men's sorrows as with magic spell.
His name was known in palace and in cot,
30   For king and peasant loved the poet well.
And why? Because he sang of human faith,
    Of human love, of human joy and pain,
The grandest thoughts couched in the simplest words,
    The lowliest mind could grasp the meaning plain.
O poet ploughman! thine the laurel wreath,
    Whose songs found answer in the hearts of men,
Thy name shall live on Fame's immortal scroll
    After his name has passed from mortal ken,
Thine the true poet soul and master mind
40   Whose lyrics touched the hearts of all mankind.

                    (1895)

FRANCIS SHERMAN

1871–1926

Born in Fredericton, New Brunswick, and educated at the University of New Brunswick, Francis Sherman worked for the Merchants' Bank (later the Royal Bank of Canada) in the Maritimes and in Cuba. A close friend of Charles G.D. Roberts, he retired from his position in the bank's Montreal head office in 1919 after service in the First World War had damaged his health. Sherman was deeply influenced by William Morris, whom he commemorated in his sonnet sequence *In Memorabilia Mortis* (1896). Issued in small volumes and pamphlets during his lifetime, his poems were posthumously edited by Lorne Pierce in *The Complete Poems of Francis Sherman* (1935).

In Memorabilia Mortis

I

I marked the slow withdrawal of the year.
Out on the hills the scarlet maples shone –
The glad, first herald of triumphant dawn.
A robin's song fell through the silence – clear
As long ago it rang when June was here.
Then, suddenly, a few gray clouds were drawn
Across the sky; and all the song was gone,
And all the gold was quick to disappear.
That day the sun seemed loth to come again;
10 And all day long the low wind spoke of rain,
Far off, beyond the hills; and moaned, like one
Wounded, among the pines: as though the Earth,
Knowing some giant grief had come to birth,
Had wearied of the Summer and the Sun.

VI

Then, suddenly, I was awake. Dead things
Were all about me and the year was dead.
Save where the birches grew, all leaves were shed
And nowhere fell the sound of song or wings.
The fields I deemed were graves of worshipped Kings
Had lost their bloom: no honey-bee now fed
Therein, and no white daisy bowed its head
To harken to the wind's love-murmurings.
Yet, by my dream, I know henceforth for me
80 This time of year shall hold some unknown grace
When the leaves fall, and shall be sanctified:
As April only comes for memory
Of him who kissed the veil from Beauty's face
That we might see, and passed at Easter-tide.

                                        (1896)

The Last Storm

From north, from east, the strong wind hurries down;
Against the window-pane the sleet rings fast;
The moon hath hid her face away, aghast,
And darkness keeps each corner of the town,
The garden hedges wear a heavy crown,
And the old poplars shriek, as night drifts past,
That, leagues on desolate leagues away, at last
One comes to know he too must surely drown.
And yet at noon, to-morrow, when I go
10 Out to the white, white edges of the plain,
I shall not grieve for this night's hurricane,
Seeing how, in a little hollow, sinks the snow
Around the southmost tree, where a lean crow
Sits noisily impatient for the rain.

                                 [1897] (1899)

The Watch

Are those her feet at last upon the stair?
Her trailing garments echoing there?
The falling of her hair?

About a year ago I heard her come,
Thus; as a child recalling some
Vague memories of home.

O how the firelight blinded her dear eyes!
I saw them open, and grow wise:
No questions, no replies.

10. And now, tonight, comes the same sound of rain.
The wet boughs reach against the pane
In the same way, again.

In the old way I hear the moaning wind
Hunt the dead leaves it cannot find, –
Blind as the stars are blind.

– She may come in at midnight, tired and wan.
Yet, – what if once again at dawn
I wake to find her gone?

(1900)

To Doctor John Donne

Those grave old men – and women, too –
Who thronged St. Paul's in your dear times,
I wonder what they thought of you
When they remembered your strange rhymes.

Did they forgive you for them then
(Because you preached so very well)
Putting them by and turn again
To hear your words of heaven and hell?

Or did they pause, seeing you there,
10 And say, "How can this man have grace?
Today, I worship otherwhere!"
And straightway seek some holier place?

(For so most men would do today
If from their pulpit you leaned down.
Yea, they would find the quickest way
To tell the scandal to the town.

How full it must have been of sin –
Your heart – had it but played with verse.
But you must tell your loves therein, –
20 Alas! could anything be worse?)

And yet, among your ancient folk,
I think there must have been a few
Who learned at last to bear Love's yoke
More patiently because of you.

I sit and see across the years
Some maiden kneeling in the aisle,
Contented now; all gone her tears
That you have changed into a smile:

Some lone poor man made rich again:
30 Some faded woman, with gray hair,
Forgetting most of her old pain:
Some grave-eyed poet, surer there.

O dim, hushed aisles of long ago,
Have ye no messages to tell?
We wonder, and are fain to know
The secret ye have kept so well.

And though we kneel with open eyes
Among your shadowy ghosts today,
Not one of us grows strong, or wise,
40 Nor find we comfort when we pray.

But they! how glad they seem who sit
And hear the voice we cannot hear.
Quietly they remember it –
The unknown thing we hold so dear.

Their faces fade with the low sun. . . .
What wonder were they dreaming of?
Surely, it cannot be, John Donne,
They think that you were wise to love?

(1935)

So, After All, When All Is Said and Done

So, after all, when all is said and done,
And such is counted loss and such as gain,
For me, these many years, the tropic rain
That threshes thro' the plumèd palms is one
With the next moment's certitude of sun.
Indolent, without change, insurgent, vain, –
So my days follow; long have the old hopes lain
Like weeds along the road your feet have run.
Now, I know not what thing is good, what bad;
10 And faith and love have perished for a sign:
But, after I am dead, my troubled ghost
Some April morn shall tremble and be glad,
Hearing your child call to a child of mine
Across the Northern wood it dreams of most.

[1901] (1935)

F.G. SCOTT
1861–1944

Born in Montreal, Frederick George Scott studied theology in England, eventually becoming canon and then archdeacon of the Anglican cathedral in Quebec City. During the First World War he served as chaplain to Canadian troops at the front. The father of F.R. Scott, one of the most important of the next generation of Canadian poets, he published more than a dozen books and pamphlets of verse as well as a memoir of his experiences during the Great War.

The Unnamed Lake

It sleeps among the thousand hills
    Where no man ever trod,
And only nature's music fills
    The silences of God.

Great mountains tower above its shore,
    Green rushes fringe its brim,
And o'er its breast for evermore
    The wanton breezes skim.

Dark clouds that intercept the sun
10   Go there in Spring to weep,
And there, when Autumn days are done,
    White mists lie down to sleep.

Sunrise and sunset crown with gold
    The peaks of ageless stone,
Where winds have thundered from of old
    And storms have set their throne.

No echoes of the world afar
    Disturb it night or day,
But sun and shadow, moon and star
20   Pass and repass for aye.

'Twas in the grey of early dawn
    When first the lake we spied,
And fragments of a cloud were drawn
    Half down the mountain side.

Along the shore a heron flew,
    And from a speck on high
That hovered in the deepening blue,
    We heard the fish-hawk's cry.

Among the cloud-capt solitudes,
30   No sound the silence broke,
Save when, in whispers down the woods,
    The guardian mountains spoke.

Through tangled brush and dewy brake,
    Returning whence we came,
We passed in silence, and the lake
    We left without a name.

(1897)

The Penalty*

The cold dawn wakes in pain
With mist and drizzling rain;
An ambulance draws nigh
Holding one doomed to die.

Heart-sick at such a death,
His comrades hold their breath,
All ankle-deep in mud
Soon to be stained with blood.

Blindfold his eyes, lest he
10 The firing party see;
Handcuff him to that stake,
Lest he some movement make.

His strength may fail the test,
Pin paper on his breast

---

* Written in Quebec. It was my sad duty on one occasion
in the War to have to prepare for death a man who was
to be shot for cowardice. The circumstances of the case
are given in my book, "The Great War As I Saw It".

I baptized the poor fellow, and gave him Holy
Communion in the prison at midnight, and then
visited two generals, interceding for his pardon. The
order, I was told, could not be changed, and he was
executed exactly as I have described the scene, at
daybreak on a rainy hillside. I am thankful to say that
the death penalty for desertion from the Front has now
been abolished. I feel sure the British Line, wherever it
may be, will hold just as well without it. The great task
before us is to abolish war itself with all its horrors.

To mark the fluttering heart
Which shirked the nobler part.

Before the shells he quailed
And lamentably failed.
Death, which he fled from then,
20 Now comes from brother men.

His wild thoughts fiercely roam
To past years, past sins, home,
And mingle with the rain
He will not hear again.

A moment more and fate
Will open some dark gate;
What will the quenchless mind
Beyond that portal find?

Somewhere he heard that God
30 The hill of darkness trod;
But in this blinding night
He gropes in vain for light.

Though sweat breaks on his brow,
He will not weaken now;
His bearing gives no sign
Of cowardice in the line.

Would God that he had shared
All that the others dared,
And braved the thunderous fire
40 Among the broken wire.

But on his bandaged face
No human eye can trace
The changes that are wrought
By agony of thought.

He sets his teeth and stands
With twitching, handcuffed hands,
His marked heart well in view;
God grant their aim be true.

A shuffling in the mire,
50 "Ready, Present – Fire."
He falls, and one man more
Has vanished from the war.

[1916]

Call Back Our Dead

Call back our Dead – the fateful feud is o'er;
   Call back our Dead, we need them here to-day,
   We need them in their freshness and their play,
Their valiant manhood ripened by the war.
Our hearts stand open; open, too, the door
   Of that still chamber where the shadow lay
   Since death's grim message came. No other ray
But their bright presence can the light restore.

Call back our Dead, they die each day we live –
10   Deep in our hearts they die the whole day long.
     Call back our Dead, the welcoming hearth is
              bright,
All that this life can give them, we will give.
   Tell them God's angels sing again their song
     And Peace hangs out her star upon the night.

(November 11th, 1925)

FRANCES JONES BANNERMAN

1855–1944

Born in Halifax and educated in Nova Scotia, France, and Italy, Frances Jones Bannerman was an active artist during the 1880s and 1890s. She was elected an associate of the Royal Canadian Academy and exhibited in Canada, at the Royal Academy (London), and at the Paris Salon. Sister of Canadian novelist Alice Jones, she married British artist Hamnet Bannerman and subsequently resided in England and Italy. Some of her verse was collected in *Milestones*, published in London in 1899. Her painting "The Favourite Corner" appears on the cover of this book.

Wolf-Head

I saw them halt at fall of night,
    I, crouching low
Where the reek of the river-mists hung white
    Over the beds of bending rush,
        In the shallow flow
        Of the rippling ford,
Where I saw the thirsting horses push
    Their nostrils spreading broad.

And I saw how rode the enemy
10   Hot on my track,
So hot he had not eyes to see
    The thing he hunted glaring back,
        From the osier-bed
        Where the green slime floats,
With eyes with famine-fury red,
    As the hunters slaked their dusty throats!

Then through the shadows I could mark
    The leader pass
Onward first from the moment's rest,
20   And to the lingering riders hark
      As they roughly jest
      On a lad with his lass,
      In the closing dark
Ere the steep of the farther bank they breast.

So the town is closed to me now!
    To me whom men hunt;
And the pious monks their sanctified vow,
To succour the needy and wayfaring poor,
Must break, or they bear the brunt
30   Of the wrath of the King
    For such harbouring,
  – Closed is the Sanctuary door!

Closed also the gates of the sea;
    As I starved in the cave
    Of the runagate slave –
Whom the price of the Wolf-head would free –
    Timely warning he brought,
    Each shipper was held in the port,
      None might brave
40 The word of the King were he balked of his sport!

Remain to me now but the hills!
    Will the gaunt grey beast
Know his fellow whom man hunts and kills
    Without law,
    For the priced head and paw,
    Or shall the pack feast
    On the starved bones that lie
On some lonely peak in the gaze of the sky?
                (1899)

Love Belated

I would have you sit as you used to do
   In the window-seat to look
Down on the square, where two and two
   Pass the students with gown and book,
And see the light touch as it used
   On the curve of your cheek and neck,
Catching a careless curl unloosed
   With a sudden golden fleck.

And I would that the harsh old lock might yield
10   To my hand with its protest vain,
That you would not hear if the Carillon pealed
   Like a burst of golden rain
From the ancient belfry you so loved,
   For the chimes that ward all harms, –
I might reach your side ere you had moved
   And turned with a cry to my arms.

And I would – oh, I would that the heart of youth
   Might be mine again for a space,
That I might annul in very sooth
20   The years that blur your face
When I try to recall your smile, your eyes,
   As they were, for now I know
That my pride had lost me so rare a prize
   In the days of long ago!

(1899)

I Would Not, Dear

I would not, dear, you might return
    To this changed world so grey and old,
Where no more from the headlands burn
    The beacons now for ever cold.

I would not have you know the weight
    Of ventureless long days I know, –
Ah, love, where once we used to freight
    The hours as ships that come and go

On all the tides the world around,
10   To wide new lands and kingdoms old,
With treasure no more to be found,
    And goods no longer bought or sold.

Dearest, when first I saw the Spring
    Send the sea-swallow by your grave,
It had an added pang to wring
    Anguish from lips that could but rave

Against all nature, you being gone
    From the bright world we loved so well;
I knew not then you were the one
20   – Not I – who should be left to dwell

For ever on the enchanted shore,
    Where youth and love had made our home,
Where on your dear face never more
    The change of the grey years may come;

While I should see unmeaning things
    Drift by through all the heavy years,
Till to strange shores the spent tide brings
    The ship that by no beacon steers.

                                        (1899)

MAY AUSTIN LOW
1863–1958

Born in Chambly, Quebec, May Austin Low spent most of her adult life in Montreal. She contributed poems to the *Canadian Magazine* and other periodicals, some of which were collected in *Confession, and Other Verses* (1909). "The Coming of the *Roslyn Castle*" refers to an incident during the South African war when the troop ship, the *Roslyn Castle*, transporting Canadian troops home from Cape Town, docked in Halifax on January 8, 1901, with a lowered flag. Two men had died of enteric fever; the wife of one, Lieutenant T.H.C. Sutton, did not learn of her husband's death until she boarded the vessel to welcome him home.

The Coming of the Roslyn Castle

Out of the night, all silently she came.
And far above, the moon, a pure, pale flame,
Lighted her pathway, on the pathless sea;
While low upon the mast hung silently
The symbol of some sorrow. Far beneath
The waiting women watched with bated breath,
And in that awful moment anguish poured
On each white soul, and voiced itself to God:
"Not mine! Not mine! Let it not be my own."
10 Wild while they waited came the sad sea's moan,
And then the name was whispered, and one life
Lay widowed of all love, and joy and light,
And one gay heart took up grief's lasting cross;
But every woman's soul had suffered loss.

(1901)

MARJORIE PICKTHALL

1883–1922

Born in England, Marjorie Pickthall emigrated to Canada
with her family in 1889 and grew up in Toronto. From 1912
to 1919 she lived in England, upon her return to Canada
settling in British Columbia. After publishing her first
story at the age of fifteen, she brought out three books of
fiction before her poetry attracted attention. Her volumes
of verse include *The Drift of Pinions* (1913), *The Wood-
carver's Wife and Later Poems* (1922), and *The Complete
Poems of Marjorie Pickthall* (1927).

Persephone Returning to Hades

Last night I made my pillow of the leaves
Frostily sweet, and lay throughout the hours
Close to the woven roots of the earth; O earth,
Great mother, did the dread foreknowledge run
Through all thy veins and trouble thee in thy sleep?
No sleep was mine. Where my faint hands had fallen
Wide on thy grass, pale violets, ere the day,
Grew like to sorrow's self made visible,
Each with a tear at heart. I watched the stars
10 Wheeling athwart the heavens, and knew thy trees,
Olive and aspen, oak and sycamore,
And all the small dumb brethren of thy woods
Awake and sorrowing with me. And so staid
Until the shepherds' songs awoke the morn.

Then I arose with tears. Yet, ere I turned
From these dim meadows to the doors of hell,
Gathered these sad untimely flowers, and found
Long beautiful berries ripening on the thorn,
With one wide rose that had forgot to die.
20 These I bore softly thence. But herewithin
This gathering-place of shadows where I wait

For the slow change, there cometh a sullen wind
Blown from the memoried fields of asphodel
Or Lethe's level stream; and these my flowers
Slip from my hands and are but shadows too.

Why should I grieve when grief is overpast?
Why should I sorrow when I may forget?
The shepherds' horns are crying about the folds,
The east is clear and yellow as daffodils,
30 Dread daffodils –
                 The brightest flower o' the fields.
I gathered them in Enna, O, my lord.
Do the doors yawn and their dim warders wait?

What was this earth-born memory I would hold?
Almost I have forgotten. Lord, I see
Before, the vast gray suburbs of the dead;
Behind, the golden loneliness of the woods,
A stir of wandering birds, and in the brake
A small brown faun who follows me and weeps.

                                    [1905] (1927)

A Mother in Egypt

*"About midnight will I go out into the midst of Egypt: and all
the firstborn in the land of Egypt shall die, from the firstborn
of Pharaoh that sitteth upon the throne, even unto the first-
born of the maidservant that is behind the mill."* – Exodus
XI : 4, 5.

Is the noise of grief in the palace over the river
For this silent one at my side?
There came a hush in the night, and he rose with his
                                    hands a-quiver
Like lotus petals adrift on the swing of the tide.
O small soft hands, the day groweth old for sleeping!

O small still feet, rise up, for the hour is late!
Rise up, my son, for I hear them mourning and weeping
In the temple down by the gate.

Hushed is the face that was wont to brighten with
                                                laughter
10 When I sang at the mill,
And silence unbroken shall greet the sorrowful dawns
                                                hereafter,
The house shall be still.
Voice after voice takes up the burden of wailing, –
Do you heed, do you hear? – in the high-priest's house
                                                by the wall;
But mine is the grief, and their sorrow is all unavailing.
Will he wake at their call?

Something I saw of the broad, dim wings half folding
The passionless brow.
Something I saw of the sword the shadowy hands were
                                                holding, –
20 What matters it now?
I held you close, dear face, as I knelt and harkened
To the wind that cried last night like a soul in sin,
When the broad, bright stars dropped down and the
                                                soft sky darkened,
And the Presence moved therein.

I have heard men speak in the market-place of the city,
Low voiced, in a breath,
Of a god who is stronger than ours, and who knows not
                                                changing nor pity,
Whose anger is death.
Nothing I know of the lords of the outland races,
30 But Amun is gentle and Hathor the Mother is mild,

And who would descend from the light of the peaceful
places
To war on a child?

Yet here he lies, with a scarlet pomegranate petal
Blown down on his cheek.
The slow sun sinks to the sand like a shield of some
burnished metal,
But he does not speak.
I have called, I have sung, but he neither will hear nor
waken;
So lightly, so whitely he lies in the curve of my arm,
Like a feather let fall from the bird that the arrow hath
taken.
40 Who could see him, and harm?

"The swallow flies home to her sleep in the eaves of the
altar,
And the crane to her nest," –
So do we sing o'er the mill, and why, ah, why should I
falter,
Since he goes to his rest?
Does he play in their flowers as he played among these
with his mother?
Do the gods smile downward and love him and give him
their care?
Guard him well, O ye gods, till I come; lest the wrath of
that Other
Should reach to him there!

(1905)

Père Lalemant

I lift the Lord on high,
Under the murmuring hemlock boughs, and see
The small birds of the forest lingering by
And making melody.
These are mine acolytes and these my choir,
And this mine altar in the cool green shade,
Where the wild soft-eyed does draw nigh
Wondering, as in the byre
Of Bethlehem the oxen heard Thy cry
10 And saw Thee, unafraid.

My boatmen sit apart,
Wolf-eyed, wolf-sinewed, stiller than the trees.
Help me, O Lord, for very slow of heart
And hard of faith are these.
Cruel are they, yet Thy children. Foul are they,
Yet wert Thou born to save them utterly.
Then make me as I pray
Just to their hates, kind to their sorrows, wise
After their speech, and strong before their free
20 Indomitable eyes.

Do the French lilies reign
Over Mont Royal and Stadacona still?
Up the St. Lawrence comes the spring again,
Crowning each southward hill
And blossoming pool with beauty, while I roam
Far from the perilous folds that are my home,
There where we built St. Ignace for our needs,
Shaped the rough roof tree, turned the first sweet sod,
St. Ignace and St. Louis, little beads
30 On the rosary of God.

Pines shall Thy pillars be,
Fairer than those Sidonian cedars brought
By Hiram out of Tyre, and each birch-tree
Shines like a holy thought.
But come no worshippers; shall I confess,
St. Francis-like, the birds of the wilderness?
O, with Thy love my lonely head uphold.
A wandering shepherd I, who hath no sheep;
A wandering soul, who hath no scrip, nor gold,
40 Nor anywhere to sleep.

My hour of rest is done;
On the smooth ripple lifts the long canoe;
The hemlocks murmur sadly as the sun
Slants his dim arrows through.
Whither I go I know not, nor the way,
Dark with strange passions, vexed with heathen charms,
Holding I know not what of life or death;
Only be Thou beside me day by day,
Thy rod my guide and comfort, underneath
50 Thy everlasting arms.

(1905)

The Green Month

What of all the colours shall I bring you for your fairing,
Fit to lay your fingers on, fine enough for you? –
Yellow for the ripened rye, white for ladies' wearing,
Red for briar-roses, or the skies' own blue?

Nay, for spring has touched the elm, spring has found
                                    the willow,
Winds that call the swallow home sway the boughs apart;
Green shall all my curtains be, green shall be my pillow,
Green I'll wear within my hair, and green upon my heart.

(1907)

The Pool

Come with me, follow me, swift as a moth,
Ere the wood-doves waken.
Lift the long leaves and look down, look down
Where the light is shaken,
Amber and brown,
On the woven ivory roots of the reed,
On a floating flower and a weft of weed
And a feather of froth.

Here in the night all wonders are,
10 Lapped in the lift of the ripple's swing, –
A silver shell and a shaken star,
And a white moth's wing.
Here the young moon when the mists unclose
Swims like the bud of a golden rose.

I would live like an elf where the wild grapes cling,
I would chase the thrush
From the red rose-berries.
All the day long I would laugh and swing
With the black choke-cherries.

20 I would shake the bees from the milkweed blooms,
And cool, O cool,
Night after night I would leap in the pool,
And sleep with the fish in the roots of the rush.
Clear, O clear my dreams should be made
Of emerald light and amber shade,
Of silver shallows and golden glooms.
Sweet, O sweet my dreams should be
As the dark, sweet water enfolding me
Safe as a blind shell under the sea.

(1907)

Inheritance

Desolate strange sleep and wild
Came on me while yet a child;
I, before I tasted tears,
Knew the grief of all the years.

I, before I fronted pain,
Felt creation writhe and strain,
Sending ancient terrors through,
My small pulses, sweet and new.

I, before I learned how time
10 Robs all summers at their prime,
I, few seasons gone from birth,
Felt my body change to earth.

[1917] (1922)

The Wife

Living, I had no might
To make you hear,
Now, in the inmost night,
I am so near
No whisper, falling light,
Divides us, dear.

Living, I had no claim
On your great hours.
Now the thin candle-flame,
10 The closing flowers,
Wed summer with my name, –
And these are ours.

Your shadow on the dust,
Strength, and a cry,
Delight, despair, mistrust, –
All these am I.
Dawn, and the far hills thrust
To a far sky.

Living, I had no skill
20 To stay your tread,
Now all that was my will
Silence has said.
We are one for good and ill
Since I am dead.

(1921)

ROBERT SERVICE
1874–1958

Born in Preston, England, and raised in Scotland, Robert Service emigrated to British Columbia in 1896. As an employee of the Bank of Commerce he was sent to the Yukon in 1904, where he composed the popular ballads collected in *Songs of a Sourdough* (1907) and other volumes of verse. After leaving the Yukon in 1912, he spent much of his remaining life in Europe as a writer and correspondent. His service as a stretcher-bearer during the First World War resulted in *Rhymes of a Red Cross Man* (1916).

The Shooting of Dan McGrew

A bunch of the boys were whooping it up in the
                        Malamute saloon;
The kid that handles the music-box was hitting a
                        jag-time tune;
Back of the bar, in a solo game, sat Dangerous Dan
                        McGrew,
And watching his luck was his light-o'-love, the lady
                        that's known as Lou.

When out of the night, which was fifty below, and into
                        the din and the glare,
There stumbled a miner fresh from the creeks, dog-
                        dirty, and loaded for bear.
He looked like a man with a foot in the grave and
                        scarcely the strength of a louse,
Yet he tilted a poke of dust on the bar, and he called for
                        drinks for the house.
There was none could place the stranger's face, though
                        we searched ourselves for a clue;
10 But we drank his health, and the last to drink was
                        Dangerous Dan McGrew.

There's men that somehow just grip your eyes, and hold
　　　　　them hard like a spell;
And such was he, and he looked to me like a man who
　　　　　had lived in hell;
With a face most hair, and the dreary stare of a dog
　　　　　whose day is done,
As he watered the green stuff in his glass, and the drops
　　　　　fell one by one.
Then I got to figgering who he was, and wondering what
　　　　　he'd do,
And I turned my head – and there watching him was the
　　　　　lady that's known as Lou.

His eyes went rubbering round the room, and he
　　　　　seemed in a kind of daze,
Till at last that old piano fell in the way of his wandering
　　　　　gaze.
The rag-time kid was having a drink; there was no one
　　　　　else on the stool,
20　So the stranger stumbles across the room, and flops
　　　　　down there like a fool.
In a buckskin shirt that was glazed with dirt he sat, and I
　　　　　saw him sway;
Then he clutched the keys with his talon hands – my
　　　　　God! but that man could play.

Were you ever out in the Great Alone, when the moon
　　　　　was awful clear,
And the icy mountains hemmed you in with a silence
　　　　　you most could *hear*;
With only the howl of a timber wolf, and you camped
　　　　　there in the cold,
A half-dead thing in a stark, dead world, clean mad for
　　　　　the muck called gold;

While high overhead, green, yellow and red, the North
          Lights swept in bars? –
Then you've a hunch what the music meant . . . hunger
          and night and the stars.

And hunger not of the belly kind, that's banished with
          bacon and beans,
30 But the gnawing hunger of lonely men for a home and
          all that it means;
For a fireside far from the cares that are, four walls and a
          roof above;
But oh! so cramful of cosy joy, and crowned with a
          woman's love –
A woman dearer than all the world, and true as Heaven
          is true –
(God! how ghastly she looks through her rouge, – the
          lady that's known as Lou.)

Then on a sudden the music changed, so soft that you
          scarce could hear;
But you felt that your life had been looted clean of all
          that it once held dear;
That someone had stolen the woman you loved; that her
          love was a devil's lie;
That your guts were gone, and the best for you was to
          crawl away and die.
'Twas the crowning cry of a heart's despair, and it
          thrilled you through and through –
40 "I guess I'll make it a spread misere," said Dangerous
          Dan McGrew.

The music almost died away . . . then it burst like a pent-
          up flood;
And it seemed to say, "Repay, repay," and my eyes were
          blind with blood.

The thought came back of an ancient wrong, and it
                stung like a frozen lash,
And the lust awoke to kill, to kill . . . then the music
                stopped with a crash,
And the stranger turned, and his eyes they burned in a
                most peculiar way;

In a buckskin shirt that was glazed with dirt he sat, and I
                saw him sway;
Then his lips went in in a kind of grin, and he spoke,
                and his voice was calm,
And "Boys," says he, "you don't know me, and none of
                you care a damn;
But I want to state, and my words are straight, and I'll
                bet my poke they're true,
50 That one of you is a hound of hell . . . and that one is
                Dan McGrew."

Then I ducked my head, and the lights went out, and
                two guns blazed in the dark,
And a woman screamed, and the lights went up, and
                two men lay stiff and stark.
Pitched on his head, and pumped full of lead, was
                Dangerous Dan McGrew,
While the man from the creeks lay clutched to the breast
                of the lady that's known as Lou.

These are the simple facts of the case, and I guess I ought
                to know.
They say that the stranger was crazed with "hooch," and
                I'm not denying it's so.
I'm not so wise as the lawyer guys, but strictly between
                us two –
The woman that kissed him and – pinched his poke –
                was the lady that's known as Lou.
                (1907)

The Stretcher-Bearer

My stretcher is one scarlet stain,
And as I tries to scrape it clean,
I tell you wot – I'm sick with pain
For all I've 'eard, for all I've seen;
Around me is the 'ellish night,
And as the war's red rim I trace,
I wonder if in 'Eaven's height,
Our God don't turn away 'Is face.

I don't care 'oose the Crime may be;
10   I 'olds no brief for kin or clan;
I 'ymns no 'ate: I only see
As man destroys his brother man;
I waves no flag: I only know,
As 'ere beside the dead I wait,
A million 'earts is weighed with woe,
A million 'omes is desolate.

In drippin' darkness, far and near,
All night I've sought them woeful ones.
Dawn shudders up and still I 'ear
20   The crimson chorus of the guns.
Look! like a ball of blood the sun
'Angs o'er the scene of wrath and wrong. . . .
"Quick! Stretcher-bearers on the run!"
O Prince of Peace! 'Ow long, 'ow long?

                                        (1916)

My Cross

I wrote a poem to the Moon
        But no one noticed it;
Although I hoped that late or soon
        Someone would praise a bit

Its purity and grace forlorn,
    Its beauty tulip-cool . . .
But as my poem died still-born,
    I felt a fool.

I wrote a verse of vulgar trend
10   Spiced with an oath or two;
I tacked a snapper at the end
    And called it *Dan McGrew*.
I spouted it to bar-room boys,
    Full fifty years away;
Yet still with rude and ribald noise
    It lives today.

'Tis bitter truth, but there you are –
    That's how a name is made;
Write of a rose, a lark, a star,
20   You'll never make the grade.
But write of gutter and of grime,
    Of pimp and prostitute,
The multitude will read your rhyme,
    And pay to boot.

So what's the use to burn and bleed
    And strive for beauty's sake?
No one your poetry will read,
    Your heart will only break.
But set your song in vulgar pitch,
30   If rhyme you will not rue,
And make your heroine a bitch . . .
    Like *Lady Lou*.

        (1951)

CHIEF K'HHALSERTEN SEPASS

1841?–1943

Renowned leader of the Chilliwack Salish in southwestern
British Columbia, Chief Sepass decided in 1911 to take the
unprecedented step of supervising the translation of his
songs into English in order to preserve them. The transla-
tor, who spent four years working with him, was Sophia
White, daughter of English missionaries, who had learned
Salish as a child. The text was eventually published as
Sepass Tales: The Songs of Y-Ail-Mihth (1963, reprinted
1974).

The Beginning of the World

Long, long ago,
Before anything was,
Saving only the heavens,
From the seat of his golden throne
The Sun God looked out on the Moon Goddess
And found her beautiful.

Hour after hour,
With hopeless love,
He watched the spot where, at evening,
10 She would sometimes come out to wander
Through her silver garden
In the cool of the dusk.

Far he sent his gaze across the heavens
Until the time came, one day,
When she returned his look of love
And she, too, sat lonely,
Turning eyes of wistful longing
Toward her distant lover.

Then their thoughts of love and longing,
20 Seeking each other,

Met halfway,
Mingled,
Hung suspended in space. . . .
Thus: the beginning of the world.

Sat they long in loneliness
The great void of eternal space
Closing in upon them.
Despair hung heavy in their hearts.
Gone was the splendor of the golden throne;
30 Gone was the beauty of the silver garden;
Their souls burned with a white flame of longing.

Up leaped the Sun God,
Chanting his love song,
The words of his love thoughts:

> "My heart wings its way to you,
> O daughter of the Moon!
> My heart wings its way to you
> Where you stand
> In your silver garden,
40 Your white face turned toward me.

> You will receive a gift,
> O daughter of the Moon!
> A gift of my great love
> For you only;
> You will receive a gift of my love
> This day, ere the dusk falls."

He seized his knife,
And with swift slashes,
Tore a strip of bark
50 From a great tree.
Still he chanted his songs
Of love and longing,

As he wrote on the birch bark
In the speech of springtime,
The language of lovers.

Then,
From his place at the gate of the Sun,
He, the Sun God,
Raised his arm high
60 And cast his message
Far into the sky.

Swift it flew,
Following an unerring course
Toward the distant garden
Where sat the Moon Goddess.

But what of the message?
Alas! It wavers in its flight;
Drops;
Falls on the embryo world;
70   Thus: the land.

Far across the heavens,
In her silver garden,
The Moon Goddess wept bitterly.
A tear was borne by the wind;
Fell on the half-formed world;
Thus: the water.

There from the love thoughts,
Longings and love words
Sprang beautiful trees and flowers.
80 Little streams gurgled through the forests;
Leaping waterfalls foamed;
Great rivers flowed to the sea;

Fish abounded;
Buffalo roamed the plains;

And through the wood paths
Sped all the wild things
Of a new world.

The Sun God left the seat of his golden throne;
Swung wide the gate of the sun!
90 A ringing shout cleft the heavens!
The Moon Goddess,
From her silver garden,
Heard the cry;
Stood,
And answered.

He of the Sun,
She of the Moon,
Stood they
With arms outstretched
100 A moment,
Silent,
Then, in the first shadow of evenfall,
They leaped into space;
Came to rest
On the new world of their love;
Thus: the first man and woman.

[1911-1915] (1963)

JOHN McCRAE

1872–1918

Born in Guelph, Ontario, John McCrae was appointed a
fellow in pathology at McGill after studying medicine at
the University of Toronto. In 1900 he joined the Canadian
contingent in the South African war, and upon the out-
break of the First World War he offered his services as a
medical officer. Written during the second battle of Ypres,
"In Flanders Fields" was first published anonymously in
Punch in December 1915.

In Flanders Fields

In Flanders fields the poppies blow
Between the crosses, row on row,
   That mark our place; and in the sky
   The larks, still bravely singing, fly
Scarce heard amid the guns below.

We are the Dead. Short days ago
We lived, felt dawn, saw sunset glow,
   Loved and were loved, and now we lie
   In Flanders fields.

10 Take up our quarrel with the foe:
To you from failing hands we throw
   The torch; be yours to hold it high.
   If ye break faith with us who die
We shall not sleep, though poppies grow
   In Flanders fields.

(1915)

HELENA COLEMAN

1860–1953

Born in Newcastle, Ontario, Helena Coleman spent most of her life in that province, where for a time she headed the music department at the Ontario Ladies' College in Whitby. She contributed poetry and prose to many periodicals, often anonymously or under one of her many pseudonyms. Her *Songs and Sonnets* (1906) was followed by several chapbooks of poetry, including *Marching Men: War Verses* (1917), and a novel.

Oh, Not When April Wakes the Daffodils

Oh, not when April wakes the daffodils,
 And bob-o-links o'er misty meadows ring
 Their fluted bells, and orchards fleeced with Spring,
Go climbing up to crown the radiant hills;
Not when the budding balm-o'-gilead spills
 Its spices on the air, and lilacs bring
 Old dreams to mind, and every living thing
The brimming cup with fresh enchantment fills.

Oh, bring not then the dread report of death, –
 Of eyes to loveliness forever sealed,
Of youth that perished as a passing breath,
Of hearts laid waste and agonies untold,
 When here in every sweet Canadian field
Are heaped such treasuries of green and gold!

(1917)

Convocation Hall

May 18th, 1917

They rose,
The honored and the grave,
The reverend, the grey,
While one read out the names of those
Who, gallant, young and brave,
Upon the field of battle gave
Their ardent lives away.

They rose to honor Youth –
What honor could they give?
10 What tribute shall we lay
Who still in safety live?
Before the shrine of those who pay
The price of honor and of truth
Giving their lives away?

They rose in reverence, yea;
But those who lie
Far on the Flanders field to-day
Had not an answering word to say;
Their silence thundered their reply –
20 They gave their lives away!

(1917)

When First He Put the Khaki On

When first he put the khaki on
    He tried with careful art
To seem blasé and casual
    And play the proper part,
But it was plain as plain could be
    He was a child at heart.

Although he talked in knowing terms
    Of what "the boys" had done,
Likewise of ammunition tests,
10   And how to load a gun,
And bragged that in his stocking feet
    He stood full six foot, one.

Yet all the while the child looked out
    With mild appealing eyes,
Unconscious he was visible
    Beneath the man's disguise,
Nor dreaming what the look evoked
    In hearts grown mother-wise.

How could he know the sudden pang,
20   The stir of swift alarms,
The yearning prayer that innocence
    Be kept from all that harms,
The inner reach of tenderness,
    And cradling of soft arms?

(1917)

FRANK PREWETT

1893–1962

Born in Kenilworth, Ontario, Frank Prewett attended the University of Toronto and later studied at Oxford. While his experience in the First World War injured him emotionally and physically, it also brought him into contact with Siegfried Sassoon, Lady Ottoline Morell, and other participants in the Georgian Movement in British poetry. After a brief return to Canada in 1920 he settled in England, where he published *Poems* (1922), *Rural Scene* (1924), and a novel, *The Chazzey Tragedy* (1933).

The Somme Valley, 1917

Comrade, why do you weep?
   Is it sorrow for a friend
Who fell, rifle in hand,
   His last stand at an end?

The thunder-lipped grey guns
   Lament him, fierce and slow,
Where he found his dreamless bed,
   Head to head with a foe.

The sweet lark beats on high,
10   For the peace of those who sleep
In the quiet embrace of earth:
   Comrade why do you weep?

                 (1922)

Card Game

Hearing the whine and crash
We hastened out
And found a few poor men
Lying about.

I put my hand in the breast
Of the first met.
His heart thumped, stopped, and I drew
My hand out wet.

Another, he seemed a boy,
10 Rolled in the mud
Screaming, "my legs, my legs,"
And he poured out his blood.

We bandaged the rest
And went in,
And started again at our cards
Where we had been.

                    [1917] (1987)

Epigram

Out of the earth I sprang
    Bewildered sore,
Gazed all around, and knew
    I lived before.

Into the earth I spring
    Bewildered sore;
So shall I rise and fall
    Forevermore.

                [c. 1918] (1987)

Burial Stones

The blue sky arches wide
From hill to hill;
The little grasses stand
Upright and still.

Only these stones to tell
The deadly strife,
The all-important schemes,
The greed for life.

For they are gone, who fought;
10 But still the skies
Stretch blue, aloof, unchanged,
From rise to rise.

                    [1919] (1921)

The Soldier

My years I counted twenty-one
Mostly at tail of plough:
The furrow that I drove is done,
To sleep in furrow now.

I leapt from living to the dead
A bullet was my bane.
It split this nutshell rind of head,
This kernel of a brain.

A lad to life has paid his debts
10 Who bests and kills his foe,
And man upon his sweetheart gets,
To reap as well as sow.

But I shall take no son by hand,
No greybeard bravo be:
My ghost is tethered in the sand
Afar from my degree.

                    [c. 1923] (1964)

Afterword

BY CAROLE GERSON AND GWENDOLYN DAVIES

In the winter of 1749-1750, *The Gentleman's Magazine* of London, England, published a series of letters, articles, and illustrations to persuade readers to settle in the newly established town of Halifax, Nova Scotia. "My dear," wrote one man to his wife, "I live as well as man can desire, I want for no victuals nor drink, nor lodging; I want for nothing but you and my dear children, and should be very glad that you would come in the fleet, the next spring, in the year 50; you shall be kindly welcome to enjoy my prosperous labour, as you may live an easy life, without labour to toil yourself." A plan of the new town gave visual reinforcement to these promises. It showed good defences, symmetrical streets, representative edifices of Church and State, a ship in the harbour, and cultivated forests. It also included North American butterflies, plants, and wildlife in a summary of images whose exoticism was tempered by sufficient familiarity to reassure both investors and future colonists. To enhance these enticements, *The Gentleman's Magazine* also published "Nova Scotia: A New Ballad," to be sung to the traditional tune of "King John and the Abbot of Canterbury" in the fellowship of the local tavern. These lively verses, appealing to a desire for financial independence, social freedom, and human dignity, could not fail to recruit the interest of those who dreamed of a continent where "all is as free as in those times of old,/ When poets assure us the age was of gold."

The lure of gold, both literal and figurative, informed the journeys of European explorers to the New World for two centuries before the founding of Halifax in 1749. By the beginning of the seventeenth century, an increasing British presence in the Newfoundland cod fishery had resulted not only in the first settlement at Cupar's Cove in 1610, but also in references to Newfoundland in poetry and prose, including William Vaughan's *The Golden Fleece* (1626) and Captain John Mason's *Briefe Discourse of the New-found-land* (1620). This writing contributed to what David S. Shields has called a "literature of empire" in which "poetry became an effective vehicle for popularizing the iconology of imperial trade." Noteworthy among these poets was Robert Hayman, whose *Quodlibets Lately Come Over From New Britaniola, Old Newfound-Land* (1628) was probably the first book of English verse written in North America. With their vision of plenty in a land "Exempt from taxings, ill newes, Lawing, feare," Hayman's epigrams struck the note of promise that was to dominate New World poetry well into the nineteenth century. Dissent, as expressed in the double-voiced satire of Irish bard Donncha Rua Mac Conmara, was safer and more effective when masked. These examples, along with Henry Kelsey's 1693 rhyming account of his journey for the Hudson's Bay Company across the western prairies, testify to the variety of experience embraced by the considerable body of English-language verse about Canada that existed by the middle of the eighteenth century.

Following the Treaty of Paris in 1763 and the recognition of the United States in 1783, the context for poetry in and about British North America altered significantly. New England Planters had moved into the Maritime Provinces in the early 1760s and approximately fifty thousand Loyalist refugees swelled the population of the Maritimes and Upper and

Lower Canada during and after the American Revolution. The subsequent arrival of immigrants, merchants, military personnel, and colonial administrators from Britain further contributed to the establishment of a domestic base in British North America from which the first locally written verse began to emerge. In what Shields calls a "mixed print and manuscript culture," poetry frequently circulated in letters or in manuscript, or was read aloud at social gatherings. Without established outlets for publishing books, poems most often appeared in newspapers, magazines, or pamphlets, the latter usually financed by the poet, either personally or by subscription. Although the hardships of emigration and nostalgia for the home country informed many immigrant works, such as Joseph Stansbury's "To Cordelia" (c. 1783) and the anonymous "Canadian Boat-Song" (1829), the majority of poems written in British North America in the late eighteenth and early nineteenth centuries were optimistic and forward-looking, focussing on domestic, social, and landscape topics. Settlement narratives such as Oliver Goldsmith's *The Rising Village* (1825), devotional hymns by Henry Alline, Hudibrastic satire by Jacob Bailey, topographical poetry by Roger Viets, and occasional verse by Anne Hecht represent the skill in prosody and the emphasis on manners, mores, and social stability that engaged versifiers of this period.

Among the Loyalists were some of the most talented poets writing in the United States. The role of the Loyalist poet at this stage, argues Thomas B. Vincent, "was not to explore or create uncharted literary worlds, but to establish a cultural base that 'meant something' to the people for whom he wrote. These people were trying to establish themselves in a variety of ways, and consciously or unconsciously, the poet worked to do his part." Although the wide geographical distribution of Loyalist poets militated against their coalescing as a literary school, their endeavours, along with the Loyalist-inspired establishment of educational institutions, reading societies, newspapers, and literary periodicals similar to those left behind in the United States, hastened the development of cultural foundations to be expanded upon by subsequent generations. Thus, the survival of the rhyming couplet or of Burnsian vernacular verse well into the nineteenth century may reflect the enduring influence of eighteenth-century Loyalist and Scots immigrants as much as it does the cultural time lag often associated with colonial societies.

By the 1820s, readers in British North America were well informed by their newspapers and magazines about the literary shifts taking place in Great Britain in the poetry of Sir Walter Scott, Thomas Moore, Lord Byron, William Wordsworth, and other poets associated with Romanticism. As the century progressed, Canadian poets such as Douglas Huyghue, Charles Sangster, and Pamelia Vining Yule evinced their reading of the Romantics in the style and imagery of their own work. What is most noticeable about the poets of this period is the versatility with which they treated subjects as wide-ranging as the War of 1812, the Rebellion of 1837, or seasonal variations in the Canadian climate. Grounded in Canadian experience, poems of the mid-nineteenth century reflected many aspects of the country's life, from industrial exploitation to politics, from intemperance to love. Although James McIntyre's "Ode on the Mammoth Cheese" (1884) may have earned him dubious distinction as one of Canada's "best bad poets," it also illustrates the degree to which the reading and writing of poetry infiltrated virtually every dimension of nineteenth-century Canadian experience, cutting across educational background, class lines, and physical locality to express individuals' responses to the landscapes and events that moved them.

During the eighteenth century, the reading and writing of poetry were among the accomplishments of cultivated men and women. By the middle of the nineteenth century, these activities had become part of the Victorian philosophy of "uplift" which saw average men and women engage in life-long quests for self-improvement and self-expression. As had earlier been the case, most poetry continued to appear in newspapers and literary periodicals, the vehicles whereby ordinary people, women as well as men, could find circulation for their verse in a society where book publication would remain a precarious endeavour for many decades to come. As poet and teacher Margaret Gill Currie caustically commented, "there is not the least shadow of danger of a Canadian author – a poet in particular – receiving too much recognition or becoming rich enough to endanger his or her morality." The ephemerality of newspapers and magazines frequently increased the frustration of poets and their readers. Often short-lived because of inadequate funding and stiff competition from American journals, these serials provide valuable insights into the breadth and complexity of the poetry written in nineteenth-century Canada.

An important milestone in bringing pre-Confederation Canadian poets to public attention was the appearance in 1864 of Reverend E.H. Dewart's *Selections from Canadian Poets.* Sharing the view of many of his compatriots that the development of literature in a new country mirrored its progress towards refinement, Dewart favoured poets in the genteel tradition. Although limited by its exclusion of aboriginal and radical verse, his anthology nonetheless cast a wide net that included most of the recognized women poets of the period. By assembling the work of several dozen currently active poets, Dewart contributed to the heightened sense of cultural identity that was to accompany Confederation in 1867, arguing in his introduction that a national literature is "an essential element in the formation of national character."

Within several decades, Dewart's predictions seemed to come true with the arrival of a new generation of poets who expressed the growing cultural nationalism of the post-Confederation era. In the rhetoric of its time, W.D. Lighthall's

1889 anthology, *Songs of the Great Dominion*, joyously proclaimed the "virility" of poets "cheerful with the consciousness of young might, public wealth, and heroism" who celebrated the virtues of "Canada, Eldest Daughter of the Empire . . . the Empire's completest type." This shift in tone derives from many factors – not just the chauvinism of late-nineteenth-century British Imperialism, but also the recent accomplishments of several younger poets that heralded a new maturity in Canadian literature.

The 1880 publication of *Orion, and Other Poems* by Charles G.D. Roberts at the age of twenty served as a beacon to many of his contemporaries. Archibald Lampman found inspiration in Roberts's accomplishment: "It seemed to me a wonderful thing that such work could be done by a Canadian, by a young man, one of ourselves." Mostly Canadian-born, Roberts's and Lampman's contemporaries strove to articulate their Canadian experience while writing within the major traditions and developments of current international poetic practice. Although some worked alone, as did Isabella Valancy Crawford in Toronto, others clustered in literary circles where they gave and received encouragement and support.

In New Brunswick and later in Nova Scotia, Charles G.D. Roberts and his cousin Bliss Carman formed the nucleus of one such community, which included Francis Sherman and Roberts's protégée, Sophia Almon Hensley. Another developed in Ottawa, where Archibald Lampman and Duncan Campbell Scott were close personal as well as literary friends. With William Wilfred Campbell, then also living in Ottawa, they contributed to "At the Mermaid Inn," a column of literary commentary in the Toronto *Globe*, which ran for a year and a half in 1892-1893. The dependence of these three Ottawa poets on civil service careers indicates that the Canadian market still could not adequately support its writers. Unwilling to take risks on volumes of verse, publishers frequently required authors to pay the production costs of their books.

Magazine publication could be more lucrative, but was often constrained by editors' formatting practices. In a letter to a fellow poet seeking publication advice, Roberts conveyed his frustration with the way in which the literary marketplace interfered with poetry: "the poem was *utterly* too long for magazine purposes. No editor would *dream* of looking at it with a view to publication. The magazine public, you know, are not purchasers of poetry, unless it be by Kipling." The options for a Canadian poet who desired a professional literary career were few: to eke out a marginal existence at home by selling poems and stories to newspapers and magazines, as Crawford attempted to do, or to move to the centres of American or British literary and publishing activity, as did Bliss Carman, Roberts, and, for a time, Agnes Ethelwyn Wetherald.

Dominating Canadian poetry of the post-Confederation period are the writings of six poets: Crawford, Campbell, Roberts, Carman, Lampman, and D.C. Scott. Although the stature of these poets is indisputable, it is important to situate them within the larger field of poetic endeavour in which they worked. The selection of writers for this anthology therefore includes some of the other serious poets active at this time, such as Wetherald, Pauline Johnson, Francis Sherman, and Marjorie Pickthall. These middle-class poets are in turn contextualized by Marie Joussaye, a working woman who spoke for a large social class that produced a considerable quantity of verse but is seldom represented in literary anthologies. First Nations Canadians, who usually appear in poetry written by non-Natives, here achieve some voice in the well-known verse of Pauline Johnson as well as in texts by two other Natives who chose to express themselves in English, George Copway and Chief K'HHalserten Sepass.

Although the lives, careers, and writings of the poets of late nineteenth-century Canada varied greatly, their work shares several general characteristics. Their presumed audience is familiar with the land, the seasons, and some of Canada's social history. Hence the aim of these poets is not to explain Canadian experience but to express it, often in syntax and imagery arising from the local landscape and its associations. Traditional forms like the sonnet endure, used by many as challenges to find new ways to work within old structures. Other poets share the aesthetic interest of their turn-of-the-century international peers in reviving such complex forms as the rondeau and the villanelle. Wetherald's tight, pithy poems reflect both her admiration of Emily Dickinson and her association with American aesthetes of the 1890s in the pages of little magazines like *The Chap Book*. The freer verse forms typical of twentieth-century modernism – in Canada usually associated with the writing of A.J.M. Smith and the Montreal poets from the mid-1920s onward – can be found considerably earlier in the work of Charles G.D. Roberts, D.C. Scott, Marjorie Pickthall, and Frank Prewett. At the same time, the popularity of a vernacular poet like Robert Service reminds us of the enduring appeal of versifiers in the tradition of Robert Burns. And both formally and thematically, several poems in this volume anticipate works by the next generation. For example, F.G. Scott's "The Unnamed Lake" (1897) stands behind the later Laurentian verse of his son, F.R. Scott. Charles G.D. Roberts, after writing the introduction to E.J. Pratt's book, *Verses of the Sea* (1930), composed "The Iceberg," which antedates Pratt's "The Titanic" (1935) by only a few years.

The First World War has often been described as an historical turning point in the evolution of Canadian society, culture, and identity. John McCrae's poem, "In Flanders Fields" (1915), drew international attention to the human sacrifice of the period, and Frank Prewett's ironic verses on the devastation of trench warfare struck the note of restrained emotion characteristic of emerging modernism. As Canada entered the 1920s, with all the self-consciousness of cultural identity and growing international commitment that was to mark that period, its poets, like their eighteenth- and nineteenth-century predecessors, negotiated the tricky position of writing both as Canadians and as citizens of the larger world. This problem would continue to intrigue and challenge Canadian poets in the decades to come.

WORKS CITED

Margaret Gill Currie to E.V.[sic] Ellis, Esq., Fredericton, July 23rd, 1897, letter folded in *Saint John and Anna Grey*, Saint John Public Library; Edward Hartley Dewart, "Introductory Essay," *Selections from Canadian Poets*, Montreal: Lovell, 1864, ix; G. Hick, "My dear and loving wife," *The Gentleman's Magazine* XX, January 1750; Archibald Lampman, "Two Canadian Poets: A Lecture, 1891," in A.J.M. Smith, ed., *Masks of Poetry*, Toronto: McClelland and Stewart, 1962, 30; William Douw Lighthall, "Introduction," *Songs of the Great Dominion: Voices from the Forests and Waters, the Settlements and Cities of Canada*, London: Walter Scott, 1889, xxi; Charles G.D. Roberts to Amos Henry Chandler, 13 November 1899, Amos Henry Chandler Papers, Mount Allison University Archives; David Shields, *Oracles of Empire, Poetry, Politics, and Commerce in British America, 1690-1750*, Chicago: University of Chicago Press, 1990, 4, 6, 15; Thomas B. Vincent, "Eighteenth-Century Poetry in Maritime Canada: Problems of Approach – A Research Report," in Kenneth MacKinnon, ed., *The Atlantic Provinces Literature Colloquium Papers*, Saint John, 1977, 18.

Copy-Texts

ALLINE, HENRY
Hymns and Spiritual Songs, Boston, 1786.

ANDERSON, JAMES
Sawney's Letters and Cariboo Songs, Barkerville, British
  Columbia: Cariboo Sentinel, 1869.

ANONYMOUS
"Canadian Boat-Song," *Blackwood's Magazine*, September
  1829, 84.
"The Fight at Montgomery's," *Mackenzie's Gazette*, 18 August
  1838.
"Nathaniel's Tilt," Cyril Byrne, "Notes on Some Early
  Newfoundland Poems," in Kenneth MacKinnon, ed.,
  Atlantic Provinces Literature Colloquium. Saint John:
  Atlantic Canada Institute, 1977.
"Nova Scotia. A New Ballad," *The Gentleman's Magazine*,
  February 1750, 84.
"A Popular Creed," *Ontario Workman*, 14 August 1873, 2.

BAILEY, JACOB
Bailey Papers, Public Archives of Nova Scotia, MG 1, vol. 100,
  428-31 (reel 14,904).

BANNERMAN, FRANCES JONES
Milestones, London: Richards, 1899.

CAMPBELL, WILLIAM WILFRED
All poems are from Laurel Boone, ed., *William Wilfred Campbell: Selected Poetry and Essays,* Waterloo: Wilfrid Laurier University Press, 1987, with the exception of "August Evening on the Beach," *Lake Lyrics and Other Poems,* Saint John: McMillan, 1889.

CARMAN, BLISS
Ballads of Lost Haven: A Book of the Sea, Boston: Lamson, Wolffe, 1897: "The Ships of St. John," "Noons of Poppy."
Last Songs from Vagabondia, Boston: Small, Maynard, 1900: "The Lanterns of St. Eulalie."
Later Poems, Toronto: McClelland and Stewart, 1921: "Before the Snow," "The Ghost-yard of the Goldenrod."
"Low Tide on Avon," *King's College Record,* 78, October 1886, 5-6.
Low Tide on Grand Pré: A Book of Lyrics, Cambridge and Chicago: Stone & Kimball, 1894: "The Eavesdropper," "Low Tide on Grand Pré," "A Sea Child," "A Windflower."
"May in the Selkirks," *The Song Fishermen's Song Sheets,* No. 12, 4 June 1929.
More Songs from Vagabondia, Boston: Copeland and Day, 1896: "A Vagabond Song."
Sanctuary: Sunshine House Sonnets, New York: Dodd, Mead, 1929: "Wild Geese," "The Winter Scene."
Sappho: One Hundred Lyrics, Toronto: Copp Clark, 1903.

COLEMAN, HELENA
Marching Men: War Verses, Toronto: Dent, 1917.

COPWAY, GEORGE (KAH-GE-GA-GAH-BOWH)
The first two poems are from *The Life, History, and Travels of Kah-ge-ga-gah-bowh (George Copway)* (1847); the

second war song is from *The Traditional History and Characteristic Sketches of the Ojibway Nation*, London: Black, 1850.

COTTNAM, DEBORAH HOW

"On Being Asked What Recollection Was," *The Novascotian*, 16 June 1845.

"A piece for a Sampler" is from "Maria Ann Smart's Extract Book St. John New Brunswick 6th August 1793," New Brunswick Museum.

CRAWFORD, ISABELLA VALANCY

Poems are from *Old Spookses' Pass, Malcolm's Katie, and Other Poems*, Toronto: Bain, 1884, with the following exceptions: "The Dark Stag," *Telegram*, 28 November 1883; "Love Me, Love My Dog," *Telegram*, 25 March 1880; "Love's Forget-Me-Not," *Telegram*, 13 March 1882; *Malcolm's Katie: A Love Story*, ed. D.M.R. Bentley, London, Ontario: Canadian Poetry Press, 1987.

GILLESPIE, GEORGE WILLIAM

Miscellaneous Poems, Toronto, 1843.

GOLDSMITH, OLIVER

The Rising Village, ed. Gerald Lynch, London, Ontario: Canadian Poetry Press, 1989.

HARRISON, SUSAN FRANCES

Pine, Rose, and Fleur de Lis, Toronto: Hart, 1891.

HAYES, KATE SIMPSON

Prairie Pot-Pourri, Winnipeg: Stovel, 1895.

HAYMAN, ROBERT

Quodlibets Lately Come Over From New Britaniola, Old Newfound-Land. Epigrams, and Other Small Parcels, Both Morall and Divine, London: Mitchell, 1628.

HEAVYSEGE, CHARLES
Jephtha's Daughter, Montreal: Dawson, 1865.

HECHT, ANNE
Grace Helen Mowat, *The Diverting History of a Loyalist Town: A Portrait of St. Andrews, New Brunswick*, Fredericton: Brunswick Press, 1953.

HENSLEY, SOPHIA ALMON
All selections are from *Poems*, Windsor: Anslow, 1889, with the exception of "Guiltless," *Woman's Supplement, Halifax Herald*, 10 August 1895, 4; "Somewhere in France," *Everybody's Magazine* 39, August 1918.
All poems reprinted by permission.

HUYGHUE, DOUGLAS
The Amaranth, December 1842.

JOHNSON, PAULINE
Flint and Feather, Toronto: Musson, 1912.

JOUSSAYE, MARIE
The Songs That Quinté Sang, Belleville, Ontario: Sun, 1895.

KELSEY, HENRY
The Kelsey Papers, ed. Arthur G. Doughty and Chester Martin, Ottawa: Public Archives of Canada and Public Record Office of Northern Ireland, 1929.

LAMPMAN, ARCHIBALD
Poems are from *Archibald Lampman: Selected Poetry*, ed. Michael Gnarowski, Ottawa: Tecumseh, 1990, with the following exceptions:
Alcyone, Ottawa: Ogilvy, 1899: "Evening," "White Pansies," "Winter Evening."
Christmas card: *These Poems, Written By Archibald Lampman and Duncan Campbell Scott, Are Now For*

The First Time Printed and Issued For Their Friends,
Christmastime, 1897: "In the Wilds."

Lampman Papers, Special Collections, Bennett Library,
Simon Fraser University: "For My Darling" [The Growth
of Love, II], "In the Wilds," "On Lake Temiscamingue."

Lampman Papers, National Archives of Canada, MG 29 D59:
vol. 2, 742, 744: "A Portrait in Six Sonnets, 1, 6"; MS
bound volume, 1045: "Winter Uplands."

"Across the Pea-Fields," *The Independent*, 14 August 1890, 1;
"A January Morning," *Christmas Globe*, 1889, 12; "Love-
Doubt" [The Growth of Love, I], *Among the Millet, and
Other Poems*, Ottawa: Durie, 1888; "A Sunset on the Lower
St. Lawrence" ["A Sunset at Les Eboulements"], *The
Independent*, 1 October 1891, 1; "To a Millionaire," *The
Week*, XII, 30 November 1894, 10.

LEPROHON, ROSANNA
The Poetical Works of Mrs. Leprohon, Montreal: Lovell, 1881.

LOW, MAY AUSTIN
Poems and Songs of the South African War, ed. Rev. J.D.
Borthwick, Montreal: Gazette, 1901.

MACCONMARA, DONNCHA RUA
Irisleabhar na Gaedhilge (The Gaelic Journal), Dublin,
Volume 2, November 21, 1885. Lines 29-32 from James N.
Healy (Ed.), *Ballads from the Pubs of Ireland*, Cork: The
Mercier Press, 1968, third edition, 48-49. Irish text edited,
and English translation, by Pádraig Ó Siadhail.

MCCRAE, JOHN
In Flanders Fields and Other Poems, Toronto: Briggs, 1919.

MACHAR, AGNES MAULE
"Rondeau," *The Week*, 27 November 1891, 830. The other
poems are from *Lays of the "True North," and Other
Canadian Poems*, London: Elliot Stock, 1902.

MCINTYRE, JAMES
Poems of James McIntyre, Ingersoll, Ontario: Chronicle, 1889.

MCLACHLAN, ALEXANDER
Poems and Songs, Toronto: Hunter Rose, 1874.

MAIR, CHARLES
Tecumseh: A Drama and Canadian Poems, Toronto: Briggs, 1901.

ODELL, JONATHAN
Odell Papers, New Brunswick Museum: Box 4, Pkt. 13: "The Battle of Queen's Town, Upper Canada"; Box 4, Pkt. 13b: "The Comet of 1811"; Box 4, Pkt. 13, Notebook #1: "Our thirty-ninth Wedding day." *The Loyal Verses of Joseph Stansbury and Doctor Jonathan Odell*, ed. Winthrop Sargent, Albany, New York: Munsell, 1860.

PHILLIPS, JOHN ARTHUR
Thompson's Turkey, and Other Christmas Tales, Poems, etc., Montreal: Lovell, 1873.

PICKTHALL, MARJORIE
The Complete Poems of Marjorie Pickthall, Toronto: McClelland & Stewart, 1927.

PREWETT, FRANK
All poems are from *Selected Poems of Frank Prewett*, ed. Bruce Meyer, Toronto: Exile Editions, 1987, with the exception of "The Somme Valley, 1917," *Georgian Poetry*, ed. E.M., London: Poetry Workshop, 1922, and "The Soldier," *The Collected Poems of Frank Prewett*, Intro. Robert Graves, London: Cassell, 1964.
Poems by Frank Prewett appear by kind permission of his daughter, Jane Youngs.

ROBERTS, CHARLES G.D.

All poems are from *The Collected Poems of Sir Charles G.D. Roberts*, eds. Desmond Pacey and Graham Adams, Wolfville, Nova Scotia: Wombat Press, 1985.

SANGSTER, CHARLES

Sangster Papers, Rare Book Department, McGill University Libraries.

SAWTELL, M. ETHELIND

The Mourner's Tribute; or, Effusions of Melancholy Hours, Montreal: Armour and Ramsay, 1840.

SCOTT, DUNCAN CAMPBELL

All poems are from *The Poems of Duncan Campbell Scott*, Toronto: McClelland & Stewart, 1926, with the following exceptions:

The Green Cloister: Later Poems, Toronto: McClelland & Stewart, 1935: "En Route," "At Gull Lake: August, 1810," "Chiostro Verde."

"Ottawa. Before Dawn," *Songs of the Great Dominion*, ed. W.D. Lighthall, London: Walter Scott, 1889.

All poems reprinted by permission.

SCOTT, F.G.

Collected Poems, Vancouver: Clarke and Stewart, 1934.

SEPASS, CHIEF K'HHALSERTEN

Sepass Tales: The Songs of Y-Ail-Mihth, ed. Eloise Street, Chilliwack, British Columbia: Sepass Trust, 1963.

Reprinted by permission.

SERVICE, ROBERT

The Complete Poems of Robert Service, New York, Dodd, Mead, 1940 (reprint of 1907 ed.) "The Shooting of Dan McGrew," "The Stretcher-Bearer"; *Lyrics of a Low Brow*, New York: Dodd, Mead, 1951: "My Cross."

"The Shooting of Dan McGrew" reprinted by permission of
the Putnam Publishing Group from *The Spell of the Yukon*
by Robert Service. Copyright © 1907 by Edward Stern &
Co.

"The Stretcher-Bearer" reprinted by permission of The
Putnam Publishing Group from *Rhymes of a Red Cross
Man* by Robert Service. Copyright © 1916 by Dodd, Mead
& Co., Inc.

"My Cross" reprinted by permission of the Putnam
Publishing Group from *Lyrics of a Low Brow* by Robert
Service. Copyright © 1951 by Dodd, Mead, & Co., Inc.

SHERMAN, FRANCIS
The Complete Poems of Francis Sherman, ed. Lorne Pierce,
Toronto: Ryerson, 1935.

STANSBURY, JOSEPH
*The Loyal Verses of Joseph Stansbury and Doctor Jonathan
Odell*, ed. Winthrop Sargent, Albany, New York: Munsell,
1860.

TONGE, GRISELDA
The Acadian Recorder, 5 March 1825, 4.

VIETS, ROGER
Annapolis-Royal, a poem, 1788, facsimile ed. Thomas B.
Vincent, Kingston: Loyal Colonies Press, 1979.

WETHERALD, AGNES ETHELWYN
Lyrics and Sonnets, Toronto: Nelson, 1931.

YULE, PAMELIA VINING
Poems of the Heart and Home, Toronto: Bengough and
Moore, 1881.

Index of Authors and Titles